THE ARCHITECTURE OF
AFTERMATH

TERRY SMITH

UNIVERSITY OF
CHICAGO PRESS • CHICAGO
AND LONDON

OF **AFTERMATH**

Terry Smith is the Andrew W. Mellon Professor of
Contemporary Art History and Theory in the
Department of the History of Art and Architecture at
the University of Pittsburgh. He is also visiting professor of architecture at the University of Sydney.

The University of Chicago Press, Chicago 60637
The University of Chicago Press, Ltd., London
© 2006 by The University of Chicago
All rights reserved. Published 2006
Printed in the United States of America

15 14 13 12 11 10 09 08 07 06   1 2 3 4 5
ISBN: 0-226-76468-0   (cloth)
ISBN: 0-226-76469-9   (paper)

Library of Congress Cataloging-in-
Publication Data
Smith, Terry E.
    The architecture of aftermath / Terry Smith.
        p. cm.
    Includes bibliographical references and index.
    ISBN 0-226-76468-0 (cloth : alk. paper)—
    ISBN 0-226-76469-9 (pbk. : alk. paper)
    1. Architecture and society.   2. Symbolism in
architecture.   3. Architecture, Modern—20th century.
4. Architecture, Modern—21st century.   I. Title.
    N72.S6S56 2006
    720.1′03—dc22

                                    2005026033

∞ The paper used in this publication meets the
minimum requirements of the American National
Standard for Information Sciences—Permanence
of Paper for Printed Library Materials, ANSI
Z39.48-1992.

Neither the sun, nor death, can be looked at
with a steady gaze. [Le soleil ni la mort ne se
peuvent regarder fixement.] François, duc de La Rochefoucauld,
Réflexions, ou sentences et maxims morales,
maxim 26 (1665)

... history, that indecent alloy of banality and
apocalypse. [... histoire, ce mélange indécent
de banalité et d'apocalypse] E. M. Corian, 1949

There is a sense of void among us. A void
that is charged with the weight of emotion,
the fears of risk and the expectation that we
can overcome. In a curious parallel, that void
is the common territory of art. It is the place
where the unexpected power of invention can
reach beyond the limits of logic and set a
new direction. Rafael Viñoly, "Fill the Void with Beauty,"
New York Times, September 23, 2001

CONTENTS

ACKNOWLEDGMENTS

My thanks to Annabel Wharton, who first posed the question of "destination architecture" to me as part of a Luce Foundation–funded inquiry into economics and the arts at Duke University in 1999. The early support of Anna Rubbo and Glen Hill of *Architecture Theory Review,* published by the Faculty of Architecture at the University of Sydney, was crucial. Tom Crow and Charles Salas enabled me to spend 2001–2 at the Getty Research Institute, Los Angeles. Much of the basis of this text was laid during the immediate aftermath of 9.11.01. My fellow Getty Scholars were valuable mostly for their skepticism, so I thank particularly those who also offered constructive support, specifically Jerry Moore, Can Bilsel, Georges Didi-Huberman, Mabel Wilson, Larry Kruger, and, later, Benjamin Buchloh. My research assistant Christina Wegel was most helpful, as were Getty Research Institute staff, particularly Wim de Witt. I owe a great debt to Nancy Condee of the Cultural Studies Program at the University of Pittsburgh for her own detailed comments and for organizing in September 2002 a consortium at Birkbeck College, University of London, and the Tate Modern, London, on "Innocence, Terror, Public Policy: The September 11th Anniversary," during which my material received useful responses from many of the participants. For invaluable research assistance during 2002 I thank Carolina Carrasco, during 2003 Rocio Nogales, 2004 Miguel Rojas, and 2005 Gerald Harnett and Morgan Hartnett. I am grateful to the dean of the School of Arts and Sciences and to my colleagues in the Department of the History of Art and Architecture at the University of Pittsburgh for their ongoing support, including Ray Anne Lockard, and the staff of the Frick Fine Arts Library. For their insights generously given I thank the following: Tamara Winikoff, David Kunzle, Jacques Derrida, Anthony Vidler, Andrew Benjamin, Shelley Rice, Roger Conover, Valerie Krips, Kirk Savage, Barbara McCloskey, Fred Evans, April Eisman, Veronica Young, Greg Shapley, Patricia Leighton, and Catharine Lumby. Many others have made useful comments in conversation, passed on clippings, or drawn my attention to helpful texts, images, and sites—too many to name, I thank them all. I acknowledge support from the Richard D. and Mary Jane Edwards Endowed Publications Fund, University of Pittsburgh. Finally, at the University of Chicago Press, I am grateful to Susan Bielstein, who saw the point quickly and then worked hard to make me do the same, to Anthony Burton, to Michael Koplow, and to the independent readers for their trenchant, improving comments.

Earlier versions of parts of the introduction and some later chapters have appeared in the following: "The Political Iconomy of Iconotypes and the Architecture of Destination," *Architecture Theory Review*, vol. 7, no. 2 (2002): 1–44; "The Dialectics of Disappearance: Architectural Iconotypes between Clashing Cultures," *Critical Quarterly*, vol. 45, nos. 1–2 (2003): 33–51; "Architektur als Ziel: Trauma und Erhabnes unter den Bedingungen der Gleichzeitigkeit," *Lettre International*, 66 (spring 2004): 34–42.

To the victims-martyrs-saviors of 9.11.01, and to those to come.

ILLUSTRATIONS

Introduction: *After Effects—Architecture, Iconomy, Contemporaneity*

If one were to slow down a videotape of the first plane approaching then hitting the north tower of World Trade Center, New York, at 8:46 am on September 11, 2001, and then zoom in to the instants of impact, one would see the word "American" slide, letter by letter, into oblivion. In what are perhaps the only three extant video films of this moment, the airplane appears as a white, sunblurred shaft. Artist Wolfgang Staehle had, since early that month, live-fed webcam transmissions of the view of lower Manhattan, seen across the East River from south Williamsburg, into the exhibition space at Postmasters, his New York gallery, intending to convey a "panorama of eventlessness," yet inadvertently, and in absentia, captured the opposite. Videographer James Naudet instinctively swung his video camera at the sound hurtling over his head as he stood on a street in Tribeca (illus. 1). At the same moment, Pavel Hlava, a Czech immigrant worker intent on making a video "postcard" of his environs to send home, captured the event by accident and from a distance—the approach to the Brooklyn-Battery Tunnel.[1] When his truck surfaced from the tunnel near the base of the towers, Mr. Hlava was one of a number of people who filmed the second attack, at 9:03 am, this time with intent. From his viewpoint, and that of others close to the building—such as Evan Fairbanks, whose video was distributed by Magnum—the second plane appears as a dark shadow or a sun-whitened streak. But to those looking from a wider angle—like Kelly Guenther, whose *New York Times* photograph of the plane as it hurtled through the skyscrapers of the financial district towards the south tower has often been reproduced—the blue and gray colors made it, unmistakably, a United Airlines flight (illus. 2).[2] As images that draw us to imagine the deaths of actual human beings, these pictures were, and remain, deeply affecting. They record, among much else, an act of spectacular terrorism—an action of one group of humans against another within a war that is conducted at both symbolic and literal levels—a raid that was, and remains, profoundly disturbing. The profundity it disturbed was expressed, through perversely exact metaphor, in the violent obliteration of the word "United."

The 9.11.01 attacks were directed, Osama bin Laden has told us, at "America's icons of military and economic power."[3] These attacks—along with the subsequent wars in Afghanistan and Iraq, directed likewise against individuals, groups, and places that were themselves both actual and iconic—have underlined the central importance to human affairs of the image economy, that is, the symbolic

1. Jules Naudet,
American Airlines Flight
11 Hits North Tower,
World Trade Center,
8.45 am, September
11, 2001. 2001, video.
Source: Gamma Presse.

exchanges between people, things, ideas, interest groups, and cultures that take predominantly visual form. In recognition of the subtle power and the all-pervasiveness of this trafficking in images, let us call it "the iconomy." This concept describes more than the dense image manipulation that prevails in cultures predicated on conspicuous and incessant consumption. If anyone required a demonstration of the immediate but also far-reaching significance of the realm of visual culture—in its distinctiveness but also entanglement with those of politics, economics and the ecologies of everyday life—surely 9.11.01 was it. If anyone doubted whether the lessons of 9.11.01 had penetrated the thinking of those at the heights and centers of world political power, then the conduct, by the U.S. government, of the media war about the War in Iraq should remove such doubts. Indeed, within weeks of the invasion it became clear that the war planners had devoted much more effort to their media campaigns than they had to planning the management of the aftermath of their lightning "victory."

In early April 2003, the American War in Iraq seemed to be reaching a speedy, and spectacular, conclusion. Real-time television footage, relayed by reporters "embedded" within tank units, showed U.S. forces racing across the desert, encountering minimal resistance, breaching key targets in towns, cities, and then finally the capital itself. To an American public conditioned by war and action movies—as well as reality—to expect at least some kind of visible fight back, the evaporation of the demonized enemy seemed at first puzzling, then confusing. One solution to this public relations problem was to target images of Iraqi president Saddam Hussein. These were not hard to find. His coercive regime was built to a significant degree around the ubiquity of his image: photographs, postcards, official portraits, daily televisual grabs, a Koran written in his blood, statues and gigantic emblemata such as his arms bearing crossed swords straddling the main

road into Baghdad. State architecture was everywhere adorned with his image, key temples were carved with his visage, and a central mosque was recalibrated so that its traditional forms celebrated "victory" in the war against Iran. In the days leading up to the arrival of American troops in Baghdad, Saddam—or, as U.S. news channels regularly supposed, one of his "look-alikes"—appeared frequently in television clips handed out by the Iraqi Ministry of Information, exhorting his people to fight back. Tit-for-tat, U.S. news cameras panned across painted images of Saddam riddled with bullet holes, posters going up in flames, and statues defaced. Still the Evil Dictator evaded capture: the nightmare of 1991—of not "seeing the job through to the end"—reappeared. An image that conveyed finality had to be found. On April 9 a crowd of Iraqis gathered in a central square, cheering as an American soldier climbed a colossal statue of the leader and wrapped the Stars and Stripes around his head (illus. 3). The cheering faltered, and the marine quickly followed orders to replace the U.S. flag with the Iraqi national emblem. Cheers welled up. The statue was toppled, and members of the crowd chased it, spat on it, shouted abuse and struck it repeatedly with their shoes, as a tank dragged it through the streets. "A typical Arab gesture of disrespect," commentators noted, gravely. Within weeks, President Bush, in Top Gun gear, alighted on an aircraft carrier and announced "mission accomplished."

The gesture that plants the flag of victory is a traditional one: hallowed by practice over time. More recent, but no less conventional, is the gesture that means to convey that the reluctant intervention force is returning an abused country to its

2. Kelly Guenther, second plane: United Airlines flight 175 nearing the Trade Center's South Tower. 2001, photograph. Kelly Guenther/ The New York Times.

3. Jerome Delay,
planting of flag
on Saddam statue,
Baghdad, April 8, 2003.
2003, photograph.
Source: AP/Wide World
Photos.

people. Both acts are readily recognizable within symbolic codes shared between
peoples all over the world. Replacing a previously prevailing visual icon with that
of the invading army says that the war is over, victory is complete, and the con-
queror is now in control. Replacing the image of a leader with a national flag is to
claim that the vanquished ruler was a dictator, that the rule of the people has been
established. It is a matter of historical record that both of these meanings proved
illusory in Iraq. It is also on the record that the placing of the flags, and the toppling of the statue, was an event stage-managed by the Renton Group, media
advisers to the U.S. government. They played a pivotal role in planning and "spinning" the American action in Iraq, from well before its commencement. In what
everyone involved knows to be, in significant part, a warring between symbolic
regimes, these performances were one of the U.S. government's weapons of mass
deception.[4]

When Saddam was finally captured, in Tikrit on December 13, 2003, visual
spin assumed command. Newspaper and television services were fed with
deflating and demeaning imagery of the crude "spider hole" in which he had been
hiding, in marked contrast to his palaces across the river. These were followed by
pictures of his meek submission while his unkempt hair and beard were searched
for lice, and his gaping mouth for ulcers, by a crew cut–sporting U.S. military doc-
tor. As the occupation of Iraq by the American-led "coalition of the willing" unrav-
eled during 2004, the randomness of aftermath surfaced in multiple ways, few
more effective than the photographs of American troops staging scenes of torture

and humiliation of Iraqi prisoners in the very cells at Abu Ghraib that had so notoriously sustained the previous regime.[5] Examples such as these point to the existence of a larger structure of symbolic exchange at work in the world today, one in which the competition between visual images—well known in most cultures when it appears in commodity advertising, entertainment, urban planning, religious ritual, and political campaigning—has spread to saturate most of the ways in which peoples, nations, religions, even civilizations relate to each other, not simply at the level of stereotype but at the deepest levels of psyche and society. The manifest presence of such a system means that we should not take it at its face value. Rather we should look through its surfaces and ask: what shape did this formation take in modernity, which shapes these days?

In many societies cultural exchange is routinely thought of as both identity defining and creatively enriching. Officials regularly promote it as beneficent in its tendency, communal in spirit, the best foundation on which to build shared values. In its greatest moments (and monuments)—it may even be redemptive. But to set out to obliterate the World Trade Center, the Pentagon, the White House, the Capitol, and a number of other structures in one action, using as one's weapons the targeted culture's ordinary means of communication and transport, is to turn a culture in on itself, and to throw into disarray what most citizens of the United States took to be the benign universalism of their routine values. Thus the astonished refrain: "Why do they hate us so much?" The attacks also made starkly clear to Americans something that is a fact of life in many embattled zones of the world: that culture, on all of its levels, across its entire reach, is not only part of the war zone, but it *is* a war zone in its own right. The operations of symbolic exchange become, therefore, a concern not only of specialists in cultural economics or the leisure and entertainment industries; understanding them becomes a pressing task for those involved in security, and of relevance to all who would grasp the world we are living in.

Iconomy

In a globalized world order, the iconomy has a pervasiveness and centrality greater even than the prominence it achieved as one of the distinctive formations of modernity during the later nineteenth then throughout the twentieth century (then, it was still specialized into forms such as advertising, commodity styling, mass media, propaganda, entertainment, and spectacle). Multinational corporations have, for decades, used it to disseminate their products, their logos, and their "style." Now, it also spreads their world picturing messages. They have rendered it flexible enough to service the niche marketing that is essential to their success. Although the look is local and casual, they continue to seek hegemonic control over current and future means of communication, forms of dissemination, and the regulatory frameworks. These include such ostensibly independent international organizations as the plethora of standard-setting agencies, as well as the most prominent: the World Bank, the International Monetary Fund, and the United Nations. Some companies have moved to control vast banks of repro-ducible images (Corbis, Getty), others to monopolize the records of sports events and entertainment (Fox), still others the flow of print and electronic information itself. The result is, as many have noted, a disproportionate Western, specifically American, cultural influence, raising fears of cultural sameness spreading every-where. Yet, in reality, hegemony is constantly fragmented, evaded, and resisted. Nation-states remain the major actors in world politics, whatever accommoda-tions they may make to globalizing forces. Local cultures have, in measurable ways, become more distinct, as they have been obliged to articulate cultural difference. And antiglobalization protest has been widespread, effective, and diverse in its manifestations.[6] The iconomy has been a field across which all of these forces have operated. It looks set to become increasingly important to their exchanges.

Certain relationships between the spectacular and the specular—above all those that had come, in late modernity, to drive both architecture and the iconomy—surfaced, fatally and fatefully, on September 11, 2001. This nexus has not been the focus of other accounts of that event and its outcomes. But I want to place these irruptions in a larger context, one that is formed by forces with much longer histo-ries. I will show that profound shifts in modernity's deepest formations had occurred (indeed, had been repressed for decades)—changes so great that they may signal the arrival not so much of a new era as of a different kind of experience of time, of being in the present, of remembering the past and of projecting possible futures. We might find ourselves naming this multivalent, inequitable, and untimely contemporaneousness by its own name: "contemporaneity."

The icons that were the subject of attack on September 11, 2001, happen to be—or used to be—buildings. A fatal convergence of architecture and terrorism occurred on that day. All buildings, built and unbuilt, suddenly attracted a shadow play of darting forces, chimera of the possibility that they could come under attack, could become target architecture. In the space they now occupy, a yawning absence became imaginable, prefiguring their disappearance. Yet this was nothing new, nor was it happenstance: from at least some of its beginnings, and certainly through-out its unfolding, architecture has had various degrees and kinds of violence built, as it were, into it. All building does violence to natural order and offers to its human occupants the bargain that they surrender to its constraints on them in exchange for its protection of them. All architecture depends on building for its foundations, its material existence, but it downgrades building to achieve its status as architec-ture. Further, all architecture has, in multiple ways, always anticipated its obsoles-cence, dilapidation, or replacement—in short, its own destruction.

The buildings under attack on September 11, 2001, were well entrenched within the iconomy. Having become key symbols within the later twentieth-century society of the spectacle, icons with the capacity to stand for crucial values, they were actively traded within it. Each of them iconized entire sectors of U.S. society, great formations of U.S. nationality. But they were more than symbols, and the attacks were not (as some commentators rushed to say) a spectacular confirmation of popular postmodern analyses of our time as one in which appearances had triumphed over reality. As I will show, the actual buildings were central, tangible embodiments of the complex functions that they housed, the most visible point of concentration of the complex array of powers associated with them. They were literal and figurative portals—gateways to, in turn, the U.S. economy, the U.S. military, and U.S. governance. The degree to which symbol and reality are embedded in each other is evident in the seismographic impact of the attacks on each of these sectors and in the differences of register between these impacts— differences that seem related to the degree of effectiveness of each attack. The special—indeed, spectacular, but also specular—role of architecture in the iconomy of later modernity (also called "late capitalism" and "postmodernity"), and in what I will show to be modernity's aftermath is the subject of this book.

In the essays that follow I will trace in detail the entry of certain architectural forms—the Guggenheim Museum Bilbao, the Sydney Opera House, the Getty Museum Los Angeles, the Jewish Museum Berlin, the World Trade Center New York, among a number of others—into the iconomy and seek to show how the imagery of them gained exchange value within the system. I will describe the circumstances of their commissioning, present the programs, note some of the technologies of their realization, and assess the degrees to which their forms met the demands of function. But my emphasis will be on their lives as icons. In each case, the prodigious (even prodigal) visual reproduction of their image achieved its intended goals of activating desire and consumption. But they also, we now know, provoked unexpectedly intense urges toward their destruction. I will treat them as instances within a system the driving energy of which is an interplay between stereotype and particularity that has tended, over time, to spread spectacle everywhere. Spectacle values are preeminent in Western societies, they seem more and more to drive their economies, and they impact on most other economies and societies across the globe. The skyscraper form is itself a measure of the rising importance of these values throughout the modern period (along with those of maximizing the bottom line). During the boom of the 1990s in parts of Asia, the skyscraper was stretched into the tower form, mostly by Western architects giving their local clients what they seemed to want: a slice of the dream of unfettered modernization. At the same time, distinct but closely related values are to be found in the creative vocabulary of the most advanced architecture being produced today, notably in the cultural and educational buildings—especially the museums—of architects as famed as Frank Gehry, Richard Meier, and Daniel Libeskind.

From a longer perspective, however, spectacular edifices are the latest manifestation of the marriage between concentrations of power and ostentatious architecture that has been so often consummated in the past. Now, as at many times before, they have been unavoidably enlisted into a war zone. They have become targets. Will the architecture of power and the imagery of spectacle survive 9.11.01? Now that certain kinds of buildings seem predestined for destruction, rather than time-traced ruination, can important architecture continue to seduce

journeying, can it still act as a destination for desire? How will the symbolic purposes of architecture be met in the future? Will architectural symbols maintain
their currency in the iconomy? Above all, the question is this: how might architecture fulfill its social contract at a time when societies are splintering, contracts
go routinely unfilled, and architecture itself has become spectacularized, a hot,
even fashionable topic, yet divided against itself, subservient to design and—
according to many critics—in a creative cul-de-sac?

Answering these kinds of questions depends on recognizing the character of
their time of asking, that is, on understanding the nature of the present and how
it stands in relation to the past. Much of the commentary on the 9.11.01 attacks in
the months that followed them expressed alarm about their unprecedented
nature. An almost equal amount of the discussion worked, with calming gestures,
to show them to be just a particular manifestation of certain long-running tendencies. A kind of dialectic of rejection and accommodation, of assimilation and
preparation for response, occurred. It was frequently mired in misunderstanding,
ideological posturing, special pleading, and, as we might expect in a situation in
which all sides were waging both symbolic and actual war, was subject to much
deliberate misinformation. In the months, now years, that followed, other
"events" occurred, and new "big stories" drove the international media. But clarity has not returned. Rather, a sense of permanent low-level crisis, of waiting
on happenstance, prevails. In the interminable aftermath of the "victory" in
Afghanistan and Iraq, this situation is becoming entrenched. I believe that we
would best tackle these issues from within a broader understanding of our contemporary condition. It is one that the concepts of postmodernity and postmodernism fail to clarify, mainly because, as I will show, it is shaped more and more
by certain forces that are persistently other-than-modern as well as others that
have passed beyond postmodernity. I characterize the current condition by the
term "contemporaneity."

What Is Contemporaneity?

In the ancient world, "modern" meant "of the current moment," the "now," that
which was "of today"—in another word "contemporary." In the modern world,
however, "modern" has become the core of a set of terms that narrate the century-
long—to some two centuries-long—formation of modernity, including its
definitive artistic currents, "modernist" art, architecture, and design. The "modern"
has, in short, become historical. In ordinary language—in English, and in some
but not all other European languages—it has surrendered currency to the term
"contemporary" and its cognates. But "contemporary" has always meant more
than just "now," more than what "modern" used to mean. The term calibrates a
number of distinct but related ways of being "of," or "with," or "in" time. The *Oxford
English Dictionary* gives four. The strong sense of "belonging to the same time, age,
or period" (1.a.), the coincidental "having existed or lived from the same date,
equal in age, coeval" (2), and the adventitious "occurring at the same moment of

time, or during the same period; occupying the same definite period; contemporaneous, simultaneous" (3). In each of these meanings there is a distinctive sense
of presentness, of being in the present, of beings who are (that are) present to
each other, and to the time they happen to be in. Of course, these kinds of relationships have occurred at all times in the historical past, do so now, and will do
so in the future. The second and third meanings make this clear, whereas the first
points to the phenomenon of two or more people, events, ideas, or things,
"belonging" to the same historical time. Yet, even here, while the connectedness
is stronger, while the phenomena may have some sense of being joined by their
contemporaneousness, they may equally well do so, as it were, separately, standing alongside yet apart from each other, existing in simple simultaneity. It is the
fourth definition of "contemporary," mentioned above, that brings persons,
things, ideas, and time together (with, in, of) irrevocably: "Modern; of or characteristic of the present period; *esp*. up-to-date, ultra-modern; *spec*. designating art
of a markedly *avant-garde* quality, or furniture, building, decoration, etc., having
modern characteristics."[7] In this definition, the two words have finally exchanged
their core meaning: the contemporary has become the new modern. We are, on
this logic, out of the Modern Age, or Era, and into that of the Contemporary.

But to leap to such a conclusion misses an essential quality of contemporaneousness: its immediacy, its presentness, its instanteity, its prioritizing of the
moment over the time, the instant over the epoch. If we were to generalize this
quality (of course, against its grain), we would see that contemporaneity consists
precisely in disjunctures of perception, mismatching ways of seeing the same
world, in the coexistence of asynchronous temporalities, in the jostling contingency of various multiplicities, all thrown together in ways that highlight the
inequalities within and among them. This is the world as it is now. It is no longer
"our time," because "our" cannot stretch to encompass its contrariness. Nor is it
a "time," because if the modern was inclined above all to define itself as a period,
in contemporaneity periodization is impossible.[8]

There is no longer any overarching totality that accumulates and accounts for
these proliferating differences. The particular is now general and perhaps forever
shall be. Certainly "master narratives" persist and continue to promise everything from continuing modernizing progress to the return of spiritual leaders.
Certainly their commanding, beguiling powers build followings in larger and
larger numbers. But they do so in ways that divide each bloc more and more from
the others. In the hearts of their spiritual leaders, there is a dawning sense that
universalism is impossible in human affairs, that not even their fundamentalism
is applicable to all humankind, that the others will, mostly, remain Other.
Differences that are as profound as this do not lie side by side, peacefully, nor do
they sit up separately in some static array awaiting our inspection. They are
actively implicated in each other, all over the place, all the time, just as every one
of us lives in them, always. Their interaction is a major work of the world, of
the world on us and us on the world. We are, all of us, thoroughly embedded inside
these processes. While many of them have become habitual, even comfortable

conventions, others are, to many, matters of survival. Too many of them are violently bent on the erasure of the other. Some, however, seek reconciliation within a framework of respect for difference. All of these elements were present in the "event-architecture" of 9.11.01. They continue to shape its aftermath.

Destination and Destiny

Early in 2001 I began an essay on the concept of "destination architecture," basing my thoughts around the cross-cultural interplay between Uluru and the Sydney Opera House, as a way of thinking about how powerful visual symbols, specifically architectural structures, become iconotypes in the social and political communications between groups within a culture, especially in the transactions between racism and reconciliation in Australia.[9] It was of interest that some of the key elements in this societal discourse were architectural—as is Uluru in the special sense that the Anangu people (a Pitjantjatjara group) understand it to have significant roles in their originary narratives, to have been created by Originary Beings in acts of purposive place making, and to be what we would understand to be a designed setting, or a set of settings. The World Trade Center had appeared in my thinking largely as a contrast case, a negative instance of building of low architectural value and little significance as a destination. Like almost everyone else I had come to the view expressed most pointedly by architecture critic Ada Louise Huxtable, that WTC architect Minoru Yamasaki had "succeeded in making some of the biggest buildings in the world ordinary and inconsequential."[10]

Yet my first experience of these buildings could not have been more different. One day in early 1973, after a lively argument with Robert Smithson about a number of matters to do with conceptualism and environmental art, I took off determined to try to see Central Park located in the city in a less Romantic fashion than his. As it happened, we had been drinking downtown, near the WTC, one tower of which was complete, and where I thought I might get such a view. Had I been in midtown, I would have gone up the Empire State Building. Distractedly, I entered the nearest elevator and pressed the button for the top floor. The shattering noise of tarpaulin flapping on all sides of the cabin was disconcerting but I thought I had entered a service elevator by mistake, and the numbers flashing on the control panel were fascinating. When the doors finally opened I was launched out onto an unfinished floor, with planks in crazy pattern, the crossbeams of lower floors showing below, building detritus everywhere, a fierce, whining wind cutting in, the open sky above and, beyond blurring perimeters, the city stretching out through a dizzying haze to an unmarked, infinite distance. I retreated in terror back to the elevator and down to the safety of the street.

Thirty years later, I had arrived, I felt, at a point where I was able to think about distance, and across distances, in a calmer frame of mind. The idea of architecture as destination had provoked a number of questions. What does it mean for an architecture to be not only functional, occasional, and symbolic (after all, these are well-known purposes) but also stereotypical? How does some architecture operate as both actual destination and desired symbol to such an extent that it becomes, in the individual imaginations of millions and in the social imaginaries of some, perhaps many, nationalities, a cipher for certain, if not universals, then generalities of global significance? Within international advertising, for example, an image of the Sydney Opera House will instantly conjure "Sydney" for most consumers, while Uluru evokes "Aboriginal Australia."

These were the kinds of question on which I was working when I came to the United States on September 10, 2001. Since then, the political situation has changed in multiple ways—sufficient, perhaps, to have precipitated an epochal shift. The 9.11.01 attacks themselves, the continuing war in Afghanistan and Iraq, the impossible attrition in Israel and Palestine—these are just some of the situations reshaping all of our lives. Responding to such changes while in the midst of them risks misjudgment, bad taste, and the appearance of opportunism. It is unusual—especially for an academic historian—to be working to grasp a situation that, along with its associated field of fact and opinion, changes every day. Sometimes, indeed, change occurs more drastically, each hour. Its overall direction is clear to few of those involved in it, however certain they may sound. Yet to fail to respond, if one believes one has something to contribute, would be cowardly. To wait for an ideal time would, I fear, be to wait in vain.

Which begs the question: why respond at all? Why not leave it to those with the competencies and the capacity to do so? To which I answer: it is the leadership of world affairs—in the White House as well as in the Al Qaeda hiding places— that has gotten us into this situation; we cannot trust them to get us out of it. It follows that everybody has something to contribute towards the large ethical effort that is needed lest the world retreat further down the path towards all-out self-destruction. To me, understanding the other, and understanding oneself in relation to the other, is the first step towards two core responses: to oppose, however one might and by whatever means, acts of terror such as the 9.11.01 attacks and the manifold others unleashed by states on their own citizens and upon others, while at the same time, somehow, eventually, and without condoning or repeating them, to forgive them. All this, in turn, is preliminary to the main task: to strive to reconstitute the world such that the causes of such actions are removed, so that the world goes forward in a spirit of reconciliation to realize the productivities of irreconcilability.

This complex ethical imperative poses a broad challenge to our interpretative disciplines, to—in this case, the history and criticism of art, architecture, and film, and to visual culture and media studies, whatever names we give them. A number of questions of method face those of us who would do visual cultural studies differently. What are the specifically significantly visual elements of those encounters and exchanges—both the important and the ordinary ones—that occur within cultures, and among them? This, in turn, sets me a concrete task in this book. It is to respond to the question: how are the visual elements at once distinguishable from and implicated in all the other relevant factors—psychological, social, political, economic, historical—at work within and around such cultural encounters as

9.11.01? What, in short, is the cultural architecture of this type of event? How do such phenomena continue to function as event sites, as image events? What can such an analysis tell us about what might happen next, about whether there will be a future? These questions bring together the two main emphases in this book: the iconomy and its various architectures—actual, virtual, and metaphorical.

The art form most discussed in these essays is architecture. This is so not because the targets on 9.11.01 were buildings, but because the conjunction of architecture and symbolism had become, during the 1990s, indicative of both the flashiest surfaces and the deepest currents of contemporaneity. Architecture had become, of all the arts, the most socially prominent, the best looking, a hot story in the media—in a word, the buzz. Anthony Vidler has defined the pleasures and traps of architecture's taking on the role of "media star" in this way:

> Over the past decade it has been used, and entirely properly, as a way to revive interest in public institutions all over the world, from the Getty to Bilbao, from the Tate in London to MoMA in New York; for the first time, architecture is receiving equal billing to its contents. In the process it has achieved star value, and it is as such a star that architecture has been called upon to address, if not redress, all the intensely imbricated problems left by the attacks of September 11. It is as a star that architecture has once again entered public consciousness— architecture as advertisement, architecture as lobbyist, architecture as witness, memorial, guide to the future and sponsor of the public will; in all these roles and more architecture is being seen as a palliative, if not a solution.[11]

Yet being a media star means playing, to some extent, by the rules of the dominant news and entertainment media. Peter Eisenman and Cynthia Davidson warn against one of these, the tendency to reduce "architecture's ideological content to a matter of style."[12] Other media crudities include a proclivity to reduce issues to personalities and to reduce complex questions to cliché. How contemporary architecture has negotiated this situation is discussed in the essays that follow. Their main theme, however, is how contemporary architecture became a "palliative" in the ways Vidler so perceptively lists, and how it needs to change in order to contribute towards a "solution."

Before and After Aftermath

Chapters 1 through 5 deal with the emergence of certain works of architecture into the iconomy. I will show that ideas of destination and pilgrimage inform much of the spectacularizing architecture of the later twentieth century, making them consummate cultural commodities. The triumph of the culture industry itself is celebrated in the work of Frank Gehry, Richard Meier recycles architecture's past, both modernist and ancient, while Santiago Calatrava naturalizes its romance with engineering. How much hubris attends these projects? Do they risk the obliteration of forgetfulness by succumbing so thoroughly to currency, immediacy, the fashion effect? Does this urge not exceed modernism's interdiction against excess, its attempts to transcend time by rejecting history, its dream of achieving a new kind of eternality through the realization of pure space? Does it not reduce these high ideals to a kind of outrageous miscegenation? I will explore how the architects involved—each of whom began as modernists—negotiated these risks.

I will show, too, that these projects had their historical precedents. The beginnings of what became Late Modern spectacle architecture appeared on the harbor front of a conservative, dependent, peripheral economy, in the shape of a building that symbolized Sydney's potential to transform itself into a global city. But it too was shadowed by a brilliant specter. The Sydney Opera House's other is Uluru, an ancient formation sacred to Aboriginal people and now much desired as a tourist destination. Despite their profoundly different origins and histories, these two vastly distinct forms are united by having been birthed during battle and by persisting in the hope of reconciliation. In contrast, the World Trade Center stamped itself on the "forest of symbols" that constitutes the iconography of Manhattan, becoming a prime example of the hubris of late modernism and globalizing capital. It provoked many specters, within Manhattan and without. In a further contrast, the deadly hand of the Holocaust—mother of all moments of irreconcilability—is absorbed into the design program of Daniel Libeskind's Jewish Museum, Berlin, and transformed into specific hope. An interrogatory architecture becomes explicit here. Between them, these buildings exemplify the major ways in which Late Modern architecture attempted to fulfill its social contracts in the conditions of spectacularity that framed the later twentieth century. Yet they contain, as well, many prefigurations of the catastrophe to come.

In the remainder of the book I explore the sense of aftermath that, I submit, pervades the architecture of contemporaneity. In chapter 6 I show that the implosion of the towers provoked an extraordinary range of responses: I concentrate on those that led to a rethinking of the nature of architecture itself, of how it has stood to humans, how it might stand. The obliterative drives of both the attacks and the clearing of Ground Zero seemed to expose what we might call—metaphorically of course—the unconscious of architecture. A domain that appears strangely misshapen, that moves in odd deformations, and is peopled by many, mostly traumatic chimeras, yet is laced with threads of hope. In chapter 7 I turn to the immediate aftermath of 9.11.01 itself: the overt evidence of its direct impact on architects, engineers, artists, and critics, and the changed relationships between architectural monuments and memorials that have appeared in the actual and symbolic realms of Ground Zero. The intense debate as to options for building on that site that occurred throughout 2002 contained many rehearsals for the future of architecture. After many months in which it seemed that the blunt instruments of money power would stunt all signs of human imagination at Ground Zero, model solutions by many of the best architects in the world went on display for public comment in Lower Manhattan. Some of them showed signs of learning from 9.11.01, especially the design by Berlin-based architect Daniel Libeskind that was eventually chosen as the basis for going forward. Whether the actual rebuilding will retain this hard-won knowledge remains to be seen. Indeed, during 2003 and 2004, the blowtorch of money and power was applied to Libeskind's vision, crystallizing it into opacity. Its eventual shape remains to be revealed. Nevertheless, for a time at least, the shattered spectacle—mark of an iconomy fissured—entered mainstream architectural practice in the United States, forcing it to catch up with the challenges facing much of the rest of the world. To catch up with contemporaneity.

In a climate of actual and impending war, of insidious misinformation and sudden violence—in a word, of permanent aftermath—keeping a broad, critical perspective is crucial. I prefer "9.11.01" as the name for what is really at stake here. The year of occurrence will remain, I believe, of more significance than its anniversary. After all, on September 11, 1973, Chilean president Salvador Allende was killed, ushering in the dictatorship of General Pinochet that only recently came to its ambiguous end. On March 11, 2004, the Spanish people were subject to what seems to have been another Al Qaeda atrocity: the bombings at Atocha station in Madrid. And on July 7, 2005, four young men detonated explosives that they believed would inscribe a fiery cross over the face of London: they imagined the city through one of its chief icons, the schematic map of the Underground, and perhaps knew that the reporting of their actions would also feature that icon, this time with their defacement of it. While I believe that 9.11.01 was, for a number of quite concrete reasons, an important event—particularly within the polity of the United States and that of the Middle East—it was not the epochal, millennial, apocalyptic Event That Changed The Entire World Forever. There were larger and stronger trajectories at work, of which it was a manifestation. The forces of globalization, deglobalization, and antiglobalization, for starters. Even more fundamental is the centuries-long pitched battle between state terrorism of the kind pursued by Russia and the U.S. in various spheres, by China, Indonesia, and countless others against their own peoples, by the European states in Africa, and by Israel in the Middle East versus the special-interest terrorism of dissident groups and sects, of which Al Qaeda is only one of the most recent. With regard to the environment, while warring to gain control of finite resources such as oil has a long and continuing history, efforts to negotiate a sustainable world economy based on renewable resources are more recent. They are, slowly, gaining ground. Another emergent dichotomy is that between the move by the European states towards tackling "world problems" through national cooperation with international agencies compared with the U.S. preference to quickly "solve" these problems by leading gerry-built, temporary alliances—usually with Britain as partner number one—or by going it alone, as it did, effectively, in Iraq. Yet gaps between the intentions of governments and those of their peoples remain open, and potent. Half a million citizens gathered in Washington in February 2003 in what both organizers and officials agreed was the largest antiwar protest since Vietnam days. Others met in protest throughout the U.S. and in capitals around the world—not least, I am proud to say, in Sydney and Melbourne—a total of fifteen million in all.

On a more general level, the evident worldwide and accelerating diversification of Islam, despite the widespread misperception of it as a monolithic religious movement, and despite the reductive insistence of Islamist fundamentalists on their version of its ancient essence, seems to be an inevitable tendency. On the other hand, Osama bin Laden remained a specter to the West, out of reach, releasing occasional, and always pointed, tapes in response to major shifts in U.S. policy in the Middle East. With an awkward yet implacable relentlessness, the U.S. intelligence and military machine has captured one Al Qaeda leader after another, chasing its $50 million prize. Yet the image of bin Laden continued its proliferation throughout the world, becoming so ubiquitous that, on the front cover of its May 26, 2003, issue, *Time* magazine visualized the nightmare haunting the West: under the header "Why the war on terror will never end" it showed serried ranks of men stretching back into infinity all holding the same bin Laden mask before their own faces. The emergence of new iconicity in the Middle East—at once contemporary and ancient—is figured here as both a fact and a fear.

The 9.11.01 attacks brought down two prominent buildings, archetypal of Late Modern architecture. Gloating over Western capitalism's recent triumph suddenly ceased, and the spread of unalloyed globalism abruptly ran up against unfathomable frontiers. The fundament of architecture, its ethical exemplarity, was shaken into instability. And its capacity to provide winning attractor images—so central to its prominence in the iconomy—turned, instantly, into a gigantic liability. Where does this leave architecture? Abandoned, in the ruins of its rapacity? Numb, in the aftermath of its ravishment? Is it, now, a time to retreat to what it is that architecture can uniquely do, to return to roots—in the housing of peoples, in the construction of community? If the roots are still there ... But architecture, to be architecture, has no choice but to do this. It is, of necessity, locked into a kind of untimely contemporaneity, a simultaneous being in time and out of time with itself and its time. Kenneth Frampton sees this as "the predicament of architecture at the turn of the century":

> Architecture is by definition anachronistic or, let us say, pertains to its own time and to moments that project beyond it, both forwards and backwards. It is this dichotomous condition that constitutes both its weakness and its strength: weak partly because of its marginality in relation to the dominance of maximizing technology, and strong because at its best it not only testifies to its time against the commodified never-ending newness of fashion but also because it is the built guarantor of the public realm as a symbolic and political arena. Such will surely remain its prerogative providing it is not seduced by either the populism of kitsch or the experimentation of empty avant-gardism.[13]

When I began, in the mid-1990s, to think about how architecture appeared within the iconomy, I did so as part of a larger project devoted to tracing the spread of spectacle values within the contemporary visual arts and the emergence of more critical responses to the conditions of contemporaneity. The multiplicity of cultures, their seemingly incommensurable differences *from* each other and the profound differences *within* them, the widespread yet everywhere different sense of being *in* but not *of* one's time, and the inequities searing through all aspects of life, thought, and the imagination—these are just the most evident qualities of contemporaneity. I began writing with as much awareness of them as I could muster, yet with hope, because I lived, like most of us, within and between them. I had generated some critical material, made my share of compromises, and have had direct experience of reconciliation. 9.11.01, taken as an event whose ramifications are still resonant, shook my world picture, as it did that of many others. Writing this text has been part of my attempt to work through the consequences for contemporary architecture of 9.11.01, and through some of its implications for world picturing as such. The major impact that I trace is the awakening of architecture to the true nature of its being in contemporaneity. As the early chapters show, this was also a reawakening. One that, I hope, will happen again.

Many passages in my account are marked with the traces of trying to make sense of events as they happened and information as it was coming in. At times, I risked falling victim to Collingwood's warning against surrendering the exacting demands of seeing "history" to the instant seductions of generating "newspapers."[14] This may be inevitable in any writing that is done from within the belly of the beast and is true to the experience of aftermath, of being both inside and pushed out of imperfect chronicle. I hope, however, that analysis surfaced often enough to make critical sense of the struggle within and against chronology. In my despair about our perhaps perpetual entrapment in the leftovers of aftermath, I discovered a lost sense of that concept, one that first came into use in English in the late fifteenth century: a crop of grass growing after mowing or harvest, one that allows a lattermath. I hope that this hope shows through.

PART 1 DISPACING TIME

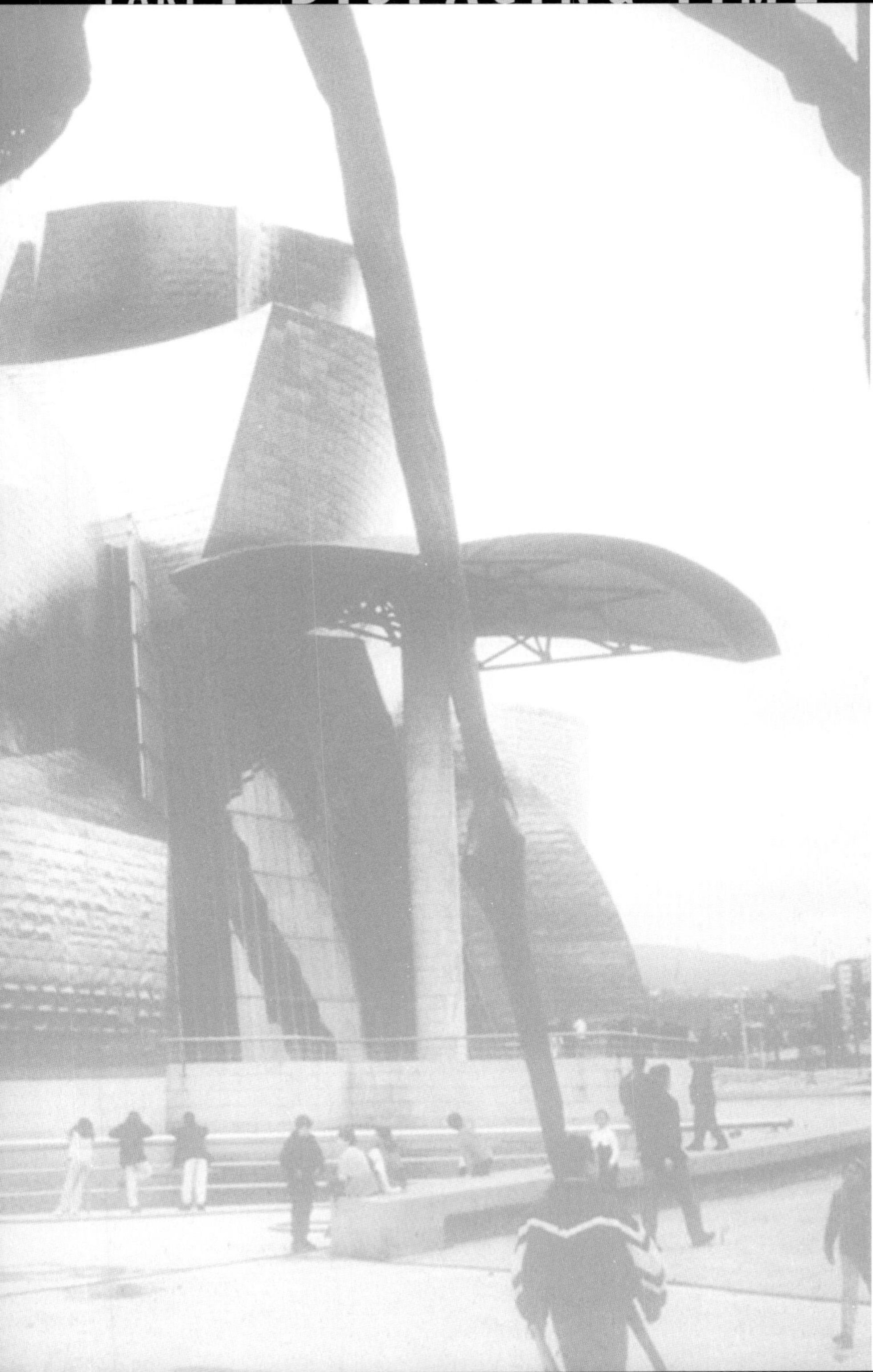

The Bilbao Affect: *Culture as Industry*

The Museum Boom

In the precincts of contemporary culture—especially in strikingly designed, architect-branded museums of art—promise is everywhere implied: uplifting experience for visitors, economic benefits for the site and its surrounds, piles of cultural capital for all concerned, and the latest, most exciting design and cutting-edge technology. At the end of the twentieth century, religious shrines, business centers, and public memorials took the back seat in the architecture of attractions. Culture was the business to be in. The multibillion dollar museum building boom was a worldwide phenomenon. Cities everywhere, especially those backwatered by globalization, made big bets on "culture-led recovery." The economic success story of the Guggenheim Bilbao was cited again and again. We will explore it in detail in a moment. Museums became the latest loci of the general spectacularization of culture, of the necessity to turn everything (history, governments, cities, new movies, heritage sites, natural phenomena, high public and private office, even media itself) into an "attraction," that is, an event site.

A worldwide survey of art museum building, conducted during 2001, although far from complete, listed eighty-four active projects. Thirty were either extensions or substantive renovations, while fifty-four were entirely new museums or new buildings near existing ones. Most were slated to emphasize contemporary art. In eight cases, the cost was not provided or was yet to be finalized. For the rest, over $4.704 billion had been committed, at an average of $62 million per project, mostly as estimates that everyone involved knew would be exceeded. In nearly all cases, funds were being raised from private sources, then matched or supplemented by public subvention—a reversal (typical of the "privatize everything" 1980s) of the century-long pattern of such cultural enterprises being regarded as primarily an obligation of governments. Projects range from the $3.5 million Palais de Tokyo—a renovation of part of the Museum of Modern Art of the City of Paris by architects Anne Lacaon and Jean-Philippe Vassal that turned the space into a mix of a rave venue and contemporary art center (its opening show was a mini-Biennale about biennials)—to the top of the range, the $650 million expansion of the Museum of Modern Art, New York, by Yoshio Taniguchi & Associates (the total cost of which blew out to $858 million). Nothing, however, came close to matching the $1.2 billion spent on the Getty Center, completed in 1997.[1]

In the midst of all this champagne popping and ribbon cutting, MoMA director Glenn D. Lowry issued a warning: "I think museums have emerged as the primary civic buildings of our time, and that has led to competition among institutions to create the most spectacular buildings imaginable. The assumption is that the building will galvanize a community and ignite the kind of financial support that would lead to a better collection, a bigger endowment. But that's a tenuous proposition. In many cases, the buildings have far outstripped the importance of the collections."[2] Some argue that the boom time of museum building and refurbishment will soon come to an end, that the focus of attraction will shift elsewhere. Despite the runaway success of recycling the ruins of the Industrial Revolution—most visibly, Herzog and de Mueron's transformation of the Bankside Power House into the Tate Modern, London—museums are, in strict economic rationalist terms, "red-ink businesses" that require constant subsidy through grants or other contributed income to survive. Their current role as attractors is accounted for by setting their costs off against income earned not by them but around them, in local real estate and business growth, in increased tax returns to councils, in accelerated tourist volume.[3] One year after opening, the Tate had to go back to the city for more funding to appoint sufficient staff to cope with the unanticipated crowds (5.25 million). But the doubts of double-entry bookkeepers were swept aside. During the 1990s, it seemed that a new museum opened, somewhere in the world, each month, while more and more were commissioned. The real excitement was currency itself: *contemporary* art, architecture, design, and fashion. The most spectacular buildings at the century's end—like the most successful art—were those in which these various visual arts worked hand in glove, mixed promiscuously, merged seamlessly or fought to a finely calibrated standoff. Each became the content, then the container, of the other. Only to reappear, transformed, as the content of a transformed container. Is it any wonder that millions were drawn to the outrageous forms and the secret interiors of contemporary architecture's magic boxes?

Bilbao Enters the Iconomy

What is the significance of the fact that, at the turn of the twenty-first century, *the* iconic building was a museum of contemporary art, and not an exposition tower, skyscraper offices, airport terminal, or opera house, still less a private building, shopping mall, or factory? That it was a museum is no surprise: the destructiveness that was the underside of the construction booms of the twentieth century—the "collateral damage" of wars, neglect, and environmental degradation—left vast tracts of the earth's surface, from central cities to national parks, vulnerable. Reconceiving them as museums or heritage sites became, in many situations, the best option for their maintenance. Nor should it be a surprise that the iconic millennial structure is a museum of *contemporary art*. After all, the cultural and entertainment industries were, along with those of service, tourism, and new technology, the growth sectors in most economies—certainly the advanced ones—in the later decades of the century. Through blockbuster exhibitions especially, the visual arts drew in millions of new adherents, not only by presenting the "masterpieces" of any art from anywhere but also through incessant retailing of the story of Modern Art, from the Impressionists to Picasso and Matisse, as wave after wave of once shocking but now quite palatable innovation. The logic of fashion was applied whole cloth to the history of modern art. Itself already woven into fashionability, Contemporary Art was next in line: up-to-date art, ready to see. Indeed, in the Guggenheim Bilbao, as in its successor, Disney Hall in Los Angeles, Gehry emerges as the chief designer of the contemporary culture industry's equivalent of the single-story sheds, such as those engineered by Albert Kahn, that were so pivotal, in the first half of the century, to mass production modernity.[4]

With art worlds everywhere going into this state of transition towards globalization, the Guggenheim Museum was uniquely positioned to lead the charge (or, in most cases, slide) toward new forms and settings. The raking ramps at the core of Frank Lloyd Wright's design for the Guggenheim in New York meant that the internal spaces of that museum were set, literally, at oblique angles to most modernist art, especially that coming into prominence at the time of its erection during the 1950s. Artists such as Willem de Kooning and Franz Kline were vociferous opponents. Ceilings and floor veered down (or up), the bays were too wide for standard-sized paintings and sculptures and too confining for murals or public sculptures.[5] It started to make sense as an exhibiting space only in the 1970s, when artists began to work against the orthodoxies of the rectangular, white cube museum, and then either took any form of museum as a challenge or took the cube for granted. Direct experience of this situation fed into Guggenheim director Thomas Krens's questioning of the typical late modernist art museum. Encyclopedic historical surveys culminating in the present made sense when people came to the great metropolitan power centers for their most important transactions, including the desire to see and learn something about the certifiably best art. By the later twentieth century, however, a much greater range and diversity of peoples were traveling everywhere, relatively readily. They had informed and specific interests or were open to general ideas about art from any time and place. Krens was clearer than most about what these audiences wanted: "a theme park with four attractions: good architecture, a good permanent collection, prime and secondary temporary exhibitions, and amenities such as shops and restaurants."[6] It will be to the lasting discredit of the 1990s that these minimal requirements were taken by most museum builders as maximal criteria for a successful operation.

Like many others, Krens was also aware that the leading edge of the strongest contemporary art—late Minimal sculpture and painting, installation art, and conceptualism—was becoming both too big in size, too quirky in concept, and often too hostile in attitude to be readily encompassed in the Modern Art museum, even one as large, quirky, and hostile as the Guggenheim, New York. He also saw that, in most countries, public funding for culture was in decline, as governments retreated from responsibility for creating national patrimony (as distinct from preserving its past monuments). As Philip Jodidio put it, "New models of resource sharing would have to be created, and the development of any and all opportunities would have to be explored."[7] Bland, programmatic amorality is the typical language of globalization. In the event, Krens applied a tried-and-true model from a rawer era: the franchise. The "brand" qualities of the Guggenheim at Bilbao reflect this purpose.

Attractor Architecture

Of the many museums constructed during the 1990s, none has attracted, and held, the extraordinary attention accorded the Guggenheim Museum, Bilbao, conceived by Los Angeles–based architect Frank Gehry in 1991 and completed in 1997 (illus. 4). Has any other building entered the iconomy so seamlessly or become an iconotype so swiftly? This occurred at a time when the competition between brands, logos, destinations, celebrities, etc. to attract attention within an economy of the image had reached such a degree of intensity that it had become apparently saturated (although it is in fact insatiable). The museum's notoriety was partly the result of a great effort at publicity by all concerned. But it was also a function of certain qualities inherent in the building itself. Many of these reside precisely in the building's success as a complex of brilliant solutions to the program set for it. Yet there is more—indeed, the Guggenheim Bilbao is a genuine case of more being more. Kurt W. Forster nails this exactly: "Before it can be considered anything else, the Guggenheim Bilbao must be reckoned overweight, overdone, and overwhelming."[8] More than merely exemplifying specularity, it seemed to embody this quality in a singular way, and to be a degree more spectacular than any other current or comparable instance. How could this be? What does it mean for excess to be excessive not only in and of itself but to be more than itself?

Spectacle, these days, is capital accumulated to the point where it exists, primarily, as a seemingly seamless image flow. This is Guy Debord's fundamental insight, the core idea of his *Society of the Spectacle*.[9] In more stable civilizations an icon is a fixed image with a clear resemblance to what it represents, an assigned meaning that changes little over time. In the classic case of Byzantine religious imagery, or that of the Greek Orthodox Church, the image is habitually taken to embody the spirit of the god or saint it depicts. In late capital, however, an *iconotype* is an image that, usually through repetition, stands out in the image flow, halts the incessant circulation, and draws fixity to itself. It maintains its iconicity, not by being different from the nature of other images in the flow, but by being more excessively like them. While singular in its configuration, it is also, and primarily, a precipitator of mobility—its own reproducibility, and that of its viewers. This type of iconic image is a generator of a variety of values: it may pleasure the eye, arouse the flesh, or stimulate the mind. With the current, globalized state of capital, however, it does these things in order to produce economic value. Not, however, simply as money—although that is a major measure of how its capacity

4. Frank Gehry,
Guggenheim Museum,
Bilbao, 1997,
approach including
Jeff Koons, *Puppy*.
1997. Photograph by
David Heald. Source:
Guggenheim Museum.

stands to other economic agents—but as itself: an iconotype spins off countless images of itself, innumerable repetitions, along with multitudes of associated images and values. Further, it promotes the iconomy itself, the entire economy of which it is part. Indeed, the Guggenheim Museum at Bilbao became, by the end of the 1990s, *the* symbol of the ascension of the symbolic to the level of major economic lever and driver in a world order that was everywhere understood as animated by spectacularity.

The merger of money and museum is right there, in front of you, and replicated in every photograph (illus. 5). The museum was expensive: its much-publicized $100 million price tag was exceeded. It looks expensive: compared to the structural solidity of much nineteenth-century building in Europe, and to the functionally articulate structures of the twentieth century, it is evidently extravagant in

its cladding in marble and titanium, its jumble of nonfunctional spaces, and above all in its deliberate refusal to repeat a shape or use a standard element thus necessitating the custom building of every piece of it. Those who celebrate Gehry's use of digital programs as overcoming "the age-old distinction between the hand that designs and the instruments that execute" are deluding themselves and their readers: these unique, eccentric shapes have still to be fabricated by workers and machines and fitted by them.[10] Excesses are out there, proudly shown off. Surplus value as a value in itself is visible, piled up right here, in spades. The broad message is that art—regarded by most as the ultimate domain of luxury beyond necessity—is now among us, that this is a world that will unexpectedly throw up such astonishing phenomena.

These abrupt appearances will, however, be authored. At Bilbao, Gehry is the artist, creator of this work, his unique originality is signaled as the most valuable of the treasures housed in this building—indeed, it is not hidden behind its walls, it is the overt fabric, the main message. Right behind this value is that of Guggenheim Museums Inc.: the second message is that this corporation is committed to the value of artistic originality and to showcasing it in its museums around the world. Signature architecture becomes brand architecture, available for franchise wherever the settings seem right.

Container Becomes Content

Like its contemporary, the Getty Museum, Los Angeles, the Guggenheim Bilbao is a much-fabled art museum that lacks a "must see" or "destination" artwork within its collections. Nor do the collections in either place add up to a "wonders of the world" treasure house, such as the British Museum, the Louvre, or the Metropolitan Museum. It is, obviously, the building itself that is the main attraction. Apart from its photogenic qualities, Gehry's design has compelled attention as a consummate architectural achievement, as worth visiting because it is emblematic of contemporary architecture—indeed, some claim, of architecture itself. It is the ultimate instance in the recent book *Icons of Architecture, The Twentieth Century*.[11] Nor is architectural historian Victoria Newhouse alone in her celebration of it as the culmination of a two-century-long search for a new form of museum, and as the most perfect realization of the type to date: "Gehry's invention of new forms, and his plurality of forms, provide a model for future museum architecture that must now be taken into account."[12] The novelty of Gehry's forms remains, despite the uncanny prefiguration of Herman Finsterlin's architectural fantasies of the 1920s and, as we shall see, the precedent of designs by Jørn Utzon, Eero Saarinen, and others during the 1950s and 1960s.

The key to the architectural program at Bilbao is Krens's statement: "The idea was that the museum had to be able to accommodate the biggest and heaviest of any existing contemporary sculpture on the one hand, and a Picasso drawing on the other hand."[13] To be, that is, a museum of both Contemporary Art and Modern Art. Its plan turns on a collision between three kinds of gallery space: the "white cube" typical of the modernist museum, the vast, open, industrial settings favored by Minimalist sculptors (especially in the now famous "fish" gallery, built around the long, curved steel corridors of Richard Serra's *Snake*) and the flexible, modifiable spaces that attract contemporary installation artists. As well, Gehry was given a free hand to make the atrium his own sculpture. This he did, with overwhelming success. And he applied an erudite and subtle sculptural imagination to the conception of the exterior forms, with the scarcely concealed ambition of

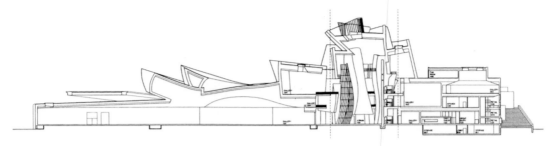

creating not only the most compelling contemporary sculpture in existence, but also the biggest.[14]

These were some of the ways in which Gehry's Guggenheim at Bilbao became an iconotype of both art and architecture. The Guggenheim Museum, New York, and the Sydney Opera House were models pointed to, often, during the planning, by both Krens and the Basque government. Krens was characteristically broad-brush and to the point: "You can think of the Sydney Opera House, the Centre Pompidou—a building that was capable of carrying the identity of a place. I told them to think in terms of Chartres Cathedral. You want a building that would have roughly the same impact at the end of the 20th century that Chartres Cathedral had in the 14th or 15th century."[15] Gehry's indebtedness to Jørn Utzon, designer of the Sydney Opera House, is everywhere evident, not least in a comparison of their longitudinal sections (illus. 6 and 10). As architecture, all three buildings seem like space ships that have arrived from the future, instantly throwing everything around them into anachronism. They invite pilgrimage for their innovative qualities as architecture. Another name for this is attractor architecture, the architecture of destination, architecture as entertainment, as a park in which the theme is Contemporary Architecture become Art. No surprise, then, that in a number of recently published textbooks, the Bilbao Museum is the cipher for Contemporary Art as such, as a category in the history of art.[16]

Instant iconicity. It is in the buildup from the specific to the global that we see the processes of spectacularization at work in their contemporary mode. In this case, the category of human desire, experience, and willingness to act that is being activated is contemporary art. It is being transformed from a set of artistic practices into the broader institution of Contemporary Art. While an actual building in a specific place is necessary to this, it is not sufficient (not any more). The building must itself embody spectacularity, and it must be locked into a system of promotion that is itself dedicatedly spectacularizing. Building and system will prioritize above all those qualities that are most readily, and effectively, projective, visualizable, imageable. This is the primary basis on which it invites those who see it to be consumers of it.

As an iconotype, the Guggenheim Bilbao is now better known than the image of the home base in New York, and at least as well known as that of the Opera House in Sydney. It signifies its city, registering it as an extremely desirable destination. Five million visitors came in the first four years, at a rate of one hundred thousand per month. Economically, it has succeeded beyond the most hopeful projections: by 2000, the city had generated $500 million in new economic activity and collected nearly $100 million in taxes. Even during 2002—*annum horribilis* for the tourism industry—it attracted 851,628 visitors and generated over U.S.$162 million in revenue to the local economy. Using the strictest economic rationalist accounting, and allowing nothing for spin-offs or cultural value, the project amortized its initial construction costs within its first three years. Sensing this straightaway, cities all over the world in similar situations to Bilbao—there are many, and their number is increasing—began scrambling to build cultural attractions: for a time, in the years around 2000, Guggenheim Inc. looked able to write its own ticket anywhere.

The Bilbao museum has spawned countless images of itself, in a bewildering variety of forms. It has become an iconotype: that is, an image that, while it represents a specific artifact, structure, person, or place, is also powerful enough to stand for a category of human experience. The degree to which it will attract addition and elaboration remains to be seen. But its summative power is well attested (just how this has been achieved is being set out in this text). It is recognized worldwide as having joined a select (and actually rather small) list of landmarks that stretches back, in the Mediterranean, to the Pyramids and the Seven Wonders of the Ancient World, in the East, to Angkor Wat, Great Wall of China, etc., etc. It is the world's latest symbol of what it is to be a landmark, and palpable evidence that such economically and culturally desirable things may be built, now, if the right architect and the right client can be brought together. In such a context, it is difficult to imagine that anyone could come to Bilbao with an innocent eye. It exists, already, for anybody with any contact with the iconomy, as an iconotype.

Gehry Builds McGuggenheim

Images in the iconomy, however striking, effective, propelling they may be as images, gain much of their potency from their embeddedness in other, nonimaged systems of power. Those who chose the targets for 9.11.01 knew this, and the impacts of their obliteration of those "symbols of American economic, political and military power" have been all too obvious.[17] This violent negativity is the opposite of the set of intentions that all concerned brought to Bilbao, but it nonetheless contains some lessons. Not least, it reminds us to look at the arrangements under which Bilbao was built, and the distribution of responsibility for its perpetuation. Taking the building as the centerpiece of its $1.5 billion regional cultural plan, the Basque administration paid out $100 million, initially, for architect's fees and costs, and accepted continuing responsibility for financing the operation, including any revenue shortfalls. The Guggenheim Foundation, for a $20 million fee, undertook to loan parts of its collections, to offshore its expertise (fewer curators, conservators, etc. than usual), and to help guide the formation of a local collection. Krens insisted that the Basque government advance $50 million to build a collection, and that it consist of the work of a few artists—Spanish and international—whose development as artists is to be shown, and followed, in depth, including the purchase of "masterpieces" by these artists. If the opening exhibitions are any indication, selection of European artists will fall, mostly, within the parameters of the New York Guggenheim's predilection for high modernism and official Contemporary Art. This includes the priorities among Spanish artists, Eduardo Chillida and Antoni Tapies. These are major artists by any measure, but are well represented elsewhere in Spain (in Madrid and Barcelona, respectively). Despite a publicist's avowal that the Guggenheim Foundation aimed to collect "the full range of 20th-century visual culture," it would be naïve to expect such scope from an institution at the forefront of defining the role of Contemporary Art within globalization.[18] Regional artists have had only a minor presence at the Guggenheim Bilbao to date, and there is little prospect of it increasing in the future. No surprise, then, that the local nickname for it is "McGuggenheim." Nor that it has been characterized as "the brightest monument to American cultural hegemony in Europe."[19]

What, then, is the fit between the Guggenheims' internationalism and local artistic cultures? Bilbao's Museo de Bellas Artes, since 1914 the leading visual arts institution in the region, was obliged to retreat from collecting and showing recent and contemporary art while the Guggenheim project was being negotiated and built. A much-bruited plan to create a center for the reinvention of Basque culture was buried. To meet local concern about being colonized by McGuggenheim, other spaces dedicated to the contemporary were established in the city. In time, they turned into precursors to the Guggenheim. Even now, at the revitalized Museo de Bellas Artes, the display of mainly regional artists, mixed with some national and international stars, declines significantly in interest as it approaches the present. Does this impression reflect a local phenomenon, or is it an impact of the presence of the Guggenheim in Bilbao? This kind of issue is key to art within contemporaneity.

Euskadi ta Askatasuna (Freedom to the Basques) has, for decades, been offering one kind of answer to the question of Basque difference. Their plan for a large explosion at the inauguration of the museum was foiled at the last minute, at the cost of the life of a security guard. Less violently, but with persistence, the Basque administration (like most other regions of Spain) has been seeking a high degree of autonomy from the central government based in Madrid. Their deal with the Guggenheim—in which they cede artistic control to the New York–based organization—is an internationalist gamble, a choice against taking a subservient place within the national agenda. (Ironically, the Basque stance was echoed—albeit in reverse—by the central government during early 2003, when it was one of the very few European states to join the "coalition of the willing" in support of the U.S. invasion of Iraq.) A related set of issues arose when Krens and the Basque administration claimed the right to exhibit Picasso's *Guernica* during the opening months. It was, after all, the bombing of the neighboring Basque town by fascist forces (the Luftwaffe in support of the Franco-led rebels) that

inspired Picasso to produce his masterpiece for the 1937 Paris International
Exposition. Gehry was asked to design a gallery with this painting and associated
works in mind, in the hope that it might come to Bilbao. Fearful of losing the centerpiece of its exhibits at the Renia Sofia Museum of Modern Art in Madrid, and
mindful of *Guernica*'s power as a symbol of a united, post-Franco Spain, the
national government refused.[20]

Much of the battle over the valiance of the Guggenheim is fought around
metaphors of shipping. A typical publicity puff reads: "Moored to the banks of
the River Nervión, the great titanium flag-ship designed by Frank O. Gehry is not
only one of the symbols of Bilbao's regeneration, but also one of the American
architect's most spectacular works."[21] In contrast, Los Angeles–based artist Allan
Sekula sees the museum as "a Los Angeles export product, a leviathan of
Californian postmodernity beached on the derelict riverfront of the economically-
depressed maritime-industrial capital of the Basques."[22] Using his knowledge of
the aerospace industry Sekula deflates those who would praise Gehry's techno-
smarts in cladding the main parts of the museum with titanium sheets, pointing
out that in the industry titanium is used mainly internally and is alloyed with
steel for elements that must be both lightweight and resistant to high tempera-
tures. Titanium is, he notes, "a *metametal*, a metal that refers to high technology
metallurgy, especially in luxury consumer products like German-designed, high-
end, auto-focus cameras."[23] His most acute perceptions arise from his approaching the building as a photographer, treating it as one of the sites within the
worldwide, densely interconnected history of maritime industry. *Bilbao* (diptych)
is part of his 1998-99 project *Titanic's Wake* (illus. 7). It shows the museum from
the hills above, framing it with both ruins and workers' apartments. In contrast,
tourist snaps promoting the Bixia (Biscay) region as a natural wonderland interspersed with astonishing quasi-natural phenomena such as the museum frame
our view of it through some carefully chosen trees (of which there are very few on
that hillside).

Reacting against the sucked-in ease of the fish and ship metaphors, Sekula
comments: "The Guggenheim Museum is more accurately likened to a giant light
modulator. It introduces a new level of specular reflectivity to a rather drab
cityscape previously restricted to tertiary hues. In effect, what it imports to Bilbao
is an aesthetically controlled, prismatically concentrated version of the high specularity characteristic of the Los Angeles cityscape, the random and ubiquitous
presence of shiny surfaces, glass and metal ricocheting sunlight in an inhuman,
migraine-inducing glare."[24] This explains the museum's two main looks: its oddity in its setting, and its perfect naturalness as an iconic image in global circulation. David van Zanten is even more caustic about such a conjunction. To him, the
unique forms of the museum, in their industrial wasteland setting, seem a nightmarish figure, a ghoulish growth, a luminous excrescence that symbolizes our collective guilt at betraying the manufacturing base of the great modern cities and
our fears that alien creatures will alight upon their shriveled, nearly stilled hearts
and spawn exotic yet specular figments of spectacle architecture.[25] Sekula

concludes his account by making an even broader point: "For this benign and restrained version of American aerospace enlightenment, for this lighthouse and control tower far upriver from the sea, the Basques, who pay all the bills for the museum, are entitled to feel grateful. Thus far, there are no Guggenheims planned for Hanoi, Belgrade, Baghdad, or Basra."[26] In his last comment, Sekula connects the potential impact of the Guggenheim franchise to that of cities recipient of sustained U.S. bombing in recent years. He could not have predicted the uncanny yet entirely unintentional prefiguration of the imploding World Trade Center that might, after 9.11.01, be read into Gehry's designs, developed between 1998 and 2001, for a new Guggenheim Museum on the East River, New York.[27]

The Perpetual Novelty of Ruination

Those who conceived the Guggenheim Museum at Bilbao set out to create a (perhaps *the*) cathedral of Contemporary Art. A capacious ambition, to be sure, yet one that has, I hope, been exceeded by the multiple elements of this analysis. A cathedral of the contemporary is what the museum aspires to be. Let me demonstrate its inevitable shortfall by taking this metaphor a little more literally. With 24,000 square meters of floor space, 10,600 square meters of exhibition areas on three levels, and an atrium that reaches up to over 50 meters (180 feet), the museum certainly has the dimensions of some of the great cathedrals of Europe and elsewhere. That such buildings were a conscious part of the program we know from comments by Krens cited earlier. Unlike most of them, it was built in just a few years, has one well-known architect as its author, its clients are all over the record

7. Allan Sekula,
"Bilbao (diptych)."
C-photographs, from
the series "Titanic's
Wake." 1998-99.
Courtesy the artist and
Christopher Grimes
Gallery, Santa Monica.

with their intentions, and everything about its conception and execution is exhaustively documented. Nor does it seem, on the face of it, to have other qualities that many find attractive in cathedrals, especially those built during the heyday of Christianity, the medieval period. A structure that stands as an expression of shared belief, esoteric interpretation, and collective will. A construction that accretes, over long periods of time, and is marked by changes of mind and style, additions and diversions. Yet a moment's reflection will show that these qualities are implicit at Bilbao. Gehry is the architect who became famous for incorporating the look of ongoing, permanent construction into his completed buildings (famously, the 1978 makeover of a standard Santa Monica house as his own). Something of this quality persists at Bilbao, above all in the restless movement of the skin, its changes of character as a building as one moves around it, its effervescence as one moves through it. But this occurs, of course, at a scale that begs comparison with the Baroque at its height, not the flats of suburban Los Angeles. As well, looking at both drawings and plan, it is evident that Gehry was haunted by the cross format of the cathedral form. His struggle with it is evident, as is his ultimate resolution: a double-crossing of two cathedral formats, that cross themselves through the atrium space. A parallel struggle occurs with regard to the various elevations. These settle into the most cathedral-like profile when viewed from the riverside. Yet the most profound parallel occurs at the level of the metaphysical. The building is, spiritually (even theologically), an instance of what it houses: the practice of contemporary art, conceived of as the legacy of early modernist painting and Minimal sculpture in postmodern art, design, architecture, and fashion—a lifestyle transformed into a generalized Contemporary Art. Contemporary style is, as many have said (believing, wrongly, that secularism has triumphed everywhere), a new religion. At Bilbao, Gehry, the Guggenheim, and the Basque administration set out to build its cathedral. Doubtless they hoped to compete with the largest tourist attraction in their region: the famous pilgrimage site at Santiago de Compostella.

No matter what its scale, attractor architecture gives the sense of a lot happening within and around it. Since the mid nineteenth century the model for architecture with buzz has been the trade fair, annual show, or, on the largest scale, the international exposition. One hundred years later, notably at Disneyland, the theme park–entertainment industry tie-in advanced the form. Soon after, shopping malls took it into the neighborhood of everyone with a car. Taking a cue from these changes, the architecture of attractions either has one standout image feature or is itself, as a whole, very jazzy to look at. Thus Gehry's preference for curving or repeat forms, incomplete shapes, off-axis ground plans—all fast-slow motivators for the eye. All of this helps when photographs are circulated, locally and around the world. They stand out amidst the plethora of signs, symbols, and brands that are thrown at everyone every day. It helps the buildings to become logos. One of the constraints of attractor architecture is to arrive at a unique yet readily readable form, a standout shape for the building as a whole (in Gehry's case) or for some spectacular part of it (the entrance lobby of Santiago Calatrava's Museum of Art in Milwaukee becomes the whole thing). So that those driving by, walking past, and, especially, those seeing images of it in the media can recognize it immediately.

This currency of distinctive appearance—this brand, or logo, quality—is, now, a design requirement of all such buildings. It has become a key constituent of destination architecture. Gehry seems to have arrived at a way of designing such buildings not by choosing a stunning gestalt and fitting his functions and aesthetics into it but by generating all of these elements, as it were, from the inside out. It is precisely a Gehry-type imagery of super-hip, eccentric funkiness achieved through the highest tech, a mechano-organic look of quasi-accidental disorder that works, now, as the most recognizable sign for "Here Is a Concentration of High Cultural Value." The Walt Disney Concert Hall, Los Angeles, conceived in its nascent form just before the Bilbao commission came in, is a consummate expression of this conjunction.[28] In the case of the Guggenheim Museums around the world, in its recent phase of energetic global franchising, Guggenheim = Gehry = Great Art = Gold. Architecture and iconomy are most perfectly met.

In Time, Out of Time

What of the Guggenheim Bilbao's continuing contemporaneity into the twenty-first century? Forster, a sympathetic interpreter of Gehry's work despite his characterization of Bilbao as "overweight, overdone, and overwhelming" cited earlier, went on to amplify his astonishment in these terms: "It is an immovable pile in the city and a sinuous creature draping its body along a narrow ledge above the river. As a luminous cave on the inside, and a metallic mountain from without, the museum appears to be both a perfect fit and a perfect stranger on its site."[29]

Indeed, its strangeness, its being at its core out of place, may lie in the fact that its perfection as architecture is achieved according to terms that are neither local nor glocal but global.

Of course, Gehry's building has qualities that remain specific, that resist translation into the relentless commodification at the core of the image economy these days. One such might be his achievement of a built form that looks as if it might behave, metaphorically, like a living being. The main ground-floor gallery, which generates the longest volume paralleling the river, was nicknamed "the fish" by the architect, who has attributed at least part of his attraction to the titanium cladding that he uses so often to its similarity to fish scales. The housing of the skylights above this gallery suggests a snake curled in on itself, while something like budding flower petals open out as the atrium roof. Yet, as noted above, neither of these is intrusive to the degree that they become a fixed association. The gap opened out here, between literalism and the hint of metaphor, is extremely interesting. From inside the atrium, one has the deepest sense of embodied architecture. Inside the atrium, one feels as if one were within a breathing eye. The atrium is a space that makes structural the idea of the body as an all-seeing eye. An organ that, above all, breathes when it sees. This eye is not the coolly rational, analytic window on the world much derided in recent theory as "Cartesian perspectivalism" and caricatured as the model of the modernist spectator of art.[30] It is much closer to the opposite of this, the "body without organs" speculatively advanced as the anti-Oedipal force in history by the philosophers Gilles Deleuze and Felix Guattari.[31] The museum in this sense might be sensed as a building without organs, built from the membranes that constitute an eye that sees itself, inside and out. In these instances, metaphor is genuinely effective, because it remains fleeting, a suggestion that does not literally metamorphose, that resists settling into literalism. [Unlike this sentence.] Yet it thematizes a spectator who is so attuned with the art that he or she has come to see that the experience is ultimately a passive one. Mobile, yes. Engaged, that too. But not brought to a state of knowledge. This happens when you step sideways, and work against the grain.

In the long term, it may be these shell-like qualities of the building, its stage-set-like aspects, that will prove uncannily predictive. Imagine an economic downturn such that the Basque administration's dream of providing a cultural reference point for the Atlantic fails. More generally, the novelty of visitation dies off if you can see the shows elsewhere. Why go back once you have seen the building once? The people of the region will return with visitors, and to see the imported shows, but will not come more often unless a major effort is made to integrate the institution within local art and culture. Will this occur when the adjacent improvements—the park designed by Cesar Pelli, for example—are complete? Or is the city—having invested in the economic productivity of the fashion edge of culture—now committed to an unending series of specular projects, to be always chasing contemporaneity? The museum becomes, then, adventitious, an event that occurs by chance. The real Bilbao effect is that the museum is itself a set of effects, that is to say, an affect. An emperor who is only clothes? Already the glistening titanium is eroding, its silver surfaces marked with streaks of black. Natural wear (the pressing of natural forces) and historical persistence (the polluted remnants of maritime industry) are taking their toll. First and second nature will not go away just because third nature has emerged on the planet. It may well be—it is a fair prediction from history—that art will develop in ways that will, in time, make even this museum look old-fashioned. But the museum itself is designed against this expectation. It aspires to be Contemporary Art of such advanced quality that no conceivable contemporary art can match it.

More generally, it announces itself as always-already present, as the ultimate expression of consumption joyfully realized, an experience of instant gratification that will last forever. This is the essence of the specular. It hopes that it will be always in time, be forever contemporary. In this, the museum internalizes the logic of contemporaneity. But this is, of course, a gamble. What if the Bilbao effect was, in futurity, another example of forgetting the lesson of Beauvais?[32] Imagine these grandiloquent spaces empty of all but the few remaining employees, nervously guarding the structure against vandalism and the homeless. Despite every intention that attended its birth, the Guggenheim Bilbao may become the preeminent symbol of the last waltz of the modernity regime, of the sunny skies during the early hours of 9.11.01. The entire Bilbao project is one that took this kind of risk. "Risk" is the buzzword of capitalism in the early twenty-first century.[33] Two decades ago, it was a challenge that few could resist. Now, it produces nothing but anxiety.

Flashback: *Uluru and the Sydney Opera House*

The Guggenheim Museum at Bilbao may have been the twentieth century's most spectacular instance of architecture as icon, but it was not the first. Many early modern buildings quickly became pilgrimage points for architects, and a number became iconic of modern architecture for people in their region, while a few came to symbolize larger-scale social tendencies and historical forces. Among buildings that have served all of these purposes, the Sydney Opera House is of outstanding interest and remains so today. It is no accident that Guggenheim director Thomas Krens, bent on selling his concept for Bilbao, reached instinctively for the great cathedrals of Europe and the Sydney Opera House to serve as compelling precedents. The opera house was a turning point in the entry of architecture into the growing global iconomy. Even before completion, it symbolized Sydney, then Australia, to the world. But it did not do so alone; it was shadowed in the iconomy by the imagery of a natural formation of striking exceptionality, one that for the Aboriginal people concerned with it is also a created form. Uluru, previously known as Ayers Rock, is a sandstone monolith that rises out of the Central Australian desert. The Sydney Opera House is located on Bennelong Point, one of the two arms of Circular Quay, the most important port in Sydney Harbour (illus. 8). Uluru began taking its current shape over 330 million years ago, while the opera house was opened on October 20, 1973, seventeen years after a worldwide competition for its design was announced. If we look at both of them together, we will see something of the prehistory of structures such as the Guggenheim at Bilbao, and, more importantly, we might grasp something of how architecture registers aftermath, that of both recent and ancient duration.

Picturing of both Uluru and the Sydney Opera House is ubiquitous in the imaging of Australia. How did they achieve this status? How do they fit within the larger circuitry of potent visual imagery in symbolic exchange, within this economy of icons, this *iconomy*? What is at stake in the huge value investment that both Uluru and the opera house represent? How might they face each other in the future? Indeed, how do the cultural orders that they represent stand to each other in Australia now, at a moment when reconciliation remains unachieved, when the nation stands undefined, uncertain, and directionless? Pursuit of such down-under questions brings us quickly to the larger, indeed worldwide, setting: one in which spectacularization wars against the details that seek to defeat it, globalization trembles always on the edge of collapse into localism, and individual

8. Jørn Utzon, Sydney
Opera House,
1956–73. 2002.
Photograph by Rick
Stephens. Rick
Stephens/Fairfaxphotos.

freedom becomes more and more exposed to powerful conformities, deep funda-mentalisms, and the fear of otherness. These recurrent conflicts, and their temporary resolutions, are the weave and warp of our contemporary condition. In this chapter I will examine how difference may be marked, and reconciliation respectfully sought, by a society that is striving to face up to itself.

To Symbolize the City: The Sydney Opera House

In his 1979 book *Great Planning Disasters*, English architect Peter Hall opens his chapter devoted to the Sydney Opera House (hereafter SOH) with these words:

> Sydney's new Opera House belongs to a select group of buildings that become immediate popular symbols. It *is* Sydney, just as Big Ben is London, the Arc de Triomphe is Paris and the Empire State Building is New York City. It could thus be argued that it put the city on some sort of mental map of great world cities. Furthermore, though residents and visitors disagree on its aesthetic merits, no one would question that it is a highly memorable building. Whether seen by day in the crisp Sydney sunlight, or at night against the reflected lights in the great harbour, its unusual sailing-ship form is a sight that no one forgets. And, despite the disagreement, there are many, both professional architects and lay critics, who think it is one of the twentieth century's great buildings.[1]

Hall does not pursue the root causes of this set of insights, as his primary con-cern is to show that the SOH was "without doubt a planning disaster. It sets some kind of world record . . . for time delay in completion and for cost escalation."[2] To grasp why the SOH did become an iconotype, and why the aura of disaster quickly disappeared from it, we need to take a longer view.

Bennelong Point, the site of the SOH, has a substantive Aboriginal history, now all but obliterated except in the name of the location and on the official website of the opera house. Aboriginal people have been present in what is now the Sydney area for at least twenty thousand years, with a relatively settled fishing, hunting, and gathering economy during the three thousand years preceding Settlement by the British in 1788. Engravings, stencils, and rock drawings in the open and inside shelters are common in the area. The language group on the southern side of the harbor, where the point it located, is the Eora. The local clan—now extinct through extermination and attrition—was the Cadigal. Bennelong Point was known variously as Tu-bow-gule and Jubgalee.[3]

British sovereignty was proclaimed at Sydney Cove, of which the point forms one arm, on January 6, 1788. A British penal colony and Pacific naval base were established by 1,500 navy personnel and convicts. Activity on the point subsequently reflected the growth of colony. It became, in turn, a cattle farm, a small artillery redoubt, the home of Bennelong (an Aboriginal man who served as a key mediator between his people and the invaders), an astronomical observatory, a salt works, a park, part of Government House gardens, Fort Macquarie, a sandstone quarry, wharves and storage, the main tram sheds, and, most recently, the SOH. The first known concert on Bennelong Point occurred during March 1791. Bennelong provided an evening of entertainment at his house for the governor and his party. Twenty-four men, women, and children danced to the accompaniment of beating sticks and clapping hands.[4]

Eugene Goossens, who became conductor of the Sydney Symphony Orchestra in 1947, most influentially mooted the idea of a concert and opera hall in Sydney. By 1954 he had convinced state premier John Joseph Cahill and in January 1956 the government announced an international competition for the design of a "National Opera House" to be erected on Bennelong Point. Requirements for the building were listed and a design brief was announced, with no cost limits imposed.[5] The site was the most prominent available in Sydney and was inevitably tied to that of the Sydney Harbour Bridge. Since 1932 the bridge had crossed the harbor from the arm of Sydney Cove opposite Bennelong Point. A scaled-up, Art Decoed version of the Tyne Bridge at Newcastle, England, it was a monument to the Machine Age that towered over a largely suburban settlement. The proposed music center had, therefore, the task of sharing the harbor with a massive edifice, one that already symbolized Sydney in the eyes of the rest of the world. Commissioners wanted a building that not only fulfilled its functions imaginatively, but also provided a silhouette to be experienced as striking from all sides, at distance and from above (that is, from the bridge and from the air).[6] Not least, it would have to compete with, and complement, what is perhaps the most spectacular natural setting for a city in the world. Sydney needed a symbol that would anchor the imagery of its competing attractions, tie them to a tangible entity, and thus draw tourists from everywhere.

These aspirations and challenges attracted 233 entries from all over the world. Judging occurred during January 1957. The judges included local architects, the City of London chief architect, and Eero Saarinen, then of Cranbrook, Michigan, and designer of a building that defined destination architecture at its time and place (and which may have been inspired by Utzon's initial drawings for the SOH), the TWA terminal at Kennedy Airport, New York. Of Utzon's winning design the judges commented: "The drawings are simple to the point of being diagrammatic. Nevertheless we have returned again and again to the study of these drawings, we are convinced that they present a concept of an Opera House which is capable of being one of the great buildings of the world. We consider this scheme to be the most original and creative submission."[7] Despite (and perhaps partly because of) its total lack of technical specification, Utzon's initial design provided an evidently aesthetic solution to what the commissioners saw as a primarily aesthetic problem. Sydney University professor Henry Ingham Ashworth spoke on behalf of the judges of the competition, justifying their choice of the proposal by Utzon. His is the normal language of destination architecture.

> All the assessors were of the opinion that it was particularly important to realize that any building placed upon the site would be seen from all around the harbor and in many cases from a high level. Thus the building must look well from almost any point of view . . . For this reason the assessors considered that the placing of a large massive boxlike building, however practical, upon this particular site would be wrong. It was felt that the building must have a unity, a sense of movement and should preferably build up towards the point thrusting out to the harbor. Thus the assessors considered that the first essential requirement should be a magnificent concept. The fact that any building must function was, of course, accepted as a *sine qua non*. Einstein once said that perfection of means and confusion of aim seems to be characteristic of our age. Our aim in this instance was to find a fine piece of imaginative architecture—the means comprise a secondary issue.[8]

Despite the office blocks that were beginning to rise in Sydney's central business district, the commissioners were not seeking a Lincoln Center type of option for the cultural domain they envisaged. They insisted on functionality but did not wish to see it prioritized, nor did they want it to dictate appearance in a modernist—or to be accurate to the time, Modern Movement—manner. Expressive monumentality was being invited back in, but not in classical garb, however up-to-date the materials. Instead, the forms had to be fresh; as untrammeled by both distant and recent history as the new country Australia still perceived itself to be.

The winning designer shared much of this spirit (illus. 9). Jørn Utzon was born in Copenhagen on April 9, 1918, trained at the Academy of Arts, Copenhagen, 1937 to 1942, after which he worked with Gunnar Asplund in Stockholm and Alvar Aalto and Arne Korsmo in Helsinki. In 1947-48 he traveled in Europe, North Africa, and the United States, visiting Mexico, where he viewed Mayan temples, in 1949. He established a private practice in Copenhagen in 1950. Utzon worked on the SOH project from 1956 until his resignation on February 28, 1966. His basic

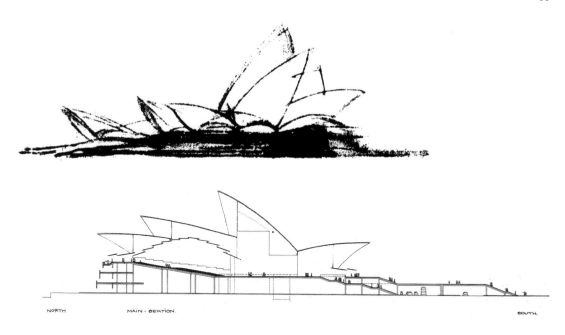

concept was to ground all the services for what became four halls in a huge podium, approached by wide steps, on top of which the halls themselves would rise freely in organic forms suggestive of bird flight and sailboats, with the effects of spiritual sonority and aesthetic uplift. "One could not design a building for such an exposed position without paying attention to the roof . . . in fact one must have a fifth facade which is just as important as the other facades . . . I have made a sculpture."[9] Frequently referring to the siting of Mayan temples, he constantly stressed the situation of arrival as a kind of procession, of the audiences being transported from the mundane and prepared for the transcendence of high culture by the architecture itself. "If you think of a Gothic church, you are closer to what I have been aiming at," Utzon said (illus. 10).[10]

The requirements of display in the setting were crucial to him, as to the commissioners: "Interplay is so important that together with the sun, the light and the clouds, it makes a living thing. In order to express this liveliness, these roofs are covered with glazed tiles. When the sun shines, it gives an effect which varies in all these curved areas."[11] Conceived to catch the eye, and to dwell in memory as a fantastic form, the opera house is perhaps the first bold step towards attractor architecture of the type that would come to dominate late capitalist modernity. In the relatively more innocent 1950s, however, the consumerist impulses that first took vibrant shape in the 1920s were just reemerging from two decades of depression and world war. In the opera house we see the embryo of buildings—such as the Guggenheim Museum in Bilbao and Disney Hall in Los Angeles—which had written into their program from the start that their primary purpose was to be an iconic image.

Engineering and fabricating the shells housing the halls became the greatest design challenge of the project, occupying most of those involved from mid-1957 to the end of 1965. In 1961, conceding that casting single forms on this scale was impossible, Utzon arrived at a solution for precasting sections of the four roofs by conceiving them as each cut out of the same sphere, the ribs following meridian curves on spheres of the same radius, "like pieces of an orange," Utzon explained. Of the fan-ribbed structure of the roof shells, he said: "If you take a palm leaf . . . that was exactly what inspired me." In Utzon's explanatory language, architectural form is conceived as emergent from the same, effortlessly natural self-replication that occurs in plant growth. Yet in her close reading of each step in the design process, Lucy Grace Ellem argues that Utzon was obliged to shift his values radically, from the organic expressivity embodied in his initial design to those of pragmatism and functionalism, resulting in a stiffened, geometrically defined edifice, a rational monument.[12] Nevertheless, the fact that solutions were found attracted to the SOH a degree of admiration for it as an astonishing technological feat, something it shares with other iconic monuments, such as the Eiffel Tower.

There were, however, substantial if not disastrous downsides. The protracted struggle to find engineering solutions to Utzon's early designs, among other factors, delayed its estimated time of opening by more than ten years (January 1963 to October 1973). Major cost overruns occurred: from an estimated $7.5 million to over $102 million. Clashes of personality and authority marked the project throughout, especially from 1964. Shortly after a change of government in 1965, Utzon resigned, and has not been back to Sydney despite many inducements. The staging of operas was switched from the larger to the smaller hall. The height of the former—conceived to house mechanisms bringing sets up from the podium level—became functionally redundant, in Utzon's words "an empty shell, a false thing."[13] The local architectural team of Hall, Todd and Littlemore completed the work, radically compromising the elaborate interiors under design by Utzon, including their erudite referencing of Islamic vaulted ceilings. Opinion on the success of these later works quickly divided, and remains so. Recent revelations as to the nature and quality of Utzon's design solutions to the interiors suggest that his forced resignation was not just a testimony to the shortsightedness of local politicians and architects; it was a tragedy for the development of modern architecture. It seems evident that he had developed a process of conceiving design solutions that was profoundly innovative, and that, in particular, he was evolving a set of unique solutions to the problems of relating interior acoustical ceilings and settings to the exterior vaults and shells.[14] In 2003, after years of pleas from a state Labor government sympathetic to architectural heritage, Utzon agreed to work with his son to restore as much as possible of the SOH interiors to his original conceptions.

In the 1960s and 1970s, however, the cost blowout of public monies taken from the taxpayers of New South Wales was met by the injections of funds from the Opera House Lottery. This lottery, created by the NSW government specifically for the purpose of financing the project, was the largest ever conducted by a government or private company in Australia. It was enormously attractive to many members of the public and, in itself, is one of the reasons that the SOH was regarded positively, as a repository of value (metaphorically, it was the money pot).[15] The lottery encouraged a highly specific, hip-pocket identification on the part of the Australian people with the image of the building. This is one strong reason why the SOH became an icon so rapidly. Each ticket was a token that enabled a small act of elaboration to occur. The lottery generated an aura of positive disposition that subsequent managers of the SOH have been at pains to perpetuate. Elaborating a summative monument through incessant invitation and constant ceremonies of participation is not just a standard strategy of publicity; it is a precondition for iconicity. In 1999, during an exhibition of the work of French conceptualist Yves Klein at the Museum of Contemporary Art, itself located just across the Quay, the sails were lit so that they took on the hue of his distinctive works, international Klein blue. Subsequently, the building has been lit many times, in a variety of signifying colors. The SOH was a key site of the millennium celebrations at the end of 2000, during which its shell roofs became the background for a performance by suspended actors from Off the Wall, a local dance company.

We have begun to adduce some of the criteria for iconicity, but there are more. Certain buildings achieve destination value, while others fail to do so. The SOH was, on its site and in its time, a large building. Not as big as the Harbour Bridge, to be sure, but powerful in scale from a distance and designed as a sequence of approach spaces that move the visitor from casual, ordinary walking through a series of ascents towards the experience of awe beneath its upward-reaching, eventually overarching forms. In its distinctive profiles, it was a building utterly unlike anything else in Australia—indeed, in the world at the time of its conception. As many at the time joked in wry admiration, it stood out on Bennelong point like a "space ship from Mars," instantly throwing all building around it back into the nineteenth century. So exceptional were its shapes and its solutions that it recast what it was for human beings to build. In this sense, it participated in a deep and profound exceptionality, one that opened out the possibility that it would be forever exceptional. The condition of brand uniqueness was fulfilled (although this, of course, is a hostage to the future: a plethora of imitations is, at least in principle, imaginable for any new proposal—and may have seemed almost upon us during the early 1960s, when concrete expressionism appeared in many places around the world, not least Los Angeles and Latin America).

That the SOH was immediately, and radically, novel is self-evident: it was instantly spectacular, and remains so for all who see it for the first time (and for many who see it often). But the perpetual novelty of the SOH rests on a complex, paradoxical foundation—indeed, it is rooted in permanence. Utzon's design, especially his first conception and model, was a clustering of shells that suggested futurity (in their "space ship" connotations they are a typical mid-twentieth-century projection of the look of the twenty-first century), yet it burst forth from a platform of a heavy solidity that had the most ancient of connotations. Is such a doubling at the level of fundamental form a necessary condition of an image's survival as an icon? Is grounding in paradox the source of an icon's capacity to generate complexity as it persists in time, as well as its capacity to absorb what the future will pour into it, surround it with, throw against it in competition? Let us keep these questions in mind in the coming chapters.

Whatever the compromises that occurred between conception and realization, the SOH was clearly conceived by all concerned as a prime instance of destination architecture. It achieved this rare status very quickly and, for millions, it remains not only a familiar icon but also a signal that calls them to come visit. Peter Hall, in the American edition of his book, had the grace to acknowledge this: "The lessons for posterity are there to see. At least, the Opera House put Sydney on the world's mental map—and that, perhaps, was one of the original reasons for the political decision to start it in the first place."[16] So begins the rhetoric of consensus building, a first sign that the mix of decisiveness, doggedness, divisiveness, and apathy that characterized the actuality of getting the SOH built would fade, gradually, into the blur of historical forgetting and that the generalities of iconotypy would eventually take over.

If, that is, you ignore the specters.

Uluru: Black and White Dreamings

Acknowledged as the largest single freestanding rock formation in the world, Mount Uluru rises 345 meters above the ground (862.5 meters above sea level) and covers an area of 3.33 square kilometers (illus. 11). It has a circumference of 9.4 kilometers, a maximum width of 2.0 kilometers and a maximum length of 3.1 kilometers. Its striking red coloration is due to rusting of the iron within its main material, arkose, a coarse-grained sandstone rich in the mineral feldspar. Its flaky surface and distinctive shapes are a result of wind, water, and gravity erosion. It is an outcrop of the Petermann-Musgrave Ranges, close to the southern border of the Northern Territory. While not, to Western eyes, a built form, it is, as I will show, a pivotal node in a world "architecture" of tourism and in an Australian "architecture" of identity.

To the Anangu and other tribes from the Pitjantjatjara language group who have lived in the area for more than twenty thousand years, there is reality as well as metaphor involved. The rock is an accretion of living forms created by the Originary Beings, originators of every thing, person, and animal in this area and all relations between them, during what is often referred to as "the Dreamtime." Very early, ancestors of the current custodians emerged and took a variety of animal, conceptual, and material forms, specifically those of the *Kuniya* (python), *Liru* (poisonous snake), *Mala* (hare wallaby), and *Kurpany* (monster dog)—all of whom are present at specific places on or within the rock. The Anangu word "Uluru" refers to the springs and waterholes around the rock's base. Details as to the rock's mythos and history were given to the anthropologist C. W. Mountford during the 1950s. They were then summarized in English and rendered in a mode of classical storytelling that, typically for its time, borders on the infantile. Presumptions as to the imminent dying out of the Aboriginal peoples, or their

assimilation into Australian whiteness, pervade its tonality. I cite it because more recent, and more nuanced, accounts are unavailable.

11. Quentin Jones, Uluru, a long view. 2001, photograph. Quentin Jones/ Fairfaxphotos. Approved for use by Uluru-Kata Tjuta Board of Management.

The two kinds of Snake people, poisonous and nonpoisonous, lived together at a waterhole called Pugabuga. The more restive members of the Kunia tribe became dissatisfied with their surroundings and decided to migrate to a flat sand hill where there was a limitless supply of water. At the end of the Dreamtime the sand hill was changed into the rock known to Australians as Ayers Rock, but as Uluru to the Pitjandjara tribe.

When the sand hill was transformed into a rock, the Kunia people were also changed into stone and can be seen as boulders and features of the Rock. Coolamons, wooden dishes for carrying water, grass-seed and other commodities, knives, spears, and grinding stones were also changed. The caves where men, women and children took refuge could be descried in the irregularities of the rock face by the imaginative tribespeople of a later age. The beards of the old men, the tracks men made to fetch water from the Uluru waterhole, all can be traced on the face of Ayers Rock.

The Liru people, the venomous Snake men, struck off in a different direction, going towards Mount Olga and preying on the peace-loving people they met.

One of the Kunia women gave birth to a baby in a cave in the Rock—a cave that was later resorted to by Aboriginal women in labour in the belief that the spirit of that Carpet-snake woman would ensure an easy and painless delivery. No sooner had the baby of the Kunia clan been born than Bulari, for that was her name, saw a party of Liru warriors coming towards her. She called to the Carpet-snake men to come to her aid, first spitting disease and death at the warriors before taking refuge in a nearby gorge. Working themselves into a fury with shouts and war songs, the Liru men attacked the Kunias. Many on both sides were killed in the battle.

The signs of the conflict can be clearly traced on the Rock. The bodies of the dead men are there, and the open mouths of the warriors who shouted defiance at their enemies. A long fissure and a shorter one can be seen in the rock face. The cracks in the rock represent places where a young Kunia warrior slashed open the leg of the leader of the raiding party. The longer one was made when the knife was sharp, the shorter one as the tip of the knife broke off.

The narrative continues in this highly specific, and yet allegorical, way. It concludes by noting the fate of the poisonous-snake people:

> After the raid on Uluru, the Liru men linked up with a tribe of men of gigantic stature, the Pungalunga. The combined force then attempted to wipe out the mythical Kunduna Snakes in the Tomlinson Range. In attempting this foolish enterprise the Liru people were completely exterminated.[17]

These sacred matters are commemorated in Pitjantjatjara law, are the subject of song cycles and rock paintings, including those in the caves of Uluru, and are relived in ceremony, often held on, at, or near the rock. While, for most visitors, the rock is a spectacularly imposing natural formation, an occasion for incidental contact with Aborigines and a unique photo opportunity, for the local people it is also the time-frozen aftermath of an ancient battle between great forces of good and evil, a moving monument to the struggles of their ancestors, a living tapestry of spiritual instruction, and a haven for the living out of everyday existence. A more immediate, and contemporary, exemplar of the past's tangible, animate presence in the present is difficult to imagine.

Explorer Ernest Giles is the first white person on record as sighting the monolith. Not so long ago, this would have made him its "discoverer." The following year, William Christie Gosse, the first white person to climb the rock, named it after Sir Henry Ayers, then chief secretary and later premier of the colony of South Australia. It remained beyond European settlement and was of no more than passing interest to Europeans until around 1950, when it began to receive some publicity as a potential tourist destination, in widely read illustrated travel magazines such as *Walkabout*.[18] Alice Springs tourist operators responded until, in 1958, the site attracted 2,300 visitors, prompting the declaration of a national park encompassing Ayers Rock and Mount Olga, a nearby formation of even more complex beauty, now known by its local name of Kata Tjuta. Tourists could see not only this staggering natural wonder but glimpse the last of the world's nomads, Pitjantjatjara, billed as "Stone Age survivors." During this period, tourism spread from Sydney to the center of the continent: Uluru and the SOH became visible together.

In the best account of the rise of white interest in the rock, Tim Rowse argues that the intent of the prevailing official policy of assimilation in this area was to progressively clear it of "these untidy displays of the unassimilated," in order to encourage the emergence of an untrammeled nature park.[19] Pitjantjatjara peoples gathered in numbers at the Docker River settlement, some two hundred miles west, during the 1960s and 1970s, while government and private enterprise built the Yulara tourist village, opening in 1984 to 149,000 visitors. Land rights agitation led to the creation of independent outstations and claims to large tracts of the desert. In October 1985 the national government made the park Aboriginal land. Shortly thereafter, the Anangu people leased it back to the National Parks and Wildlife Service for management purposes under a power- and skill-sharing arrangement that also nets the Anangu 20 percent of the park entry fee as well as a $75,000 royalty each year.[20]

Meanwhile, nonindigenous interest in the rock increased exponentially. Uluru was accorded world heritage listing in 1987 for its "natural value." In 1994 the Uluru-Kata Tjuta National Park was listed for its cultural value in recognition of the continuing relationship between the Aboriginal peoples and the natural environment. In December 1993 the Australian government had enacted recognition of Aboriginal and Torres Strait Islander priority over traditional lands. The Uluru model had, it seemed, heralded a nationwide reconciliation between black and white cultures. In March 1996, however, a new conservative government took office. It quickly dismantled a range of structures supportive of Aboriginal people, including the land rights legislation. In this new climate, Uluru resumed its more abstract, figurative status.

For conservative historian Geoffrey Blainey, in his lecture marking the centenary of Australia's Federation, changing attitudes to Uluru have been an indicator of how "the sense of belonging has grown for the typical Australian." It is a marker of how "the average Australian's concern for the environment has been transformed," a linchpin of a nationalistic "feeling for affinity with a whole continent." Reflecting on the swing from the "little appeal" of the 1950s, Blainey remarked "today The Rock is one of the best-known Australian symbols, possibly ranking with the Sydney Opera House."[21]

Carrying the weight of stereotype can be hard to bear. On January 6, 2001, Uluru was again on the front page of local and national newspapers. The *Sydney Morning Herald* ran a story headed "Don't snap the Rock: custodians say Uluru is turning into Disneyland." The coordinator of the Uluru-Kata Tjuta National Park—the Aboriginal-run agency responsible for the care and management of the rock and its surrounds—was quoted as saying, "A lot of people do want to use Uluru as a backdrop, without regard for the values of the place, and particularly the cultural values. There is concern about that. What we are trying to do is protect its integrity. If you turn it into Disneyland you just lose that." During the year 2000, for example, the board of management received three hundred requests for commercial film visits and photography shoots. It deals with four hundred thousand visitors per year, most of whom stay at designated accommodations. Like other iconotypes, Uluru is both reproduced as a stereotype and individuated each time a visitor takes its photograph. Photo opportunities are a highlight of most, if not all, tourist visits.[22] The plethora of photographic images of the rock is generated not only by the professional spectacularizers, those with a hard economic interest in its continuing pulling power, but by all of us seeking an anchor for our experience of the place itself. The visual image of the southwestern face of the rock, as seen from the prescribed viewpoint of "sunset strip," becomes a record, a souvenir, and a memory token. The northeastern face is excluded, as are a number of specific sites at the base. In this way, custodians seek a compromise between the invaders' thirst for recorded spectacle and their own need to preserve sacred sites and sights. By controlling the interplay between summative singularity and specific particularity, they seek to elicit a "respectful representation" from visitors. In exchange, they offer guided tours to those seeking a somewhat more detailed introduction to their history of the site.[23]

The front page story on the January 6-7, 2001, *Weekend Australian* was headed "Plague on dark side of the Rock." The color image shows a concerned, gray-haired Aboriginal father and mother bent over their teenage son, who weakly tries to brush away flies as he sits collapsed in a wheelchair. In the background, Uluru dominates the skyline. "Tourists don't get to see the tragic toll that petrol sniffing takes in the shadow of Uluru," the subhead told us. Indigenous people in Australia have lived for two centuries in the aftermath of the occupation of the continent and its islands by foreigners, people from over the seas who have come to stay for what they see as the future. Other signs of stress include the dying out of tribes and peoples, the extinction of their languages, the fading of custom, and the evaporation of memory. Yet there are signs of survival, even growth, as well. Of the 18.3 million inhabitants of Australia in 2001, approximately 400,000 were Indigenous peoples: 265,000 Aborigines and 135,000 Torres Strait Islanders. Low percentages, but steadily increasing numbers over the past thirty years. This is paralleled in the extraordinary growth in production, quality, and popularity of indigenous art. And by an enlarged—indeed, central—political presence.

These kinds of disjunction remind us that the stereotype is achieved only and always at the cost of the particular. A more consensual vision of the conjunction of cultures at Uluru has spawned a diverse architecture, ranging from backpacker accommodation to a five-star hotel. Phillip Cox and Associates has produced award-winning designs for accommodation at Yulara, which is featured prominently in advertising directed at attracting tourists to the area. In contrast, Greg Burgess has worked with Anangu people to create a striking visitor and craft center, Bambruk. Both designs meld indigenous design motifs with nonindigenous technologies in interesting ways. Yulara is also the base of Maruku Arts and Crafts, a successful art and artifacts center, specializing in pokerwork and carved woodcrafts.[24] Contemporary Aboriginal art has, since 1970, generated a number of pathways through the fissures, voids, and bridges between black and white cultures in Australia.[25] What would be an architectural equivalent? Perhaps Peter Myers's Knockabout Walkabout house: standard parts, made from recyclable woods, slide-in metal fenestration, separate toilet and kitchen sink, clip-on or simple air-compressed nail gun assembly, repairable rather than fixed and disposable, no dependence on external parts or power, everything transportable on a normal-size truck, and easy to disassemble for transport to another site for reassembly (illus. 12).[26]

Faces of the Nation

Uluru and the SOH relate to the theme of the architecture of aftermath in specific, local ways. Uluru has its own internal history of violent, epochal struggle and eventual resolution. Within today's iconomy, it is the most general image of Aboriginal Australia and thus carries in its chain of associations the history of the violent occupation of the continent, the memory of the massacres, the dying out by unknown diseases, the attrition of the land, the alienation of country, the enforced relocations, the breaking up of families, the acts and occasions of resistance. For Aboriginal people, this history is overwhelmingly negative, although laced with hope. For other Australians, it occasions guilt, but then the response is divided between regret and the urge to make reparation, and denial and the refusal to accept the obligation toward reconciliation. For many, there is a grieving for those who were victims of past injustice, a desire to assuage the effects of trauma, and a sense of mourning for a social contract carried out badly. Others vehemently deny these feelings and any such obligation, labeling it a "black armband view of history."[27]

In contrast, the opera house has, from its inception, embodied hopeful striving, faith in the future, and—in its evocation of sails on Sydney Harbour—hedonistic pleasure, a ready escape from care that is, in principle at least, available to all. Its

12. Peter Myers, Knockabout Walkabout house, Northern Territory, Australia. 2001. Courtesy Peter Myers.

internal history was, as we have seen, one of struggle. Yet it is also a story of creative inventiveness on the part of both architect and engineer meeting the constraints imposed by politicians and accountants, an encounter that resulted in a building that became at once soundly functional and strikingly original. This internal reconciliation continues to define it and is the basis of its force as an icon, one that is both well grounded on its site and in the local economy, as well as always attractive to those who see it afresh.

So, in the cases of Uluru and the SOH, we have two architectures of destination, two structures with undeniable and seemingly limitless pull as destinations, each figuring core values of their respective cultures, each acting as symbols with valiance in each other's cultures, and each with a definite and growing presence in the visual esperanto of international communication. Both are pivotal in the histories of created/built form of their respective cultures and have the capacity to serve as the site of a wide range of relationships between the cultures, from confrontation to (at least the possibility of) reconciliation. Each has accumulated a history, particularly in recent decades, such that their present iconic power seems almost predestined. Each is more than capable of attracting further meaning, and of occasioning transformation. Future connections and disjunctions between the two icons will probably be characterized by much continuity, a deal of repetition, and, one hopes, some surprises.

Striking parallels . . . but what has brought the *pairing* of Uluru and the opera house into such intense focus these days? Something more, surely, than the coincidence of form that triggered the multicultural happy mix in Ken Done's popular paintings of these two icons blending into each other.[28] But the populist artist was on to something. As gestalts, both formations have qualities that declare singular profiles, when seen from distances, and that draw viewing into subtle complexity, multiple internalities, when experienced close by. Both are place markers from afar, while at the same time giving strong, unmistakable impressions of their uniqueness as places (their genius loci) to those who approach them closely. And both of them are emphatically doubled: ancient and modern at once, classical and streamlined, rooted in the earth (of it) and molded by winds, naturally given and manmade. Les Murray, articulate proponent of convergence, saw this, and showed it to us in his 2001 poem "Clothing as Dwelling as Shouldered Boat":

> Propped sheets of bark converging
> over skin-oils and a winter fire,
> stitched hides of furry rug-cloak
> with their naked backs to the weather,
> clothing as dwelling as shouldered boat
> beetle-backed, with bending ridge-lines,
> all this, resurrected and gigantic:
> the Opera House,
> Sydney's Aboriginal building.[29]

Within the aesthetics of the iconomy, these elements—when added to all those accumulated from their separate histories—go a long way towards explaining why Uluru and the Opera House became iconotypes, why they have eclipsed other contenders, and why their power as icons persists, in parallel. But their pairing within the contemporary iconomy is explained, perhaps, by how they link two levels of what is basically the same difference. The dynamic cities of modern Australia versus the fragile pastoral industries, the sparse populations and the not-modern otherness of the bush and the outback. And the outer-directed inter-nationalism of European Australia in contrast to Aboriginal Australia's commit-ment to country. They are paired because, for all their similarities, and for all their differences, they face each other in a facing—at times a sharing, at others a face-off—that constitutes Australia as a nation. This is inseparable from the fact that they also appear as a pair because they face outwards to the world as Australia's two faces, facing it sometimes together, sometimes looking away, at others simply side by side. All of these exchanges converged, symbolically, during the New Year's Eve celebrations that ended the "year of disaster" 2001, and ushered in the next. At the moment when the fireworks display culminated with Roman candles exploding from the top arc of the bridge—in a burst that illuminated everything around it, including the opera house—a large electrical image of Uluru appeared in the center of the structure, and then glowed quietly through the rest of the night (illus. 13).

13. Ben Rushton, "Year of Disaster Ends with Peaceful Message." 2001, photograph. Ben Rushton/Fairfaxphotos.

The Past-Modern Present: *Empire Redux at the Getty Center*

The Museum as Culture Mall

If there was one building that competed with the Guggenheim Bilbao for the attention of both the architectural and the popular press during the mid and later 1990s it was the Getty Center, Los Angeles (illus. 14). Pictures appeared in all the professional journals, along with detailed plans, designs, interviews, discussion of building practices, etc. These two projects seemed to embody, in their different ways, both the institutionalization of postmodern architecture and a precipitous shift into something perhaps new and different. Well before completion, they became—separately and together—a red-hot topic in public sphere imagery, from newspaper magazines through television to long insider essays in the *New Yorker* and elsewhere. Both opened to their publics in 1997.

Given the length of their gestation (fourteen years for the Getty Center), the near-mythic stories of conflict and resolution surrounding their realization, and the cultural sexiness of their purpose, it is no surprise that they received so much play. A huge investment was made in promoting the architecture of the museums as itself well worth visiting, as much—and perhaps even more so—than the art within the walls. Thomas Krens remains unabashed about this approach. He nominates the Frank Lloyd Wright building on Fifth Avenue as the "greatest work of art" in the Guggenheim collections. He refuses to have built the partition walls designed by Gehry for Bilbao's interiors, despite the advantages that this would bring to the experience of the artworks, on the grounds that they would reduce the impact of the overall spaces, of the building as a work of art.[1] He is right about this. In these cases, and with increasingly greater rapidity, exceptional architecture amounts to more than an attractive housing of the end point of a pilgrimage; it becomes the object, the point, the completion of the journey, it becomes a meeting with destiny. Architecture is, in itself, the attractor, the draw to a destination.

Faced with the challenge of creating, in their own words, "a museum for the new century," those involved in the planning of the Getty Center came up with this: "a new museum devoted equally to tradition (well-displayed collections, exhibitions, scholarly publications) and the forward-looking (a strong commitment to education, a broadened audience, a setting designed for visitors' comfort and pleasure)."[2] Putting on a happy face, the Getty Center promotes itself as a site of attractions, a place to come for an enjoyable day in its ambience. The people come in droves. Visitors love Robert Irwin's garden, the architectural tours of the site, and the chance to eat and wander and take in the views. Some, in fact, never

get to the art collection. David Carrier draws the obvious conclusion: "The Getty, one may infer from the published information, realized that it has started too late to collect a truly world-class collection. Today it is very hard to import old masterpieces. And so it chose to construct an extremely expensive showplace."[3]

When, in the seventeenth century, the need to house the princely and cardinalic art collections of Europe arose, what a dilemma faced the architect: how to match in one's own design a body of artistic achievement that he or she could not possibly hope to eclipse? By the nineteenth century—through powerful models such as the renovation of the Louvre and Schinkel's National Gallery, Berlin—a rich response had been found. An imposing façade to attract the punters while at the same time acknowledge past centers of power, celebrate the beneficence of donors, and inspire national pride, followed by tasteful restraint on the inside, to satisfy the aesthetes and the professionals. At the Getty, however, Richard Meier had, from day one, an opportunity to outshine the artworks. To his credit, he did not do so—at least, not in one big bang. Rather, he divided the collection up into easily digestible chunks and located these in separate pavilions, so that moments of pleasant contemplation could be experienced easily, between breaks for coffee and the views of Los Angeles, a city rarely seen from above. In this design he was merely following the program, letter for letter. Objecting to the overwhelming size and the synoptical, art history textbook internal divisions of most museums, the

15. Richard Meier, the
Getty Center. 1983-97,
axonometric. Source:
The J. Paul Getty Trust.

Getty trustees insisted on a "relatively modest" size and scale—a condition met
at Brentwood if you compare the site to, say, the pyramid complex at Giza or the
entire Washington Mall—and a building that would "subordinate itself to the
works of art in the galleries, assert itself with dignity and grace in the public
spaces, and contribute logic as well as pleasure to the visitor's progress." As to its
look, they hoped that "the building can give modern form to the well-proven
virtues, aesthetic and functional, of the great museums of the past." At the same
time, they required an interior design that echoed the original contexts of the
works, making them "look at home—albeit in a home of the 1990s." They
stressed, finally, the need for visitors to have spaces in which to relax and recover
from the intensity of their art experience.[4] Rather than deliver all this in one
edifice, Meier came up with six double- and triple-storied buildings, arrayed
around a courtyard, and set on top of a labyrinth of service floors. Plazas and garden areas connect easily to centers for research, conservation, education, information, and grant disbursement, and to make space for a garden (illus. 15). Meier
went for an imagery of place with multiple outlooks rather than one standout
image form that demanded to be looked at and admired.

No subversion of the brief here. Nor the chrysalis of the museum of the future. The Getty Center is the art museum as mall, except that everything, save the food, souvenirs, and parking, is free. In his autobiography, *As I See It*, J. Paul Getty contrasted his total subsidizing of the Malibu museum (the predecessor to the Getty Center in Los Angeles), particularly the parking, to Joseph Hirshhorn's insistence that the U.S. Government meet all costs of housing and maintaining his collection when it undertook to build the Museum of Sculpture in his name on the Washington Mall.[5]

Museums sometimes label their most visited icon—Gainsborough's *Blue Boy* at the Huntington, Seurat's *Sunday Afternoon on (the Island of) La Grand Jatte* at the Art Institute of Chicago, and the vapid David Hockney panorama painting of *The Grand Canyon* in the National Gallery of Australia—their "destination painting." But what if an architect were to turn this concept inside out and project the building itself as the destination? More, what if he or she created an architecture as beautiful as the artworks within it? Indeed, as *more* aesthetically accomplished than them? Somewhere here is the ambition for an architecture that will be, not just one of the arts, however brilliantly so, but an architecture that *is* contemporary art like other contemporary art, particularly sculpture, installation, and performance art. Despite his fulfilling the brief to the letter, Meier at the Getty was no less intent than Gehry at Bilbao on creating an architectural work of art that would be, at once, utterly contemporary and for the ages.

The center is no replication of a past building, nothing like the first Getty Museum, with its careful effort to reproduce as accurately as possible the Villa dei Papyri at Herculaneum on Ocean Boulevard, Malibu. Getty had been impressed by William Randolph Hearst's creation of a medieval setting at Saint Simeon, but wanted to go one degree up the scale. The original villa consisted of a set of plazas overlooking the sea and was the house of Julius Caesar's father-in-law. It was buried under the lava mud that flowed from the eruption of Mount Vesuvius in A.D. 79. Getty's own account of his motivation is of interest. He abhorred current museum buildings as "Penitentiary Modern" and regarded art world luminaries as "doctrinaire and elitist . . . Artsy-Craftsy" types. Instead, "I thought it worthwhile to create one building in the Roman tradition. The Graeco-Roman buildings that remain to us have had hard usage during the past couple of thousand years. I suppose that 99.99 per cent of the buildings of Imperial Rome have disappeared. The precious few buildings left are all more or less incomplete. They have been worn by time."[6] By taking "meticulous care" to "ensure fidelity to the architectural spirit of the original," Getty could provide a building that was, at once, a historical (even archaeological) document, and brand new. It would evoke an ancient time, but not be old. His collection of antiquities would look at home in it. And it would be unlike anything else that existed anywhere, even that which it replicated. It would be the product of scholarship and the best current technologies. And parking would be provided free.

The Malibu trustees were in tune with the trend to attractor architecture in the early 1970s. "The Trustees did not want to commission a modern building, numerous examples of which—both good and bad—already existed among

museums. Neither were they satisfied with the usual design concept whereby the structure would be a mere backdrop for art objects. They felt that a museum building should be a statement in itself—that is, be of interest for its own sake—as well as provide a harmonious setting for the collection."[7] As we have seen, those commissioning Meier felt the same. And to make sure that they got the right mood inside the galleries they took that task away from Meier and gave it to an accomplished, if somewhat Rococo-inclined interior designer.

The Museum of Architecture

Meier's design goes beyond its program in one important sense—a sense that, I will show, is indicative of its entering the age of specularity. It is, above all else, a built visual essay in architectural memory. Its aggregated forms are made up of multiple allusions to masterworks of early modernism, making it thus a spectral Museum of Modern Architecture (illus. 16). At the same time, the site plan evokes the ur-forms of urbanity, echoing back through the medieval village on an Italian hilltop to the forums of imperial Rome and the acropolises of ancient Greece. More specifically, it conjures those magical precincts, such as the Alhambra, where campaigns to create a locus of strategic and symbolic power have waxed and waned between civilizations, over centuries.[8]

The Getty Center is not a museum that houses architecture. It is unlike the Pergamon Museum in Berlin, with its installations of great structures from Hellenistic times, and from Babylon and elsewhere. Nor is it like the Metropolitan

Museum, New York, with its Cloisters and its room encasing the Egyptian Temple of Denur. In these cases, the museum becomes a mausoleum for the monuments of earlier, finished or conquered civilizations, a prison-house of their chief symbolic images. Their main gateway, for example, their most prominent landmark or their most sacred inner temple—that is, their destination architecture, their iconotypes. Such deep complicity between the museum and colonization, its ancient purpose as a treasure house of spoils taken in war, must not be forgotten. It parallels the other great purpose of museums: to monumentalize their own societies, nations, or at least leading elements within them, as civilized (and victorious). The Louvre is, of course, the great early modern exemplum. Much twentieth-century modernist museum building seeks to strain out these associations. By washing the acquisition of artworks through money, through the connoisseurship of applied art history, their genesis in other, conquered societies and cultures is laundered out of the picture. In the most recent revamping of the Louvre, which occurred during the 1980s under President Mitterrand—the Grand Louvre project—this history was repackaged as an endless journey of consumption, "a continuous museological landscape linked by a mall."[9]

Meanwhile, at Brentwood, the specters of previous architecture haunt the shapes of the Getty Center buildings, figures of earlier canonical modernist buildings appear in the heat haze before your eyes, like Corbusian mirages, and the inflection of pastness shades all of its surfaces. An echo here of the ethos of the original Getty at Malibu, with its "meticulous . . . fidelity to the spirit" of a lost and unrecoverable original Roman-style villa, yet generalized. This is heritage in the broad—and now widely accepted—sense of a contemporary use of a monument that existed in the past.[10] Although it is presented as a token, or instance, it is actually a re-creation of a type. Thus it evokes an ersatz past, as gratifying as fast food.[11] An Acropolis ambience would have been stronger if Meier's proposed aqueduct-style open wall linking the museum to the research institute had been built. And if his idea for a garden arrayed on the terraces of an amphitheater had not been sacrificed, after much struggle, to sculptor Robert Irwin's design (itself a sequence of historicizing replays of past gardens and imagined natural settings woven through a Minimalist schema).[12] In general, however, the new Getty Center recycles the past, not as a replication, nor as a set of type forms, but in its use of its setting, and the fossilized marble, to evoke a generalized sense of the Past. These evocations waft alongside the story of modernity as told by the shades of modernist architecture, the chimera of World's Fairs gone by. It is the most developed realization of the idea of the Past-Modern to date.[13]

The stale breath of spectacle insinuates itself into Meier's more generally high-minded, and high modernist, aesthetic at such moments of lapse into generality. If one looks up from the far side of the garden towards the museum, a panorama of new/old building types unfolds (illus. 17). The tracking shot is calming, but is also interrupted by staged incident. The exhibition building lurches forward with all the instability of a robot character from *Star Wars*. Half of it is picked out in rough-cut marble slabs (the other half flows along in familiar neo-Corbusian

17. Charles S. Rhyne, panorama of the Getty Center showing Getty Research Institute, Garden, and Museum of Art. 1997. Photo Charles Rhyne.

manner and reads as another, adjacent building). These slabs cover it as if they were the scales of a stone monster from outer space. Its upper, boxlike form is raised on spindly columns, themselves sheathed in the same uneven slabs. The overall effect is one of fictive instability. It is an effect caught with the broad-brush sketchiness of indicators of place that one finds, usually, on theater or film sets. This is Los Angeles, after all.

Acropolis Now?

As you walk past the entrance to the Getty cafes and restaurant, an elegant, white stone rectangle frames a view of the nearby houses perched on mountains. This is only the most explicit instance of something that happens all over the site: picture-perfect scenes are everywhere. According to David Carrier, this is the Getty's answer to its self-imposed 1900 terminus: it has added to its collection "one additional, absolutely contemporary work of art—Los Angeles as viewed from Meier's building. With windows framing the landscape, the Getty turns its vistas into art, completing its collection with these cityscapes."[14] Looked at this way, the Getty buildings become an elaborate, ornate oculus, a device for looking, a picturesque machine activated by both perambulation and pausing to look. This is an eighteenth-century inheritance, recalling a time when museums were relatively exceptional, where they might take the form of pavilions in gardens. How does this experience substitute for the absent art of the twentieth century? Carrier's instinct is that Meier's gesture is a Duchampian one; he "treats the vistas as readymades, which need only have attention called to them to become art."[15] I am not so sure that Meier escapes the eighteenth century, or even the Roman sequencing of spaces—as at the Roman Forum, for example—that he avows inspired his planning of the Getty site.[16] Duchampian irony is not a common attribute of Getty visitors and anyway is not necessary to persuade them to pause to take in the views. Meier has given them a grand-scale version of what some locals, at

least, would have in their own house: the picture window. The views show Los Angeles as it is now, as it has developed over time, primarily during the twentieth century, in mostly distant vistas of suburbs punctuated with clusters of tall buildings rising from the crossing of freeways or rimming parts of boulevards. One needs to bring a lot of love of LA to one's viewing to take these prospects as, in any sustained way, matching the modernity of experiencing the city through a much more appropriate viewing apparatus: the car. This is an obvious point that has been made by many, not least Reyner Banham.[17] But it is only the first of many to be made about Los Angeles.[18]

Overall, it is as if the Getty Center were a materialized book about architecture. Not a textbook, more a manifesto. Like Le Corbusier's *Vers une architecture* of 1923. The English title of this polemic, "Towards a New Architecture," emphasizes the modernist line of Corbu's arguments, and was a reasonable translator's/marketing nuance given his program as manifest in his long-running journal of advocacy *L'Esprit Nouveau*.[19] If Meier did have it in mind as he conceived the Getty Center, it was less the chapters celebrating the pure functionalism of the anonymous engineers of industrial structures in the U.S., more, probably, those pages that matched photographs of the clean, thrusting lines of the latest Buggati to pictures of the Parthenon's splendid prominence when profiled against a brooding sky. Moderate in tone, then, but vauntingly ambitious in its substantive propositions.

Or perhaps Meier was paying homage to the ur-text of postmodernist thought, *Complexity and Contradiction in Modern Architecture*, written in 1966 by his fellow architect, Robert Venturi.[20] This was a counterhistory of modern architecture, one that pointed out, delightedly, how impossible it was for architecture to follow the precepts of the International Style as formulated in the work of Walter Gropius, Ludwig Mies van der Rohe, Le Corbusier, and the other Modern Masters in the early years of the century, and turned into a program by Henry Russell Hitchcock and Philip Johnson in their Museum of Modern Art, New York, exhibition of 1932.

Instead, in *Complexity and Contradiction*, and in the equally influential *Learning from Las Vegas*, Venturi advocated multiplicity, striking contrasts, historical allusion, and a dynamic differential between the façade and the body of a building, with the whole or key parts of the structure operating as a sign—a "decorated shed," not a "duck," to use his still-striking central metaphor.

How could Meier respond, so astutely, and at the same time, to the central values of these classics of *both* modernist and postmodernist architectural thought? What ever happened to the supposedly total, unbridgeable antithesis between them? One might argue that, on the level of architectural taste, the gulf had vanished because both tendencies, once they became learnable, repeatable styles, had been overrun by the relentless march of architectural fashionability, so that Meier was obliged to work within a "post-post" aesthetic. Indeed, he had been doing so since the 1970s.

Meier's own developed style was by then utterly neo-Corbusian. The real precedent to the Getty Center is his Athenaeum, a center for visitors to the remnants of the utopian colonies of New Harmony, Indiana, erected 1979. Seeking a way of creating senses of passage, of harmony and flow, and of circulatory return, Meier set his Corbusian shapes and spaces to work on each other. The tight skins of early modernism are reoriented, and split asunder, by internal spaces, particularly staircases placed externally and glass-framed outside areas relocated indoors. These ideas are taken still further at the Getty Center, and spread—with greater success—between a number of buildings. They can also be felt in the disposition of buildings, their address to each other around and across the site.[21]

Did Meier incorporate contemporaneity into his design? Not at all in his plan, nor in the main weight of architectural allusion. The ground plan of the research institute stands in subtle opposition to that of the main gallery building. In contrast to the simple circle of the gallery's great hall, it spirals inward and down, in a protracted effort of self-examination that enacts spatially the scholarly journey that its library and archives invite. It also echoes the obsession with the spiral form in the work of artists such as Robert Smithson. Mostly, however, contemporary art appears in the details, as quotation of aspects of post-Minimal, post-conceptual art, especially sculpture. Skylights recall Donald Judd sculptures, window fixtures the paintings of Jo Baer. Most arcane, perhaps, is the echoing of the form of Dan Graham's transparent collective experience environments—such as that which defines the roof area of the Dia Foundation in New York—in the revolving doorways and entrance areas of many of the Getty buildings: the research institute, and the conservation institute. Such usage—along with the much more overt, indeed (at Disney Hall) whole-scale, adaptations of Frank Gehry—shows that those aesthetics of the 1960s that did *not* continue down the pathways opened by conceptualism have had a continuous, and very powerful, life in the most advanced architecture. This is Meier's best answer to the Getty Trust's refusal of the high arts after 1900, a policy that visitors experience with bafflement when their art historical tour terminates, abruptly, with James Ensor's terrifying and crazy painting of 1888, *Christ's Entry into Brussels in 1889*. In mitigation, Meier supplied huge hints of twentieth-century modernist architecture in his built forms and, in the spaces between each building, spectacular views of its urban formations. Plus a sprinkling of deft allusions to contemporary art.

But it is not enough. These small and esoteric incorporations of the contemporary will become even less adequate as time goes on. To lock the collection behind a 1900 gate—however much the outstanding photography collection, the enterprising temporary exhibitions, and the activity of researchers burst out from behind it—is to freeze the artworks in a premodern time warp, one that will inevitably send them backwards in time. At the same time, this policy pushes those who care for these collections, interpret and display them, forward: into postmodern ambiguity. It places the architect where we have found him: in a historical revolving door. But it leaves the center as a whole where its masters wanted it: a museum on a hill, the climb to which offers, as its reward, a respite from complexities of contemporaneity in general, and those of modern art in particular.

Esybilt Aftermath

By the end of the 1980s, modernity and its posts had (as Jacques Derrida among others noted) been subsumed under another logic of aftermath: the large-scale work of mourning for the failure of modernity, of both capitalist progressivism and communist sociality, that European societies, and those culturally tied in to them, had, necessarily, to undertake.[22] In Europe itself, this mood became pervasive and continues to echo as if the continent were in a perpetual state of shock. In the U.S., this logic of aftermath could, during the 1990s at least, be perceived as a puzzlement, a pause, a toy to be played with—these were, after all, the Clinton years.

But the condition of aftermath has continued, and seems to be settling in, but for who knows for how long. In such circumstances, every material thing in the world falls into one of two categories: a monument to loss and thus an object of mourning or hope, or a place to hide within the chaos. Often, it is both. If the fall of the Berlin Wall became an instant symbol of liberation, of a wide-open future full of possibility, the collapse of the Soviet Union provided a sickening demonstration of what chaos looks like on the other side of the now-absent defenses. In such desperate situations, preservation is widely urged as the best bulwark against chaos. Museumization marches to the forefront as the ideal embalming procedure for anything deemed worth preserving, indeed, of anything that stays still long enough to be preserved. It becomes an important work of social maintenance to attract great crowds to historical monuments—to, in Getty's words, reduce the number of cultural barbarians. But this might amount to nothing more than increasing the number of those bemused by culture. More to the point is this: in a state of sporadic but relentlessly increasing devastation, how else will we know who we are? In the condition of aftermath, preserving anything can seem a heroic act of human continuity. But this Terminator logic may also work as a restraint on invention, ingenuity, and creativity. This is the paradox of heritage, one that haunts the urge to preservation.

The Getty is, in these circumstances, another new and living monument to European art and civilization before this fall. That is to say, the fall has imposed on the center as a whole—its research, archival, and grant program as much as its art collection—the project of historicizing Europe, of mourning its lost opportunity to continue to generate history. Or, at least, of holding its heritage in reserve in the unspoken hope of its renascence. This has been America's broad task since it became, increasingly throughout the twentieth century, so unevenly but inevitably, what many see as a new kind of Empire, or Imperium (to me, "Emperium" gets it right). In which context, it comes as no surprise that while the first Getty Museum, the imaginary Villa dei Papyri at Malibu, has undergone a multimillion-dollar refit, the original edifice—subject of major excavations between 1991 and 1998—has fallen into such a ruined state that it now requires emergency work to save it.[23]

From the Scholar's Terrace at the Getty Center—and from the east pavilion, across the cactus garden—you can look down the hill and take in as much of the city as the smog allows. On a clear fall day, you can see snow on the San Bernardino Mountains, the sprinkle of modest skyscrapers downtown in sharp profile, the factories of Segunda, the sun glinting from the procession of airplanes in their two-minute queues above LAX, a string of sand dunes with the letters "LMU" prominent, the beach line, the infinity of houses, small high-rises and the occasional school, above which poke the clusters of Westwood and Century City, including Yamasaki's Century Plaza Hotel. You are drawn, inevitably, to sharp lines of the streets, especially the caterpillar crawl, both ways, of the 405 freeway. And its transection, along Wilshire Boulevard, by what could become the fault line of an earthquake.

Imagine, as of course an entertainment specter, the last scene from *Planet of the Apes IV*, in which a lone rider surveys the postapocalyptic landscape after the final, great shift of the Fault. As a result of the extreme measures taken to make it earthquake-proof, is it not possible that, after the Event, the Getty Center might be the only set of structures left standing, the only surviving built forms on the West Coast, perhaps on the American continent, maybe even—shock, horror!—the world? Was it Meier's hubris that the Getty Center might, in these fantastical circumstances, be the mother of all architecture, of architecture to come after such an Event? It would be an extraordinary academicism, an anticipation of future ruin value unmatched since the epochal phantasms of the 1930s. Yet, in truth, the buildings are locked in, through deep steel struts, to the largest single rock formation in the area. The 295,000 chunks of travertine that face most of the walls are individually suspended, the better to withstand earthquake shock. The center, in this deep scenario, anticipates its future as the resource for the architecture of the postapocalyptic future. It is, already, the object of antiquarian interest, that of the anticipated posthumans. This nightmare is driven by narcissism without bounds, unlimited even by time, locked into a narrative that wishes only to repeat its self-absorption.[24] For now, however, it offers a fascinating tour of itself as a relatively new, yet already classical, heritage site.

Contracting the Future

Bilbao and the Getty are spectacularly successful as destinations, as innovative and erudite architecture, and as icons of their moment—that between the Fall of the Berlin Wall and 9.11.01, a time of post–Cold War euphoria, when capital stood alone as the world's answer, when global reach seemed that it might override the limits of nations, and culture could be offered to visitors from everywhere, gift-wrapped. Let us ask of them a more difficult, longer-term, and exactingly concrete question: are these two solutions, inspired as they doubtless are, examples of architecture that holds out an improved social contract, that suggests the shape of a better form of life? By this high criterion, the Getty Center, although it has grand, even transcendent ambitions as architecture, falls short of greatness. Mainly because of its overreliance on size, spread, and expense, its all-inclusive striving. It is, as we noted, an architecture of instant eternality, of manufactured heritage. Because it monumentalized itself from the outset, it does not permit monumentalization to occur to it, to be added, piece by personal piece, by those who come to it, pass through it, return to it. In a perverse sense, its Rieglian mood of being immersed in all times while at the same time as being above time is the modernist legacy in it. In contrast, Gehry's design solutions use only contemporary forms, specifically those of contemporary art, as well as their own internally generated fresh solutions, and employ the latest cutting-edge technology, while eschewing quotation of earlier architecture (except occasional echoes of the 1950s, the funky '60s fish shapes, etc.). Does this enable them to provide spaces in which desirable kinds of sociality may be experienced?

Certain architectural writers celebrate Gehry's work above all for a quality of this type: its democratic spirit. In this, they echo Gehry's own, oft-repeated characterization of Los Angeles as a postwar, Free World city, and of his own instincts as those of a rugged individualist free to work with others on projects of collective value.[25] Responding to the Guggenheim retrospective exhibition, *New York Times* critic Herbert Muschamp praised it as "a tribute to the ideal of service: to an art form, to the City and to the continuous reconstruction of a democratic way of life."[26] *Los Angeles Times* critic Nicolai Ouroussoff defends Gehry against critiques of Bilbao by drawing out an implied contrast to the Getty Center: "But the power of Bilbao stems from its desire to aggressively engage contemporary realities, rather than retreat to a sentimental version of the past. It is a museum of the people, and as such, it makes art seem accessible and relevant, a fundamental part of our everyday lives."[27] Anthony Alofsin exposes this as wishful twaddle by asking, "What is this democracy ... and whom does it represent?" He answers: "a democracy defined by the tastes and values of an international assortment of corporations, major museums, cultural and educational institutions ... [or] Gehry's work can be seen as democratic in the sense that Disneyland is democratic, motivated by an intention to entertain and ultimately to sell ... It may be more accurate to claim that artists such as Gehry are champions of an 'artocracy' rather than the renovators of democracy."[28] Hal Foster insightfully relates this issue to the key formal struggle within Gehry's work, a battle between the residuals of the critical regionalism of his early designs (famously, the 1978 renovation of a Santa Monica tract house as his own) and the demands of the spotlight:

> What is at stake here is the difference between a vernacular use of chain-link in a house or of cardboard in a chair and a Pop use of giant binoculars as an entrance or of a fighter jet attached to a façade (as in his Aerospace Hall, 1982–84 in L.A.). Equally at stake is the difference between a material rethinking of form and space, which may or not be sculptural (here Gehry is influenced by Richard Serra), and a symbolic use of a ready-made image or commodity object (here again he is influenced by Oldenburg). The first option can bring elite design in touch with common culture and renew stale architectural forms with fresh social expressions. The second tends to integrate architecture, on the model of the advertisement, to a public projected as a mass consumer.[29]

Foster notes that Gehry "surfed" this dialectic into the early 1990s, and that his adroitness in doing so "propelled his jump from L.A. architect to international designer." Like Meier at the Getty, Gehry avoided being pigeonholed as either a late modernist or postmodernist. Yet the dialectic wreaks its revenge, it cannot be conjured away by the use of digital design programs. Despite the overwhelming impression of a skin that expresses its interiority, given by Gehry's exciting interplay of swirling surfaces and random breakouts, this, like all late capitalist imagery, is an illusion. Foster sees the "disconnection between skin and structure" in Gehry's recent work, such as Bilbao, as problematic because it leads to mystifying rather than inspiring spaces, and, as in the proposed New York Guggenheim, tends to set the building against its context. "The Wall Street Guggenheim would be even more anti-contextual than the Bilbao, which has come home to roost, swollen to twice the size and propped up on super-pylons like a giant metal dodo." Returning to the issue of the purported democracy of Gehry's approach, Foster observes, "The great irony is that Gehry fans tend to confuse this arbitrariness with freedom, this self-indulgence with expression." The result, for the spectator, is gawping awe, or nothing. Echoing Guy Debord's aphorism that was mentioned in chapter one, Foster notes that the reverse is true of Gehry and his compatriots: "Spectacle is 'an image accumulated to the point where it becomes capital.'"[30] Thus the convergence of mall, theme park, and cultural center in the cities of today. And in the designs of Robert Venturi, Frank Gehry, Richard Meier, Santiago Calatrava, Daniel Libeskind, and many, many others.

Actually, Gehry's ability to synthesize Venturi's "decorated shed" and "duck" (in effect, by incorporating the values of the former into an open gestalt that became the latter) had its precedents in the work of a number of LA architects active during the 1940s and 1950s, notably John Lautner. A pupil of Frank Lloyd Wright, Lautner is best known for such one-shot, stand-out structures as the Chemosphere on Mulholland Drive (now owned by publisher Bernard Taschen) and the Bob Hope House in Palm Springs (of which Hope said, when shown the plans, "Well, at least the Martians will know where to come, and will feel at home

when they get here."). Lautner is also the chief author of Google Architecture, those drive-to eating houses that were decorated sheds long before Venturi coined the term. In setting a Norm for that type of purpose, they became ducks. Lautner's Desert Hot Springs Motel, designed and built for Hollywood-based clients in the mid-1940s, prefigures Gehry in its use of industrial forms to create intimate domestic space, but does so within an aesthetic of restraint that does not persist in this type of architecture.[31] Indeed, it is the accelerating spectaculariza-tion of our culture, the widespread internalization of the values of the decorated shed that, along with the aging of modernism, has enabled Gehry to effect his synthesis. To, in effect, present a decorated shed as a duck.

Not that he is alone in this regard. Engineering design as itself spectacle motivates the work of Santiago Calatrava, who was, during the 1990s, the fast-emerging alternative designer of choice for big-splash structures. His Quadracci Pavilion for the Museum of Art in Milwaukee, situated at the point where the city's main street meets Lake Michigan, features two huge brise-soleils of such size that they dwarf the rest of the building (illus. 18). They are of so striking a form that they eclipse any perception of the building as having a purpose other than to be. This technological marvel is flamboyantly in excess of its function as the covering of an entrance hall to a museum. Galleries and other services are essentially confined to rooms off the corridors that lead from it and to other buildings on the site that, although relatively undistinguished, had to be retained. While it might have its inspirations in sources as wide apart as the wings of a pterodactyl and Vladimir Tatlin's wacky *Letatlin* of 1929–32, an avant-gardist archetype, its most evident purpose is to be an unforgettable image. A logo for the city.[32] A somewhat more subtle deliverer of this kind of "wow" impact is Rafael Viñoly, creator of massive, unimpeded public spaces, huge extents under graceful roofing and mostly transparent walls, such as the Kimmel Center for the Performing Arts in Philadelphia and the David Lawrence Convention Center in Pittsburgh. Their external form is less important, less logo-like than their jaw-dropping internal spaces, and the rapidlike flow of people through them.

The City Core Implodes

During the 1990s the architecture of authority was also rethought from another angle than that of spectacle, one that followed on from the downgrading of city centers during the 1970s and 1980s. If the complex cultural center was the most striking kind of singular spectacle architecture to appear at the time, the more deeply emergent urban form was the domestic landscape, the "post-suburban" city, the highly structured community plus mall domains such as—to use only U.S. examples—Orange County, California, or Fort Lauderdale–Palm Beach, Florida, and "mininucleated metropolitan regions" such as Suffolk County, New York, and Santa Clara County, California.[33] Sharon Zurkin demonstrates that "postmodern suburbanity" is shaped by the liminality between the demands of *market* (for constant change, obsolescence, and repeat consumption) and those of *place* (for stability, rootedness, and concentrated value).[34] Perhaps the destination architecture we have been reviewing is a Late Modern synthesis of this dialectic. No longer the Eiffel Tower echoes of the Canadian Railway Tower in Toronto and other thin and desperate place markers of the 1970s. Rather, an array of dazzling instant worlds is placed before the spectator/consumer. The high-end Past Modern of the Getty Center, or the glitzy shambles of Gehry's Guggenheim on the edge of the old city of Bilbao and his Disney Hall, in Los Angeles's still tenuous downtown. On this reading, Meier and Gehry's fabled designs are upmarket, high-culture attractor features in what are, in effect, upmarket, high-culture malls. At Bilbao, such boutiques have swarmed like bees around sweets melting in the sun. What is ignored by these developments is architecture's other traditional function: housing the people. With some honorable exceptions, this core mission has been, by and large, surrendered to developers driven by quick-return greed and to builders operating below the radar of architecture. Their gerry-built monuments proliferate in the abandoned industrial zones that had become interstices between downtowns pervaded by a museumlike quietus, the faux heritage and picture postcard imaginaries of the postsuburban gated communities.

Perhaps this is also why, in order to stay at market, modern cities from Berlin to Kwangchow have to be constantly rebuilding at least one zone at or near their centers. These are black holes of Manhattan-style incessant excavation, around

whose rims rise instant monuments to economic expansionism and internal diversification. The edifices that arise from them consume in their creation ever more complex engineering, increasingly compacted hardware, and ever more refined software. They represent the maximum possible property value and the highest concentration of capital value. They attract, at once, the most rapacious energies and the best minds of their generation. They exercise the most far-flung influence around the globe. Are not these precincts of destruction/creation in themselves a transitional architecture, a zone of always arriving/departing?

It is a contradiction quite typical of contemporaneity that the most successful architect of the late modern moment was one who taught us to read the architecture of "deconstruction"—of structures in a state of apparent constant construction—as if it were the most vividly prefigurative and hopeful imagery around. In a project that was postmodernism's swan song, Frank Gehry's proposed $678 million Guggenheim New York on the East River, there was, as the museum's publicity puts it, a conscious effort to respond "to the urban landscape that serves as its backdrop, and to the East River. The rigid forms characteristic of a skyscraper— the quintessence of New York architecture—are fractured and recombined with a curvilinear body suggestive of the water's fluid movement and the energy of the city" (illus. 19).[35] In its massing, the design is contextualism taken to Baroque extremes: its horizontal configuring replays the festive gateways and theater settings of the seventeenth century, while its verticals draw shape from earlier modernist box forms at the lower levels and from skyscrapers towards its center. The viewpoint of the photograph of the design model at its site, that is, set among

19. Frank Gehry, installation view of current design model, proposed Guggenheim Museum New York, 1998-2001. From *Frank Gehry Architect, 2002 Guggenheim Museum* (calendar) (New York: Guggenheim Museum, 2002). Photograph by David Heald, 2001. Source: Guggenheim Museum.

block forms of all adjacent buildings, features the Twin Towers of the World Trade Center as its apex. So does the angle of the "installation view," a simulated photograph of the future building, to scale, with downtown in the background. These photographs imply that the most vertical element of Gehry's model, in which the central cluster of "skyscrapers" are thrown against each other, with glass curtain walls collapsed into and through solid walls, the whole angled crazily against the perpendiculars of the buildings behind it, was intended as a meditation on buildings such as the WTC, as an imagining of them, or their modernism, perhaps their corporate rigidity, put awry or "fractured."

Coming to the huge final model for this building after walking around the exhibition of Gehry's work at the Guggenheim Museum in August 2001, I read the major elements of its design as a joyous double play between two energetic unfoldings. On the one hand, in its vertical dimensions, it is a rehearsal of the well-known trope of the modernizing city as an explosive ruin that is always already in the process of constantly destroying and rebuilding itself; on the other, along its horizontal register, organic forms of time passing, clearly simulated cloud-shapes, a kind of speeded-up cinematic scudding that pays homage to the site's natural environment. A dynamic meeting of construction site and cloud-burst clearing, both as seen by a mobile viewer, perhaps in a seaplane, a traveler who sheens through city space.

Gehry's design, like that of Meier at the Getty, does project into the future in the sense that it rehearses the idea of the modern city as a graceful ruin. That is to say, it posits a future in which this building would eventually become a museum of itself (and, it was clearly hoped, do so as gracefully as the Frank Lloyd Wright Guggenheim on Fifth Avenue has become a museum of itself as a museum that was always, also, superb architecture). As well, it retains elements of a typical Gehry theme, one that has persisted in his work since his refurbishment in Santa Monica. That is, it symbolizes architecture as the product of the construction site, as a place of constant self-renovation. As to the social contract on offer, that is not so clear. The sense that this building needs us, its users, to complete it, is a generous invitation. That we do so, as minnows within a multitude that has come to gawp, wonder-struck, and that leaves with nothing transformed, is hardly a model for democratic participation. It does not give us much in the way of tools to start building what Hardt and Negri would call a "counter-Empire."[36]

Remembrance Now: *Architecture after Auschwitz at the Jewish Museum, Berlin*

Since the Fall of the Wall in 1989, Berlin has been Europe's most visible stage for the large-scale testing of architecture that has, as its basic building blocks, the hard facts of social division *and* the high hopes of spiritual redemption. For the average citizen and visitor no try at this is more prominent than Sir Norman Foster's dome on the Reichstag. The refitting of the entire building alternates between acknowledging a number of violent, totalitarian, and revolutionary pasts while opening out each space to the dream of a democratic future. The see-through Chamber of Deputies is ringed by memorials of various kinds, ranging from graffiti inscribed by Soviet soldiers during their occupation to rooms dedicated to contemplation of past atrocities and future hope. Throughout the complex, specially commissioned artworks appear. Some fade into the decorative: Gerhard Richter's glass panels painted in the colors of the German flag. With more subtlety, Christian Boltanski offers a subterranean archive, a narrow corridor of cremation boxes of dead deputies. In a courtyard, Hans Haacke stages *Die Bevolkerung*, the word itself made up from earth drawn from Germany's many regions by their living deputies. By stressing "The Population," Haacke creates a counterhomage to the various peoples of Germany, which stands in pointed contrast to the much-disgraced concept of "Dem Deutschen Volke," words that still adorn the building's façade, despite the disgrace brought upon them during the Nazi period.[1]

The new Reichstag's democratic reach culminates in the great dome. Visitors circle its interior via gradual ramps, where they may see the city's rooftops receding if they look out and the deputies at work if they look down. As a constantly present Eye of God, their positioning enacts collective conscience. As a people, they perform oversight, literally looking over the shoulders of their representatives. Foster clearly aspired to reverse modernity's oppressively panoptical political structure—to which Michel Foucault has famously drawn our attention—by stripping bare its backstage machinery. (The architect overlooks the fact that the surveillance state's effectiveness always depended on its machinery being visible—as a threatening glimpse—to all.) From both inside and outside, then, the dome is intended as at once a literal, highly visible, transparent form and a symbolic declaration of accessibility and transparency. Yet the best intentions cannot vanquish the shadows of history. For many Berliners, and for visitors with any depth of social memory, the uncovered dome triggers recall of famous photographs—now, indeed, iconic—of the skeletal frame of the original dome, the

20. Jewgeni
Ananewitsch Chaldej,
"Ruhe Berlin, April
30, 1945." 1945,
photograph. [public
domain]

building's skull, its covering blasted off by the advancing Soviet army in 1945, with the airplanes of the conquerors passing overhead. In Germany, as everywhere else, democracy is a fragile form (illus. 20).

Impossible Poetry

To Theodor Adorno, inclusive gestures such as the Reichstag renovation would be, in the aftermath of the Holocaust, acts undertaken in the most perverse bad faith— or, at best, in an ignorance so profound that it would betoken a world that had lost its memory altogether. His declaration, "To write poetry after Auschwitz is barbaric," is the most unequivocal challenge yet formulated to the possibility of art and culture in our time. In its absolute negativity, it draws, unambiguously, the line up to which art and ethics, if they wish to amount to anything more than delusory cowardice, must step, and, in doing so, face the improbability of their ever again merging to create culture. Furthermore, and crucially, it offers no exits from this standoff.

It did not, however, take the Holocaust to bring Adorno to a trenchant dismissal of Hegelian metaphysics and of the role for art as the progressive realization of the *Geist* of History at a certain stage of its development that was the key to Hegel's aesthetics. An aesthetics that remained, in Europe at least, perhaps the most elaborated and influential outline of how art might serve society.[2] Yet the Holocaust drove Adorno, and later his parents, from Germany, and claimed the lives of many of his colleagues and friends—not least Walter Benjamin. It became, and remained, the signal, most vivid instance of the quality that he found most hateful in modernity, yet most characteristic of it: its implacable drive to administer everything and, in so doing, reduce all living beings to things.

In this context, Adorno's statement joins the novels of Primo Levi, the photo-montages of John Heartfield, the photographs of Margaret Bourke-White and Lee Miller, and a delimited number of other efforts to express through art and criticism the specificity of the impact of the genocidal policies and practices of the Nazis. These latter were, in themselves, an extreme example of the redirection, through the twentieth century, of campaigns of terror and death dealing away from soldiers battling in relatively defined theatres of war toward campaigns against selected, and largely civilian, populations, usually in the neighborhood or country of the murderers. Adorno's remark channels these effects to the problem of what it takes, in such circumstances, to create works of art and to construct civil culture between citizens. It would, he believes, take a denial that the Nazi barbarism was ever visited upon us—itself a barbarism. Any effort to create a high-cultural artifact would, in these circumstances, be an act of the utmost complicity in murderous vandalism. As would be any generalized affirmation of art's redemptive grace—which would be simpleminded to boot. All artists can do is contemplate, in immobile silence, the enormity of the devastation that has been wrought. The same applies to critics and to those seeking a radical critique of contemporary culture. Art and criticism have forgone their right to exist. The depth of Adorno's pessimism is clear in his first statement of this proposition, made in 1951:

> The more total society becomes, the greater the reification of the mind and the more paradoxical its efforts to escape reification on its own. Even the most extreme consciousness of doom threatens to degenerate into idle chatter. Cultural criticism finds itself faced with the final stage of the dialectic of culture and barbarism. To write poetry after Auschwitz is barbaric. And this corrodes even the knowledge of why it has become impossible to write poetry today.[3]

What of that art that takes Auschwitz as its subject and seeks to show its horror? In his subsequent writings, Adorno rejected most attempts at this, especially those—such as Schönberg's operas and Brecht's plays—that took committed, engaged, transparently critical forms. Music and theater such as this risked, he thought, the danger that their very artistry might provide pleasures, however indirect and inadvertent, to those receiving the political messages, thus blunting the artists' obligation to the victims of the Holocaust: to show that it was, above all, unthinkable, inconceivable.[4] Only one work of art met his (impossible) demands: Samuel Beckett's play *Endgame*.

> *Endgame* trains the viewer for a condition where everyone involved expects— upon lifting the lid from the nearest trashcan—to find his own parents. The natural cohesion of life has become organic refuse. The national socialists irrecoverably overturned the taboo of old age. Beckett's trashcans are the emblems of culture restored after Auschwitz.[5]

Adorno understood that Beckett had deliberately refused to represent the Holocaust directly, and that the postapocalyptic dreamscapes in which his plays, especially *Endgame*, were set, were, in fact, its aftermath. His last comment on this topic, in *Negative Dialectics*, returns to this very point. In a major expansion of his ethical penumbra, he acknowledged that "perennial suffering has as much right to expression as one who is tortured has to scream; hence it may have been wrong [to have said] that after Auschwitz no more poems may be written."[6] He acknowledges, belatedly, that the survivors of the Holocaust deserve the compensations—or at least the companionship—of representation, as do, in varying degrees, those of us condemned to live in its infinite shadow. But these compensations are hard ones—indeed, they are the hardest imaginable: "Beckett has given us the only fitting reaction to the situation of the concentration camps—a situation he never calls by name, as if it were subject to a strict image ban. What is, is like a concentration camp."[7]

The sequence of quite concrete, carefully circumscribed claims as to permitted aesthetic/ethical conjunctions in the aftermath of the Holocaust that we have just reviewed have had an enormous impact on cultural practice throughout the world, particularly since the 1970s. Gene Ray sums these up in a useful way:

> Adorno's very specific demands that art should refuse positive representation, aesthetic pleasure and the possibility that Auschwitz could be mastered or redeemed eventually attained the status of a dominant ethic of representation. Today we can recognize the decade following the mid-1980s as the period in which this ethic came to dominance and was gradually conventionalized. While artists who produced early responses to Adorno would include Beuys, Anselm Kiefer, Christian Boltanski and, in film, Claude Lanzmann, this ethic would be elaborated more fully in the 'counter-monuments' developed by Jochen Gerz and Esther Shalev-Gerz, Horst Hoheisel, Maya Lin and Daniel Libeskind. The more general and less rigorous demand that any aesthetic treatment of Auschwitz be handled with high seriousness, ethical rigor and scrupulous respect for the victims and their memory is a popularized legacy of Adorno's reflections that critics such as Susan Sontag have sought to vigorously enforce.[8]

The Architecture of Auschwitz

One question that most of these commentators seem not to ask is: what was Auschwitz, as architecture? This small Upper Silesian city was redesigned from 1942 as a model town, a Garden City surrounded by efficient industry, of a kind ideally suited to the New Germany, above all its *Drang nach Osten* (illus. 21). Many of those Germans who settled it (there being virtually none living there before this occupation) did so in the belief that they were contributing, in their modest way, to building the *socius* of the New Germany, its ordinary groundwork. This may explain part of their reluctance to recognize the perversion occurring both in the center and on the outskirts of town, in nearby Birkenau and the surrounding

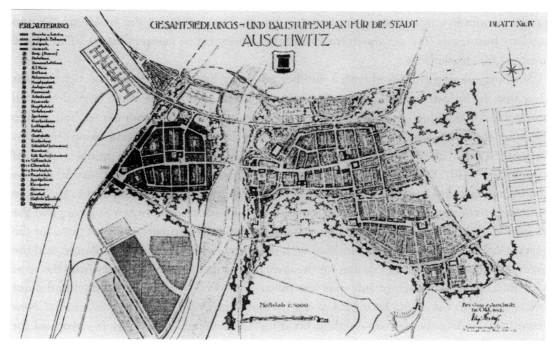

areas, the death industry that was booming there. Another factor might have been the dawning realization that they too had all along been cogs in the death-dealing machinery of the Final Solution, that its relentless evacuation of their sham morality had made them victims too. Yet, as van Pelt observes, "by the early summer of 1942 Auschwitz-Birkenau had become the site of mass-murder by means of two primitive gas chambers in adapted peasant houses. A year later the same camp contained four modern crematories with advanced killing installations and fourteen incinerators with a total of forty-six cubicles. For one million people these buildings proved, indeed, the end of the world."[9]

As the regional headquarters of the SS, the entrance to Auschwitz was intended to symbolize the power of the organization, a goal it achieved even more emphatically in the aftermath of the Nazi defeat, when it became iconic of the Holocaust itself. Its medievalizing style, chosen by Himmler, sought to root the new era in that of an earlier unifier, Heinrich I. Yet, as architecture, the majority of the structures at Auschwitz, Birkenau (Auschwitz II), and the related camps were modern industrial structures, of no distinction as architecture, and certainly not modernist in any sense. Local and Berlin-based architects strove to relate the disposition and servicing of these camps to the urban plan of central Auschwitz. But their singleminded purpose—to extract the maximum labor power from the inmates and to dispose of them by the most minimal means when they became useless—was a reversal of the lifestyle hymned by the main city's attractive, suburban variegation. Rows of barbed wire hemmed the camps in: they were, in this bizarre sense, the visible manifestation of the walls of war that surrounded Germany itself and that its armies fought to extend outwards.

21. Dr. Hans Stosberg, final master plan for the expansion of Auschwitz, September 14, 1942. Provincial Archive, Katowice, Collection Landesplanung Gau Oberschlesien.

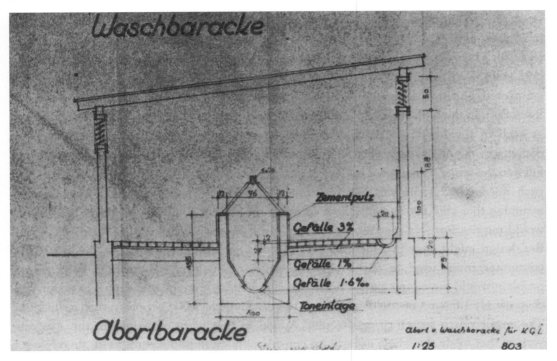

22. Karl Bischoff and
Fritz Ertl, latrine for
Auschwitz-Birkenau,
section. 1942.
Provincial Archive,
Katowice, Collection
Landesplanung Gau
Oberschlesien.

These camps fell short of their own presumptions of order and efficiency in
ways that are at once devastating to recall and most revealing of the shortcomings
of modernity as a social model. Many of these are by now well known and were
typical across the entire concentration camp system (it had begun in 1933, and
had served many political and economic roles under the expanding Reich). Chief
among them was the assignment of vastly more people—at first Russian prisoners of war and then, after 1942, Jews—than could be accommodated, even when
the death dealing was at its most efficient and least disguised as the unfortunate
by-product of an exhausted labor force. This exacerbated the arbitrary rule of
camp commandants and other officers. There was, as well, the imposition of
internal discipline, often carried out, on the false promise of their survival, by
inmates against their fellows. Medical experiments on inmates went beyond the
limits imposed by the profession for research involving human "patients." Less
known, but in the event even more deadly, were Auchwitz's architectural shortcomings. Van Pelt presents in factual detail the nauseating miasma of organizational inefficiency, deliberate underresourcing, official cowardice, design
incompetence, and bad judgment that attended every aspect of this ghastly industry of death. I confine myself to citing one example from this architecture of hell,
the toilet and sewerage arrangements (illus. 22):

> First, there is the spatial arrangement: the "privy" meant to serve 7,000 inmates
> is a shed with a single concrete open sewer, 118 ft. long by 3 ft. wide, without seats
> and with one long beam as a back support. The design was adapted from a model

latrine for large units in winter quarters and was first published in a leaflet on wartime emergency construction. Like the model latrine, the camp latrine could be accessed from walkways at both sides. Neither in Auschwitz, nor in the model on which it was based, were the walkways connected; but in Auschwitz this proved catastrophic, for each of the walkways was 118 ft. long. Both in the built version and in the model, doors at each of the building's short sides provided access to the walkways. Imagine 7,000 inmates at sunrise, suffering from diarrhea or dysentery, and trying to enter, find an unoccupied place, defecate, manage not to fall into the sewer, and get out in the ten minutes or so allocated by the camp's regulations to such necessities. Assuming that 150 inmates could find a place at the one time, and also assuming that all 7,000 inmates were able to move their bowels with the requisite precision, it would require forty-six successive "seatings," with all the traffic jams involved . . . One sewer, supplied with an anemic supply of water and a drop of only 1.6 percent could never flush the discharge of 7,000 people in such a short time. The result was a secretory catastrophe. Added to that were the omissions in the Auschwitz version that made the whole experience considerably more unpleasant. First, there were no seats. Second, the system of support was based on the minimal design of the field latrine, only to be used at the front. Third, the "shame-walls" were removed, which might have provided at least some physical privacy for those who had to defecate next to each other. Finally the separate aeration for the pit was omitted (it had become superfluous since the pits at Auschwitz were open), which meant an insufferable stench.[10]

Building Being and Not-Being

Since 1967 the Berlin Museum has been housed in the Königliches Collegienhaus, a former Baroque palace reconstructed in an elegant Rococo manner in 1753 that later served as a major Prussian courthouse. This building is located on one of the city's main axial streets, Lindenstrasse, close to its intersection with the Wilhelmstrasse and the Friedrichstrasse—that is, in the Friedrichstadt area, since the late eighteenth century often touted as an alternative center for the city. Through the nineteenth and into the early twentieth century the Lindenstrasse sector was a focus of Jewish life. During the 1930s its southern sections became the spoke of the Nazi terror system that was managed from SS Headquarters and other local buildings. In 1988 the museum trustees announced a competition for a design for an extension that would meet their institution's needs for additional "exhibition space and storage and other functional space," and "because the Jewish Museum Department has to be enlarged and fully integrated into the Berlin Museum."[11] The city was ready, at last, to take a further step in recognizing and repairing the barbarisms of its recent past.

In 1989, from among fifty entries, the jurors chose that of Daniel Libeskind, declaring it "an extraordinary, completely autonomous solution."[12] A decade of complex negotiations followed—no surprise given the conflicted nature of the project, the profound political transformation of Berlin itself, and the radical nature of the architect's proposal—before the building opened in January 1999.[13] Even then, it stood empty for two years while the architect was given the opportunity to allow his building to speak for itself.

What did it say? There is no shortage of statements on record as to the architect's intentions. Let us review some of them before turning to his drawings, and then to the building itself. Libeskind stunned the judges by submitting as his competition entry a philosophical program typed onto music paper. Titling the entire project "Between the Lines," he began by noting, "A Museum for the City of Berlin must be a place where all citizens, those of the past, of the present and of the future, must find their common heritage and individual home."[14] So far, so platitudinous. But then, this radical architectural challenge: "To this end, the Museum form itself must be rethought in order to transcend the passive involvement of the viewer, actively confronting change." To begin this rethinking he immediately goes to the nub of the philosophical problem that Adorno had highlighted: "The extension of the Berlin Museum with a special emphasis on housing the Jewish Museum Department is an attempt to give voice to a common fate: common both to *being* and what is *other* than being. The museum must serve to inspire poetry, music and drama, (etc.) and must give a home to the ordered/disordered, chosen/not chosen, welcome/unwelcome, vocal/silent." (We may take it that "etc." includes architecture.) Libeskind's language hints at the depth of his reading of German philosophy, especially Heidegger and Adorno. His ambition here is nothing less than to use aspects of Heidegger's ontology to solve Adorno's deontological impasse. In full awareness of the force of the impasse's dialectical negativity, Libeskind sets out to create a post-Auschwitz architecture, and to do so poetically. He knew that he had to take on the presenting of unpresentability, the presencing of nonbeing, as the problem's only solution, as the building's only possible program. His hope was that, if he succeeded—that is to say, if his solution failed in a negatively dialectical way, if it enabled the world to be present to itself in perhaps the most extreme forms of its impossibility—the Jewish Museum would not only be a solution to the problem of making architecture after Auschwitz, it would inspire an after-Aftermath kind of art. His ambition is signaled in the conclusion to his "Between the Lines" competition entry. After sketching the mobility of usages and spaces within the museum to come, he says: "A Museum ensemble is thus always on the verge of *Becoming*—no longer suggestive of a final solution." The moment when Berlin imagined itself without its Jews forever is pivotal in the history of Berlin, and is the core content of the museum. It established history and contemporaneity as existing above all before and after it. Yet if the museum was not to become stuck in an eternal return to this moment, it had to avoid being a Holocaust museum per se. Thus the necessity of building into the museum open-endedness, a state of permanent incompletion, of always becoming. This is hopefulness beyond Adorno's pessimistic imagination—or the wishful thinking of a (divine) fool. It might, of course, be both.

What *chutzpah!* To aspire to forge—in the design impulse for a Jewish museum, in Berlin—the basic insights of the philosopher of Being who notoriously succumbed to Nazism and those of the Jewish philosopher who famously argued the impossibility of philosophy—indeed, of any kind of responsible being—after the propositional eradication of the Jews. But Libeskind did this consciously. If you reread these preliminary statements, you will see that they turn the profound admonitions and prohibitions uttered, in turn, by Heidegger and Adorno, back on themselves, each of them separately, then as a pair. Heidegger's insistence on the always-becoming of the world is set against the Nazi Final Solution. Building an artwork that embodies from its ground plan up the thrall of its own impossibility is to enact Adorno's prohibition as a road map. This is the substantive content of the architect's claim that he set out to complete Schönberg's unfinishable opera *Moses und Aron* (a work that could not, in its own and Adorno's terms, find its resolution) "architecturally."[15] Libeskind took these philosophical steps not only consciously, but conscientiously. Heidegger's and Adorno's passages through their times were, for all their differences, contemporaneous. Libeskind saw this as consequential not only for Berlin but for the rest of humanity. Thus the double pathways, the doubling of void and "not-void" throughout the museum. Yet this contemporaneity was not adventitious, not for the philosophers, nor for any of us. Disjunctive parallelism just is what it is like to share, as the architect never tired of pointing out, "a common fate."

The references to "passage" here, and in Libeskind's notes, alerts us to the presence of another philosopher, the quintessentially conflicted Berliner who chose suicide rather than fall into the hands of fascists, Walter Benjamin.[16] To resolve the dialectical tensions between Heidegger and Adorno's irreducible demands, Libeskind's design thinking drew on four of Benjamin's key concepts. The complexities of modernity, the contending forces of modernization, Benjamin vividly showed, have created—in cities and in the minds of men—mobile, contingent *passages* of connection and disconnection. The conflicts of modernity, including the incessantly accumulating history of these conflicts, constantly transform these passages into *ruins* and memory into ruination. The experience of this passaging is felt first, as *shock*, then as melancholy, later as trauma, while to some it serves as an inspiration to revolt. Finally, if one is to grasp what it is to live, critically, in modernity, it is necessary to apply dialectical materialism not as a mechanical Marxism but with a *collage* consciousness.[17] Libeskind made his debt to Benjamin quite explicit by dividing the visitor's movement along the zigzag of galleries into sixty sections, representing each of the "Stations of the Star" described by Benjamin in his notes about Berlin and modernity, *One-Way Street.*[18]

It is this set of existential/ethical challenges that is at the core of Libeskind's response to the idea of a Jewish Museum in Berlin in the aftermath of the Holocaust. While the philosophers, as we have seen, expressed them in philosophical terms, the challenges themselves were fundamental to what it was to exist in mid-twentieth-century Europe. It is to Libeskind's enormous credit that he did not begin from convenient softenings of these challenges, those that have become the liberal ideology of post World War II German officialdom, but took them on at their most intractable. A hard question to ask of the museum, then, is whether, despite the best intentions of its architect, the compromises necessary to get buildings built have meant that the museum does, ultimately, end up as a monument to such soft thought.

Collage Consciousness

The tendency of Libeskind's training as a musician, at the Lodz Conservatory, and architect, at Cooper Union, New York, was avant-garde modernist. As were his attitudes. An early manifesto is his 1987 "Architecture Intermundium: An Open Letter to Architectural Educators and Students of Architecture," in which he asks:

> Why spend time tediously applying gold leaf onto a pinnacle of a tower (impressive!) when the foundations are rotten? Before that delicate task will have been completed, the entire edifice will collapse, destroying both the work and the worker. Invisible disasters precede those that can be seen . . . No amount of research, discussions on "relevance," or compiled information can disguise the fact: Architecture as taught and practiced today is but a grammatical fiction. Enough to see the gulf that separates what is taught (and how!) from what is built (and why!) to understand that somewhere a lie is being perpetrated. Only a sophistic method could mask a situation where so many spend so much to do so little—with such damaging results.[19]

The Jewish Museum was his first major project, and the first of many conceived during the 1980s, to be actually built. Some of its architectural ideas had been first advanced in a raw form in a set of twenty-eight drawings done in 1983 entitled *Chamberworks: Architectural Meditations on the Themes from Heraclitus*, and in such urban planning concepts as his *City Edge* competition entry of 1987.[20] In 1989 he proposed, unsuccessfully, an extension to the Edinburgh Museum of Art that would have consisted of a complex of radical, raking shapes erupting into the street beside the restrained neoclassicism of the existing buildings—as if the ur-form of early modernism had suddenly landed in this eighteenth-century city center. During his decade of work on the Jewish Museum, Libeskind spun off a number of other powerful projects and proposals, including the 1995-98 Felix-Nussbaum-Haus, a small museum at Osnabrück, Germany, which he entitled *Museum without Exit*.[21] In Berlin, Libeskind was clear about "the three basic ideas that formed the foundation" of his Jewish Museum design:

> First, the impossibility of understanding the history of Berlin without understanding the enormous intellectual, economic, and cultural contribution made by its Jewish citizens. Second, the necessity to integrate physically and spiritually the meaning of the Holocaust into the consciousness and memory of the city of Berlin. Third, that only through the acknowledgement and incorporation of this

erasure and void of Jewish life in Berlin, can the history of Berlin and Europe have a human future.[22]

There are gentle allusions here to various forces that were then in contention for the cultural imaginary of Berlin's citizens, including those that sought to redefine the city—above all, and typically for their moment, through spectacular architecture and related forms of iconomic repositioning—as the capital of the united Germany, as a powerhouse of the European Community, and as a key economic and cultural vector of the new globalization. Thus the great renovations of major buildings along Unter den Linden, of the entire Mitte district, and the techno-mall wonderland at Potzdammer Platz. In pointed contrast, Libeskind is saying: if you don't get the recent past right, these aspirations, however worthy they may be in themselves, would amount to nothing more than gold leaf appliqué over rotten foundations.

Libeskind's very first sketches for the museum show him to be contemplating different kinds of human movement through a four-story building. These include the shuttering of film frames related to distinct times and distances. He quickly breaks the profile of this structure into disaggregated units of distinct sizes and planes, a la Malevich, or Rodchenko. Another early idea shows steps leading up to a closed wall—presumably the Berlin Wall (which will reappear in stronger form later).[23] These turn into a series of drawings of volumes standing erect, leaning toward and away, as if they were an ensemble of Minimal sculptures—those with the symbolic presencing of a Tony Smith rather than the withheld muteness of a Donald Judd. The goal here seems to be an exploration of the external massing of a possible building or pair of buildings.[24] But it was the ground plan, as always (because it moves the user through the building and is, therefore, the shape of their social contract), that was pivotal. Libeskind rightly named the entire project for his core insight: "The official name of the project is the 'Jewish Museum,' but I have called it 'Between the Lines.' I call it this because it is a project about two lines of thinking, organization and relationship. One is a straight line, but broken into many fragments, the other is a tortuous line, but continuing indefinitely."[25] To his credit, he never names one of these lines "German" and the other "Jewish." Instead, the internal multiplicity of both cultural formations swarms between the two forms.

It is here that we start to see the deepest relationships between this museum and a main theme of this book: contemporary architecture's implication in the iconomy. The museum's external gestalt is deliberately broken and odd in outline, too well disguised by its cladding, and so bunkerlike and tangential in its address to its neighborhood that it resists every attempt to read it as iconic. Indeed, despite its moments of attractiveness, its striking beauty when seen from certain angles, the design refuses to settle for spectacle. Its exterior, at least, is anything but "overweight, overdone, and overwhelming"—Kurt Forster's admiring first impression of the Guggenheim Museum, Bilbao.[26] The zigzag shape of the underground passageways, shaded by a broken straight line, is foregrounded in museum publicity as its signature logo—but we have seen that Libeskind explicitly refutes this as an iconic reduction: yes, it is precisely this "German-Jewish" coupling that is to be emphasized, but only in its implicated, open-ended ambiguity. However distinctive the penetrated zigzag may be as an architectural form, and as a gestalt, it is, to him, an anti-icon, at best. After all, it symbolizes movement into darkness, into death, and the invisible connections between Germanness and Jewishness. This is the underside of the iconomy, a tracing within its spectral unconscious. Very hard to trap in a stereotypical image, to render as an iconotype. If the spectacle pervades the Getty as a Hollywood style pastness, and shiny, techno-organic complexity is the newly won logo style of Gehry's cultural creations, then the iconomy enters the Jewish Museum in a different, and deeper, way. It does so by rejecting not iconomy as such but its contemporary, spectacle array. Instead, the architect resists consumer spectacle from a long-term perspective, through constant recourse, in developing his design thinking, to the symbols of regimes past and recent, to their logos, their icons.

The ground plan of the museum has been frequently read as an exploded Star of David. This seems a simple two-step, absolutely appropriate to a Jewish Museum in Berlin: the symbol of Jewishness, used both by Jewish communities throughout history and by the Nazis to identify those they held to be Jewish, is registered as shattered, emblematizing the Nazi's prodigious but ultimately failed attempt to eradicate Jews from the world as they saw it. The implication here is that fragments, however ruined, can be reconnected; and a broken culture restored, however slowly and painfully. At such a level of generality, this would be a liberal architecture. Yet I have argued that Libeskind did not take this soft option. How did he use this well-known, stereotypical image, specifically? In the publicity surrounding the project Libeskind employed a "compressed and distorted" Star of David as a graphic device to connect the two lines mentioned above, creating a "Star Matrix" that joined those German Jews— "Certain people, workers, writers, composers, artists, scientists, and poets who formed the link between Jewish tradition and German culture"—who lived and worked in what was, when he began on the project, East and West Berlin.[27] Exploding the star triggered the idea of plotting an "irrational matrix" based on the addresses of these people, the locations of their houses on a map of Berlin, the lines between which he then used to generate the disposition of the slatted windows and other tears in the exterior walls of the museum. So the streets in Berlin where Jews were made to wear the identifying insignia, one that separated them, marked them out for exile to the unhuman, is now a place where this sign has expanded out to draw in the possibility of a culture of integration and growth. Indeed, a hint of the star, shattered, may be glimpsed in the window slits on the stepped-back front of the museum, to the right of the Collegienhaus entrance (illus. 26).

One page of felt-tipped pen drawings stands out for the intensity of its exploration of the possibilities of this one motif (illus. 23).[28] We can follow Libeskind's mind-eye-hand as he works over the basic shape: emphasizing some parts, fading others out, subtracting sections, turning them different ways, adding others of the same type, turning the figure in space, rotating it, separating its parts,

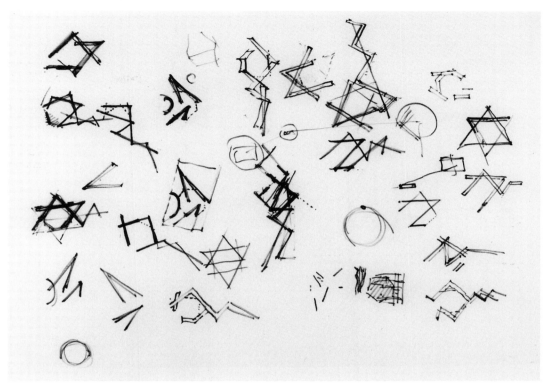

reconfiguring them within a frame or in space. These are no mechanical set of formal exercises, nor have they a mathematical character. He is searching the shape for its expressive potential, for the kinds of connotative power it might retain, or surprise, when put to work channeling human movement through space. Shape is being reshaped into orientation (not yet entries, passage, obstruction, exit). He is clearly attracted to unfolded versions of the form: these predominate on the page. As he pursues this unpacking, however, he seems careful to avoid a shape that hovers as the Star of David's other: the Swastika. In some of the drawings, it seems almost as if one has become the other, but the Swastika never emerges as a distinct figure. Instead, the designs cluster near the top center, where he stretches the loosened form into three dimensions, making it a set of interlocking walls. Then, at page center, doubles it into a quasi-Constructivist figure, echoing El Lizzitsky's famous collage *The New Man*, an image on the cusp of revolution in Russia. The joining of the "two lines"—a zigzag cut by a straight line, both of them broken—with the Star of David and the absent Swastika, is the moment that generates the plan of the underground passageways in the Jewish Museum. In the most elegantly rendered of these drawings, entitled "Void—voided void ('Jewish Dep't')," a number of axonometric projections of the volumes generated by the underground passageways, the galleries and the voids between them are disposed as shards in space (illus. 24).[29]

    Collaging the incompatible to generate synthetic meaning is typical of the way iconic images are treated throughout Libeskind's drawings. Not as isolated

23. Daniel Libeskind, concept drawing for Jewish Museum, Berlin. 1993, pen on paper. Research Library, the Getty Research Institute, Los Angeles [920061 box 31*.3]. Credit: Daniel Libeskind.

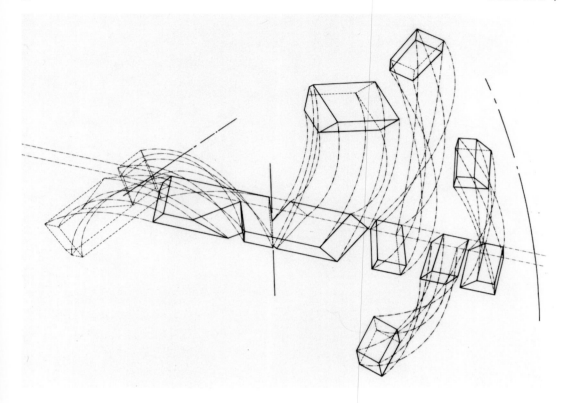

24. Daniel Libeskind, "Void–voided void ('Jewish Dep't')." 1993, ink on tracing paper. Research Library, the Getty Research Institute, Los Angeles [920061 FF 15]. Credit: Daniel Libeskind.

emblemata, nor as place-holding signs. Rather, they are thrown together, into a collage of contending and symbiotic forces and made to work against their narrowness, their exclusionary powers. Another related drawing shows him rendering the hammer and sickle, symbol of Communism, and of workers' power in general, then separating the two elements before breaking them up in the ways he did the Star of David.[30] At this point one feels that he is testing his basic design for its capacity to absorb every ideologically loaded image that human beings have ever dreamed up. The most extraordinary of these is a drawing that configures the museum ground plan, across a double-page spread, into cursive Arabic script evoking the sacred calligraphy of the phrase "Allah is merciful!"[31]

Not only symbols, but also architectural forms that have themselves acquired a symbolic force, are grist to his incorporative mill. A number of drawings show him contemplating the interplay between open and closed spaces, and between different kinds of enclosure and escape. In one sketch the entire above- and belowground project is imagined as if made from sections of the dismantled Berlin Wall.[32] Typically, these are linked with others in which the stacked shapes of the museum are thought of as sets of volumes of the Torah, tied together, and penetrated by shafts.[33] In another drawing, the ground plan is projected into three dimensions and imagined as a mini-history of architectural styles, from classical colonnades to a skyscraper and an angular projection labeled "Cloud Breaker" (illus. 25).[34]

In these drawings we can trace how Libeskind mobilized the almost unimaginably negative elements that came, during the 1930s and 1940s, very close to

Cloud
Breaker

River

expunging not just Jewishness from Berlin but also history itself. The voiding of
Berlin's Jews is registered as something that is irredeemable, a statement made
architecturally in the straight but broken line formed by a series of actual voids
that pierce the center of the zigzagging museum building, intruding into all its
exhibition spaces. The memory of Berlin's Jews, however, is regarded as recover-
able, as is the return of Jews to Berlin, not least in the form of this museum. The
historic Collegienhaus has been reduced to an elaborate gatehouse (illus. 26).
Once inside, visitors assay an abyssal entrance, down steep steps to a space that
has no externally anticipated layout and is, in this sense, unbuilt. You stand facing
a choice between a set of three underground streets; none marked for preference,
and nobody insisting on your following an official itinerary (illus. 27). As you
gradually discover, each one does have a single—indeed, singular—destination.
Turning right up a short passage, the Holocaust void is entered only through a
heavy concrete door, which is then closed. The unheated, uncooled space inside is

25. Daniel Libeskind,
concept drawing for
Jewish Museum, Berlin.
1993, pen on paper.
Research Library, the
Getty Research
Institute, Los Angeles
[920061-8]. Credit:
Daniel Libeskind.

26. Daniel Libeskind, entrance, Collegienhaus and Jewish Museum, Berlin. 1993-99. Bitter+Bredt Fotografie, Berlin. Libeskind Studios.

shaped into a sharp wedge by twenty-seven-foot-high unadorned concrete walls. You can just make out the sounds of the city outside as it goes about its business. Above, a thin strip of white light, reflected from some unseeable source, rims the top of one wall. An air vent? Divine Light?[35] Another passage, signed with the names of places to which Jews were exiled or emigrated, leads out into the E.T.A. Hoffmann Garden. Set on a sloping surface, forty-eight raked, minimal rectangular concrete columns contain Berlin earth and signify the birth of the State of Israel in 1948, while one isolated column, filled with earth from Jerusalem, signifies Berlin. From the top of each a pomegranate tree grows. Divided cities, joined here, in this Jewish Museum in Berlin. The third passage is a Stair of Continuity that rises high into the uppermost part of the building, allowing access to the exhibition spaces on different floors of the museum. Above you, as you climb, the building seems to crumble down. There are no windows until you reach the platform at the top: light floods in through a narrow, raking slit, and you can look out across the low skyline of the city.

Voiding the Labyrinth

Responding to Libeskind's ambition, architectural writers from all over the world celebrate the museum as meeting the most serious contemporary standards of

27. Daniel Libeskind, underground passageway, Jewish Museum, Berlin. 1993–99. Bitter+Bredt Fotografie, Berlin. Libeskind Studios.

meaning and beauty. Let me illustrate this by drawing on the comments of Anthony Vidler. His immediate reaction was one that should be, by now, familiar from our accounts of the impact of aftermath architecture:

> As a work and as an experience it stands as testimony to the power of a certain kind of phenomenological stance before the world, a spatial evocation that, through brilliant and deeply thought out moves, resonates with an aura of the terrifying sublime, and that, perhaps more than any modern work of architecture I have ever seen, manages to hold the visitor in spatio-psychological suspense, the closest experience to what I imagine religious experience of architecture might be.[36]

Awe, to be sure, but something is different here from similar-sounding reactions to other recent architecture. Vidler contrasts the museum to projects such as Meier's Getty Center, and many other museum renovations and heritage reconstructions (including the Reichstag dome), with their generalized evocation of pastness, their allusions to what was once an order of immense, concentrated, and civilized power but is now tamed for manipulated consumption as mass entertainment. Ignasi de Solà-Morales labels this preoccupation with architecture's past glory a "weak architecture," one that induces delighted recollection, mild historical fantasy, and, perhaps, bemused rumination on time's passing and the follies of human aspiration.[37] To me, this is "after architecture" rather than an "architecture of aftermath." The Past Modern trades on a generalized sense of resonance from the past; it offers an imaginary proscenium for the spectral replay of events of consequence that happen to have happened beyond some fabled horizon. It does not take up history in its actuality as part of its working materials. In the aftermath of the Holocaust, and especially in a museum in which the Holocaust is at the core of its program, "after architecture" simply would not do.

What were the "brilliant and deeply thought out moves" by means of which Libeskind achieved "an aura of the terrifying sublime" and brought the visitor to a "religious experience of architecture" of a kind that is present in the great destination buildings of the past but missing from the work of his Past Modern contemporaries? Vidler summarizes them as the result of the architect's careful reading of the most advanced thinking around the issues involved, results that expressed themselves, above all, in concrete design decisions:

> Its materiality is powerful in metal-clad reinforced concrete and does not hide its pretensions behind weak structure ... Its routes of passage are firm, defined by the darkest darks and the most brilliant lights: its disregard for the "normal" functions of museums, for the requirements of exhibitions spaces, the modesty demanded by background spaces for foregrounding exhibits is more or less contemptuous; its ignoring of spatial economy—the prolific insertion of meaningful voids—absolute. There is no effort at all to "fit into" its context as it denies completely through scale, mass and surface the Baroque pavilion to which it is nominally an extension, but which is turned into nothing more than a traditional portico to the new structure. Yet this strength holds nothing of the "miserable monstrosity" decried by Weber; part fragment of city wall, part bunker, part storehouse, it retains its own identity in the face of the wasteland that surrounds it.[38]

Defining the strengths of Libeskind's "moves" by what they do not do, Vidler highlights the architect's refusals of both conventional expectations as to the briefs of such buildings and the (in contrast) easy solutions to similar problems adopted by his contemporaries. Functionality, legibility, a spectacular external gestalt, deference to the higher arts, contextualism—all are rejected, emphatically. Invoking Heidegger and Sartre, Vidler argues that, instead, the Jewish Museum plunges us into "bodily and mental crisis, with any trite classical homologies between the body and the building upset by unstable axes, walls and skins torn, ripped and dangerously slashed, rooms empty of content and uncertain or no exits and entrances."[39]

Is the building, then, an induction into chaos, to the traumatic, nightmare scenarios so characteristic of life in the twentieth century—never pursued more grotesquely and rationally, nor on such a scale, than during the Holocaust? It is this, but even more precisely it draws us into a tactile and emotional awareness of the incessant, incoherent interplay between irrationality and the pursuit of order that represents, in Vidler's words again, "the fundament of contemporaneity, its reason for being."[40] He glosses this insight: "In such a world, Libeskind's ellipses, his wandering paths and warped spaces without perspective and ending blindly, can only be seen as so many tests of our own abilities to endure the vertigo experience of the labyrinths that, as Nietzsche had it over a century ago, make up the form of our modernity."[41]

I would make a distinction between modernity and contemporaneity: it is the aftermath of the former that constitutes much of the substance of the latter. It is this constitution that Libeskind was striving to represent. This emerges when Vidler argues that, to Libeskind, the void is not a way out of the labyrinth (that being impossible) but "a provisional path . . . which through habitual and piecemeal encounters, by unexpected and suddenly revealed shocks, and through touch and feel in the dark as much as by clear vision in the light, might in some way domesticate what for Pascal, as for us, has been a rather stern, uncompromising and certainly terrifying 'horror vacui' (horror of the void) in a world of apparently endless space and no place."[42]

Modernity would frame this kind of experience with myths of progress, or with attacks on their reductiveness. The deepest program of the museum responds to this definitively modernist doublet. It recognizes the vacuity of dreams of progress and the relative ineffectiveness of radical action against it. It aims to concretize a hope-filled negativity, the small consciousness of surviving in the void. One way of measuring Libeskind's success or failure would be to ask: is the museum's negativity of a kind that would have secured Adorno's approval? The question that has been posed and tested throughout this chapter is one step harder. It asks: does Libeskind succeed in creating an architecture that takes us beyond Adorno's question, that succeeds in transforming the architecture of aftermath into an architecture of hope, and does so, furthermore, without lapsing into liberal sympathizing?

The Jewish Answer

Libeskind's answer is a peculiarly but also particularly Jewish one. It is offered on two levels: that of overt contestation and that of subliminal negotiation. The first is evident in the forced contingency of the two aboveground buildings, the Collegienhaus and the Jewish Museum, and in the initial shift of the visitor through the older building to the underground passageway into the new one. Both of these initial orientations seem to announce the sharp division between

Germanness and Jewishness as the starting point. Their combined effect is to vanquish the Museum of Berlin, leaving us to take the entire ensemble, Collegienhaus included, as, now, the Jewish Museum Berlin. This latter certainly seems to be the experience of the visitor: the Rococo structure functions as no more than an elaborated entrance. In fact, in the course of planning and construction, the project underwent a succession of name changes that seem to reflect these shifts: beginning as an Extension to the Berlin Museum, one which included expansion of the Jewish Department, it became an Extension to the Berlin Museum with the Jewish Museum, to the entire project being one of the Jewish Department of the Stadtmuseum, then the Jewish Museum in the Stadtmuseum until finally it became the Jewish Museum Berlin. A new kind of museum, a Jewish kind, has, it seems, not only gained autonomy from its parent, the Museum of Berlin, it has eclipsed, even absorbed, its progenitor. This is some reversal of the final solution.

Yet there is a more profound, and fitting, sense in which this is a Jewish museum. The idea that we all share, like it or not, a "common fate," in which the obliteration of one type of those among us has been contemplated, has often been systematically pursued, and may well be again, is, in a special sense, a *Jewish* idea embodied in this museum, yet one offered to humanity. In his interpretation of this museum, Andrew Benjamin draws attention to an important distinction, underlying the project at its deepest levels, between the identity of being a Jew and Jewish being as such.[43] The first is an imposed Jewishness, never more thoroughly pursued than by the Nazis. While developing his thinking for the museum, Libeskind was permitted to see a *Gedenkbuch*, a two-volume listing of the names, addresses, dates of birth, dates of deportation, and presumed destinations of those sent to their deaths during the fatal years of the Holocaust.[44] Benjamin points out that these people were listed, in this book, in a way that they—as mostly secular Jews who believed that they were assimilated into the cosmopolis around them— would rarely have thought of themselves and would never before have been associated, not even by Jewish organizations. They became Jews because of "a special occurrence . . . to be named in a book that marks their mass death."[45] In this form of identification, identity amounts to closures of an increasingly horrific and ultimately terminal kind: submission to administration, reification into a cipher, reduction to a name and some dates on a list of those to be executed. Jewish *being*, on the other hand—as the philosophers cited in this chapter amply attest—is a matter of putting identity into question, of opening it to the productivities of perpetual interrogation. Neither oneself nor the others can alone decide the question of who one is, the matter of what it is to be. In the face of the forces of closure, this is the offering, to all, from the experience of being Jewish: the unanswerability of being, its decisive undecidability. Benjamin sees precisely this as the deepest inspiration and the most powerful effect of the Jewish Museum Berlin:

> Here is a building that guards the question of representation, refusing it finality and thus necessitating its retention as a problem to be investigated, while allowing

at the same time for presentations; a building that questions display while allowing for display; a building that, in its effectuation as a building, holds open the question of remembrance as a question, enjoining humility while providing—because of the question—the necessity for a vigilance that can be identified as present remembrance . . . in being an architecture of the question, the Museum allows identity to endure as a question; this is a way of interpreting what Libeskind may have meant by hope.[46]

Warring between Museum and Exhibit

During the two years it was open prior to the staging of exhibitions within it, the museum attracted 350,000 paying visitors. Many were architects, and those interested in architecture as such. Since September 8, 2001, when the exhibitions were finally installed, some have objected to them as a distraction, as a lesser experience than the building itself. The exhibits have been devoted to a broad narrative of the history of Jews in Berlin, and to some special individuals—including, of course, Walter Benjamin. When I visited in May 2002, it was bursting at its seams with tokens of memory, each a small, poignant monument. So many, however, that the implacable negativity of the museum was obscured and its equally trenchant yet demanding hope was returned to a more easily accessible hopefulness. Who could blame the curators? When you have been silenced for so long, a visual cacophony on first outing is to be expected. But this was no natural outpouring: it fell subject to the current most fashionable style of general-purpose museum exhibiting. Designer Ken Corby was also responsible for the Tin Pan Alley populism of the opening displays at the Te Papa National Museum in Wellington, New Zealand.[47]

Reversing the positive response by architecture professionals, many visitors have complained that the building is unfunctional, frustrating to curators of exhibitions, and confusing to the public. The opening exhibitions were overloaded to the point that a feeling of quiet chaos and desperation was induced. But this sense of too much is not a consequence of the architectural design itself. Libeskind, as we have seen, created a memorial/museum, that is, a building with a complex, always doubling, set of purposes. And within these two goals, a myriad of pathways. Each in its own way, the architecture and the exhibitions tell a story of integration, forced removal, and redemption that is first hard to take and then profoundly moving. This is the classic narrative of a memorial to the dead, to loss of any kind. The exhibitions did this by means of image and text, objects and explanations. The architecture, as we have seen, and have heard attested, did so by means of a series of extraordinary spatial sequences.

If a series of raking corridors culminating in a heavily concrete void transports you into a sense of being a victim of the Holocaust, who needs to be directed into a mock-up freight train to trigger the same emotions? When seemingly endless staircases lead to nowhere, to the blank walls around from which one turns to see that towering over one's path are collapsing supports, rubble, further voids and splits of light, who needs to walk through a mock-up concentration camp? Nor do you need the visage of a smiling survivor when you reach the outside, and enter a "garden" that consists of gigantic boxed columns, each enclosing a pomegranate tree that nevertheless grows wildly from its upper opening, the whole pitched at an unearthly angle. Here is a fascinating paradox: a building that fulfills not only the purpose of being an appropriate house for, in this case, a museum of Jewish history but one that became, in itself, in its shapes and spaces, a site of Jewish experience. An architecture that induces this experience in all of its users, Jews and others at once (but not, of course, alike).[48]

Is the museum, despite its architect's consciousness of the relativity of time, and the complexity of the movement back and forward in time necessitated by its core purpose, nevertheless marked by its own time of conception and creation and its position within the history of architecture? Of course it is, as much as, in its exceptionality, it pushes, partly, past those constraints. Vidler is, again, the best guide to this aspect of the building:

> If we cannot characterize this building as either "posthistorical" or yet fully historical, we can nevertheless understand it as a kind of terminal state of space, a millennial closure so to speak, that stands as a paradoxical statement of the twentieth century problem of monumentality: how, without history (the clothing of which afforded such security in the nineteenth century), and without ostentatious pretension and empty theatricality, can an architectural object imply a strong status, while constructing itself out of space—the one medium that, as the high modernists perceived, was opposed to monumentality from the outset.[49]

It does so, he suggests, by capturing space, holding it hostage by its "impermeable walls"; thus it "preserves space, as a traditional museum would preserve art." In this sense, he concludes, "it is a museum of and in architecture." This is a conclusion that echoes our account of the Getty Center, but with a difference, one that goes back to the distinction between "weak" and "strong" architecture noted earlier. As Vidler has elsewhere shown us, modern architectural space was fraught with anxieties of the most Freudian kind.[50] At the same time, for modernists space was opposed to monumentality, because they wished for its purity, its potential as the domain in which a utopian future might be lived. After Auschwitz, this is revealed to be what it always was: an impossible naïveté. Space in the Jewish Museum, especially when its rooms are emptied of displays, is filled, palpably, with the anxiety induced by the question: how is it possible to be human after the enactment of systemic inhumanity? These spaces are also split by shafts of light that shine back on the questioner—who is, after all, the only hope of an answer.

Aesthetic Occupation

The battles for Jerusalem, and the systematic unbuilding of Palestine by the Israeli army, were specters that filled public discourse during the construction of the Jewish Museum Berlin. By filling a column in the garden that symbolized Berlin with earth from Jerusalem, Libeskind gestures, rather weakly, at this connection.

Nevertheless, the core message of the museum, as we have interpreted it—that the labyrinthine openness of perpetual self-questioning, rather than the citadel-like closures of fundamentalism, is the human way forward—is one that has to be the basis for any hope of peace in that region.

Indian architect Romi Khosla has imagined an architectural "solution" to the Palestine-Israel problem: one structured around a train that performs transportation, socializing, and museum functions as it travels incessantly along a water pipe that connects a proposed new sovereign state of New Canaan.[51] This kind of quasi-fanciful proposal would, perhaps, infuriate those, such as Daniel Monk, who, in connection with the current warring over religious sites in Jerusalem, raise the issue of whether the very identification of architecture with a nonarchitectural value—that of nationality, for example, or of spirituality—is not itself a violent fusing of elements that reason, if it is to be achieved, must keep separate.[52] Yet architecture is made in a world of contradiction, of competing demands, and is always an act of dialectical reasoning laced with intuition. If the shapes of peace and reconciliation are to be discerned within the visual cacophony that is the contemporary iconomy, they must be prepared for symbolic contestation. As we have seen, this requires the mobilization, through architectural form, of meanings that go far beyond the limits of an autonomous architecture, one defined in either modernist or heritage terms.

Minimalist Memorials: The Contemporary Cult of the Antimonument

It is no coincidence that the kind of language used by Vidler to account for his direct experience of the Jewish Museum is, at first glance, scarcely distinguishable from that which many visitors—myself included—have been moved to utter when striving to describe their feelings upon entering the atrium at the Guggenheim Museum, Bilbao. Yet Gehry's building is, as we have seen, a cathedral of Contemporary Art, not a Holocaust monument: how could the experience of both have anything in common? One reason is that, to secure many of his effects Libeskind, like Gehry and Meier, used the by now international art language of Minimal sculpture and post-Conceptual installation art. This has in turn become a lingua franca of contemporary architecture. And it has proved particularly effective in the design of public memorials—indeed, it has been indispensable to what might amount to a post-modern (although, to be accurate, it is a contemporary) cult of the antimonument, or better, the unmonumental memorial.

Maya Lin achieved extraordinary public success when she recycled the form of a Richard Serra steel piece as an earthwork in her Vietnam Veterans Memorial in the Mall, Washington.[53] For some, this disqualifies the memorial as a serious work of art. It would thus fail the test of being an architecture that was so compelling in its architectural logic that it became an attractor for its quality as art. But this judgment puts a premium on originality at the level of signature style. Like Gehry, Meier, Koolhaas, Libeskind, and a number of others, Lin's success as a communicator is based in her ability to deploy Minimalist art strategies to maximal public, palpably lucid, symbolic purpose.[54]

Lin's originality, we can now see, was to create a piece of public art that brought together, around an independent critical consciousness, the elements of the program given to her. As we descend the path alongside the marble wall, noting the list of American casualties, all 58,158 of them, we experience the fact of death, the irrevocability of specific human lives. Against the shock of this actuality, the venal and arbitrary politics of that war quickly shifts off to another, differently valid, register. From within the black, reflective marble, our own specter shadows us, offering an irresistible invitation to reach out and touch a name. We see ourselves doing so. We pause, at its base, immersed in the immensity of this kind of dying, aware at once of its pointlessness as a generality and its particular point for those who died and those who mourn them. This connection of self-to-other, enacted privately yet out in the open, in this fold in the earth, is the experience that is at the core of the memorial. It is an act of remembrance available to everyone. It is a gesture of healing that echoes the memorial's own form: its closing a gash in the earth, a slash in parkland. War seems impossible from such a place: thus the antiwar sentiment at this memorial's core, its audacity. Small wonder that, while most veterans and most everybody else is evidently satisfied with the memorial, certain organized vets and others pushed for the subsidiary memorials that kitsch up the site.[55]

> Ms. Lin's sculpture confronts the visitor with the greatest controversy of the Vietnam war: body counts. More and more soldiers die as you walk down. Just like the war planners in the 60's, you are literally in over your head with all the death. But Ms. Lin's sculpture also offers you a narrative. After you walk in, you have to walk out. Ms. Lin's thinking about the exit is her genius. Either route tells the story of Vietnam that is still hard for Americans to think about. The war ended, not in a military victory, but a democratic one. The American public insisted that the officials shut the war down, and they did. The two paths Ms. Lin inscribed in the earth point to the twin exits of all of America's great constitutional battles: to the east is the Washington Monument, the symbol of Liberty; to the southwest, the Lincoln memorial, dedicated to the promise of equality. Back to first principles. Back to the Constitution. This was the way out of Vietnam and the only way out of Ms. Lin's memorial. It is what redeems all of those deaths and moves the narrative Ms. Lin is telling.[56]

These words, by journalist Jack Hitt, rightly stress the importance of narrative to the experience of the memorial, and, in his evocation of the Gettysburg Address, its larger political point from an American perspective. He omits, however, any reference to Vietnamese and other victims. To some of us at least, their deaths too are marked by this memorial.

As a result of its extraordinary success, the Vietnam Veterans Memorial has become canonical. It has established the international language of acceptable memorials. Its movement down through mourning then up through redemption echoes in many of the V-shaped wedges that proliferate through Libeskind's Jewish Museum notebooks. Raked angles dominate the museum's garden, as we have noted. Similar shapes appear in Peter Eisenman's Berlin Memorial for the Murdered Jews of Europe, completed after much acrimony and hesitation, in

2004. If representational forms are used in recent memorials, they tend to appear in schematic, minimal form: thus the chairs symbolizing each of the victims in the garden of the Memorial to the Victims of the Bombing of the Oklahoma Federal Building, and the benches for each victim set into the park outside the Pentagon along the illuminated path taken by American Airlines flight 77 on 9.11.01. A similar mix characterized all finalists among the entries for a memorial at Ground Zero. It was no surprise that the design that employed the most minimal aesthetic was the one chosen: Michael Arad's concept "Reflecting Absence" (illus. 56).

Berlin Free Zone

Berlin is, of course, not the only city where these issues have become pressing. New York-based architect Lebbeus Woods traveled extensively in Europe during the Yugoslavian wars of the 1990s. His notebooks include anguished drawings of the attrition visited upon Sarajevo. One that shows an implosive conflagration, seen as if from above and below at once, is captioned *Who can forgive the crime? Abandoned to die*, and is accompanied by these comments: "The crime whose guilt is in two parts—first, the Serb gunners and their commanders—second, the so-called Great Powers, which let it happen and continue. WHO CAN BELIEVE, AFTER SARAJEVO, IN THE HUMANITY OF GOVERNMENTS, IN THE GOOD INTENTIONS OF AUTHORITY?"[57]

Another drawing, made on June 10, 1992, is captioned *Imagine the Towers, Burning* (illus. 28). A paragraph from Woods' 1993 pamphlet *War and Architecture* sums up his perspective in words that sound, in the aftermath of 9.11.01, uncannily prescient, but actually update his long-held view that war and architecture have always been partners in both crime and reconstruction:

> The towers are now burned in Sarajevo. The steel and glass monuments to enlightened progress in an age of industrial society are gutted hulks and with them the ideologies and values they embodied. Sarajevo's skyscrapers were prime targets of gunners in the hills together with the minarets and domed mosques, the great library, the post office, the university buildings, and all the others that symbolized reason and its promise of humane civil life. Once set afire by incendiary shells, there was no way to save them. Not only had the infrastructure with which to do so been destroyed, but also the delicate tissue of reasons to do so. The burning towers of Sarajevo are markers of the end of an age of reasons, if not reason itself, beyond which lies a domain of almost incomprehensible darkness.[58]

Following this experience, Woods developed a way of imagining buildings that incorporated their destruction within them, yet still kept functioning as livable environments (or at least as settings for survival). Against heritage restoration as a form of aestheticized social amnesia, he proposed that building occur in ways that recognized that ruins should retain the marks of their historical suffering. He devised a sequence for reinhabiting the ruins: "scab" shapes that would be added to the half-destroyed structures to allow for essential shelter and minimal

28. Lebbeus Woods,
Imagine the Towers,
Burning. 1992, pen on
paper. From Woods'
"Notebook 28 Mai 92
to 15 June 92."
Research Library, the
Getty Research
Institute,
Los Angeles, and
Lebbeus Woods
[970081, box 1].

I MAGINE THE TOWERS, BURNING —

services, were followed by "scars" that would integrate the marks of destruction, the surviving fabric and new construction, itself of the most basic, materials-to-hand sort. Financing would occur through barter, not institutional borrowing. Regulation would be at the disposition of the occupiers, not the authorities—they having been shown up as complicit in the destruction, prone to corruption and enslaved to either modernist clear-felling followed by the building of new barracks (the East German model) or the faux-pastness of heritage restoration. The consequence for urban planning of Woods's approach is, precisely, an avoidance of planning. It is the creation of "free zones" in the shards of war-torn cities.

Woods has applied these ideas in this 1990 Berlin Free Zone project, among others (illus. 29). Many of his drawings show huge missile-like bombs embedded

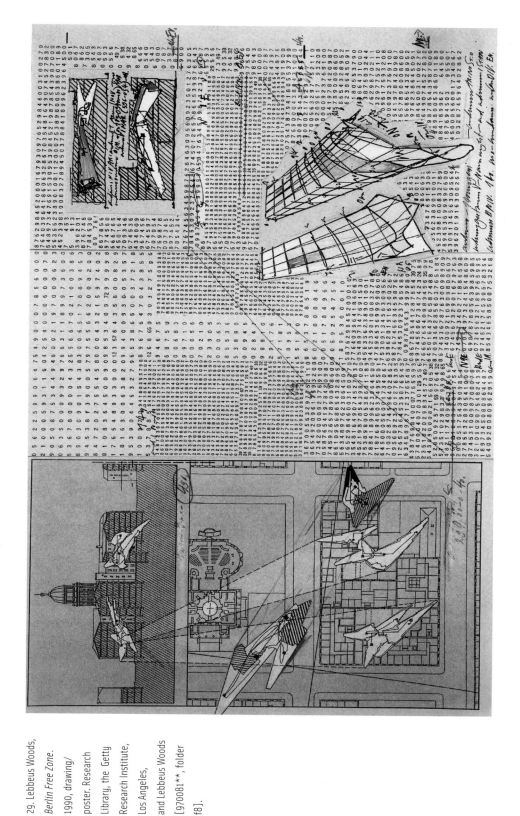

29. Lebbeus Woods,
Berlin Free Zone.
1990, drawing/
poster. Research
Library, the Getty
Research Institute,
Los Angeles,
and Lebbeus Woods
[970081**, folder
f8].

in apartment blocks, both together being transformed into living spaces by squatters and others who wish to build lives within them. The concept of "living ruins" gains new meaning. Similarly, he imagines the entire Mitte district—since the 1990s subject to much heritage restoration and infilling by global chains of expensive boutiques—as a zone cut and carved by swooping spirits that have flown in from who knows where. They are, at least, not bombs, nor are they attack planes. Their payload is freedom.

PART 2 TARGETS AND OPPORTUNITIES

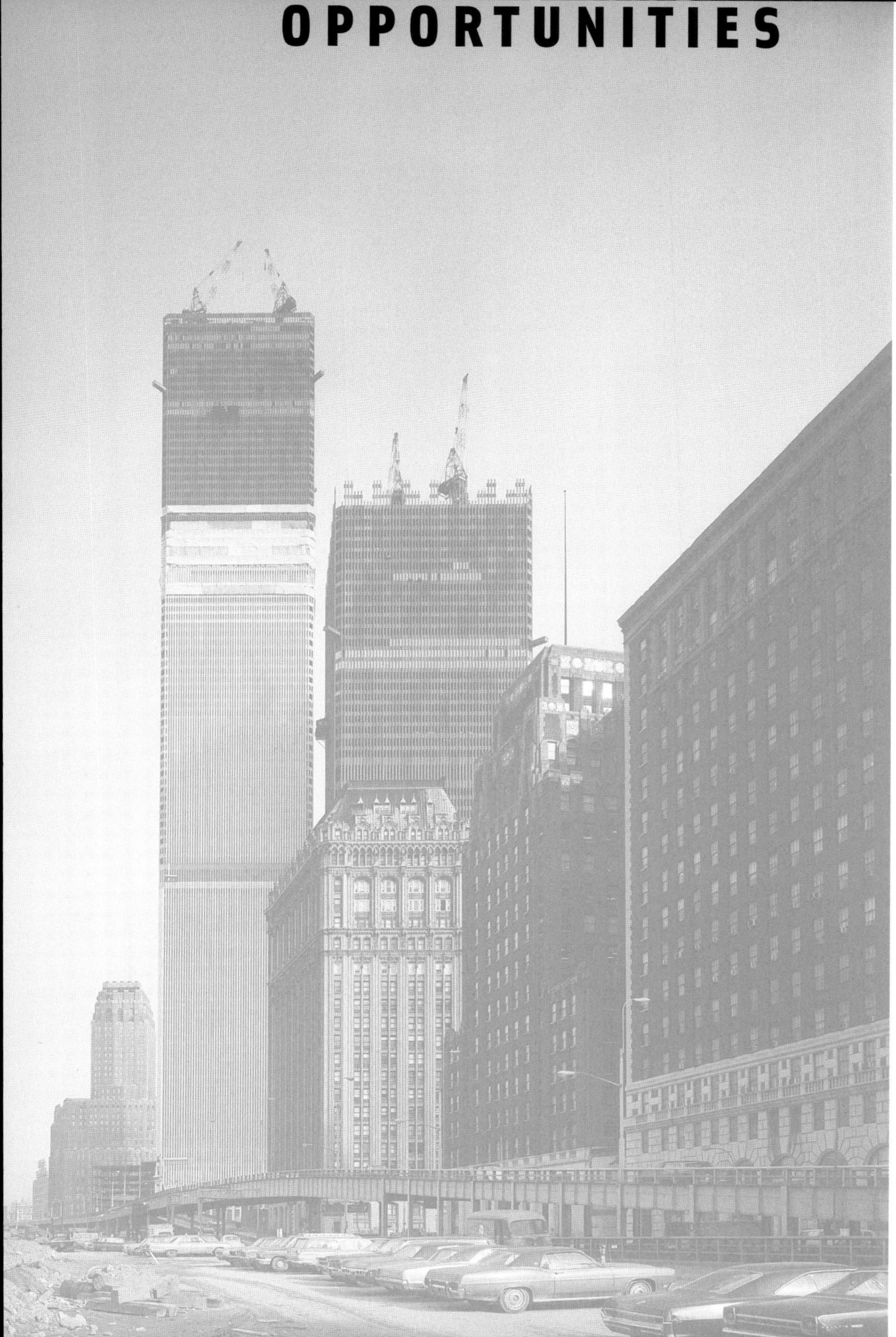

Fast Forward: *Skyscrapers on the Isle of the Dead*

The Iconography of Manhattan Island

When, towards the end of the twentieth century, modern Manhattan was celebrated as a "forest of symbols," the meaning of this metaphor was immediately apparent: the skyscrapers that crowd its Midtown and Downtown, the skyline that they animate, and the unmistakable profile of the city. Taken together these elements amount to a unique image: New York City, the world's home base of modernity as a way of life.[1] Standing tall among architectural forms, the skyscraper had come to symbolize most emphatically the alliance of thrusting capital and adventurous technology that, to many, was the driving force of modernity. Ada Louise Huxtable opened *The Tall Building Artistically Reconsidered* with these words: "The skyscraper and the twentieth century are synonymous: the tall building is the landmark of our age. As a structural marvel that breaks the traditional limits on mankind's persistent ambition to build to the heavens, the skyscraper is this century's most stunning architectural phenomenon. It is certainly its most overwhelming architectural presence."[2] Philip Johnson, himself a producer of many striking examples, put his finger on why the skyscraper flourished in Chicago and New York, and later in Asia: "Our commercial skyscrapers are the result of the pushing and shoving of the competitive commercial world . . . Masses of towers together represent a cultural age that strives for fame and recognition—standing. I've got a bigger [   ] than you have."[3] In New York, skyscrapers were in-the-face-of-God expressions of the city's surges of economic energy, worn with pride and without ambiguity, not just on its sleeve but all over its seemingly irrepressible body. NYC became the corporate headquarters of Modernity Inc., and the skyscraper its iconic visual manifestation. For those who came to the city from outside, or who saw it through the distances of reproduction, the skyscraper skyline has long been its symbolic portal.

Even those who had no love for modernity's achievements, no taste for its attractions, formed their views with reference to this bustling cluster of built images. Writing on September 12, 2001, the editors of *ArchitectureWeek* had no doubts about the face that the city presented to hostile encampments abroad: "The skyscraper targets in New York City were prominent symbols of our civilization, buildings of American invention that all over the world expressed the spirit of a will to soar above the earth in creations of steel, concrete and glass. The terrorists chose very carefully. They discerned those skyscrapers as the cathedrals of our age and aimed at their heart."[4] This reading of the enemy's intentions might seem confirmed if we recall Sayyid Qutb's dismay at what he found in America.[5] Or Osama bin Laden's warning: "To America and its people, I say a few words: I swear to God, who raised the sky without pillars, that America and those who live in it will not be able to dream of security before we live it on the ground in Palestine, and before all of the infidel armies leave the land of the Prophet, may peace and God's blessings be upon him." Indeed, in his videotape intervention into the 2004 U.S. election campaign, bin Laden confirmed that the idea of launching bombing attacks against the towers of American cities came to him after he witnessed the 1982 Israeli invasion of Lebanon and the bombing of Beirut high-rises by the cannons of the Sixth Fleet.[6]

Whatever else is going on in these exchanges—and a lot is going on—they take the form of a palpable trading in visual stereotypes, in images of destruction and symbols of power, aimed at creating certain quite specific effects in the minds and hearts of others. But the world picture has never been starkly black and white, nor is the iconomy a simple field on which encapsulated intention, put out there into the glare, guarantees an expected impact. Just as cultural stereotypes are the most reductive versions of vast quantities of habitual particularity, visual icons are the most visible tips of mountains of contending representations. There is resistance, and counterexample, everywhere. The interplay of generalities and specifics drives these ensembles forward, pushing them into configurations that we see, often, as spectacle's tapestry, while at other times they disappear into the plain shadows of the ordinary. Most images hover in half-lit spaces between these two textures.

When Marshall Berman used the metaphor with which I began this chapter, he did so from the inside, and from within an expansive vision of democracy, seeing the city as having been consciously shaped into a "Baudelairean forest of symbols" that included not only the famous skyscrapers but also expanses such as Central Park and Coney Island and districts such as Greenwich Village and Times Square. This kind of openness as to what counts as iconic, and to the mobile meanings of how icons iconize, is the counterpoint to both market and millennial reductiveness, to the stereotypes of spectacle society. Openness was the spirit of the 1960s, as consumerism grew and colonial empires crumbled, and of the 1970s, when critical questioning found wide voice. But something changed, for the bigger but the lesser, in the 1980s, when the markets and the dictators grabbed power. Architecture stands out in these kinds of contexts, or it retreats and disappears, all in its own special ways. In the previous chapters we have seen some of its icons shining forth, or hiding in the light, at the end of the twentieth century. Let us turn to the most prominent building type of them all: the skyscraper. Especially the pair that were, for a time, not only the tallest buildings anywhere, but were also, in the retrospective summary of two *New York Times* journalists, "the biggest and brashest icons that New York ever produced—physically magnificent, intimately familiar structures."[7]

The Erasures

During the late 1960s, twelve blocks of downtown Manhattan were obliterated to provide the sixteen-acre site for the series of buildings that constituted the World Trade Center. This was the most extensive erasure in the site's volatile human history. It took out an area known as the Syrian Quarter. A diverse Middle Eastern neighborhood, including Arabic people from Egypt, Iraq, Lebanon, Palestine, and elsewhere, it was also an internationally known, thriving bazaar. Community leaders promoted it as a model immigrant community, driven by "ethnic trade," and as contributing something distinctive to the American Dream. Radio Row also fell under the hammer: fifteen bustling blocks devoted to the manufacture and retail of electronics, textiles, garments, and dry goods. The disappearance of the nearby Washington markets was another ghostly consequence. The layered ironies of such dense concentrations of people, especially Middle Eastern, engaged in innovative international trade, gathering on this site, and then being abruptly dispersed from it, scarcely need underlining. Various versions of the WTC story were told before its destruction; even more have emerged since.[8] I will highlight those elements that were crucial to its times, and remain vital to its continuing life as an iconotype.

The early history of the place is characterized by patterns of Indian and European usage and settlement, ebbs and flows interrupted by sudden moments of violent destruction, and periods of energetic rebuilding. These are gathered in the extraordinary archive, *The Iconography of Manhattan Island, 1498–1909*, collected by the Reverend Isaac Newton Phelps Stokes early in the twentieth century.[9] Two hundred years before then, much of the site was underwater, the North (later Hudson) River flowing along the edge of what is now Greenwich Street, the shoreline turning slightly inland at what is now Dey Street and then running south again to meet the end of what is now Broadway, once a typical Dutch canal, the major one in New Amsterdam. Munsee Lenape settlements were nearby, suggesting that the site may have been a landing point. Any possible ritual use is not reported in published histories, yet it was part of land created by Kishelemulong—the creator deity of the Munsee Lenape—and held by his descendents in common trust. It was not part of the original Dutch West India Company's trading post on the island, "purchased" by Governor Minuit from the Lenape Indians (for trinkets worth approximately a pound and a half of silver).[10] Under tribal law, hunting and planting land might be shared or temporarily transferred; it could not be sold or owned. As in other settler colonies, cooperation between Indians and Europeans soon descended into violence and exploitation. Systematic "clearing" of the Munsee occurred during the 1640s.[11] Meanwhile, the fortifications at what became Battery Point continued to grow, in anticipation of threats from other European powers. They indicate the strategic military and commercial value of the island as a whole to its colonizers, its early role as an outpost of the New World. Historians of Manhattan emphasize the violence that has been inflicted on its peoples for centuries, their "sense of exposure, of precariousness, of vulnerability," along, of course, with their fabled energy and aggressiveness. Manhattan, it might be said, has always been at war.[12] A sense of outpost continued to define the symbolic role of New York as the city that seemed, for much of the twentieth century, to be leading Western civilization—indeed, the world, it so often, so loudly, said—into the future.

The Dutch West India Company established a thirty-three-acre food-growing area in 1625: one of its corners overlapped the future WTC site. A decade later this land was sold to a Dutch farmer and was in turn sold to a British captain in 1671. Resumed by the Crown, it was leased and then, in 1705, given to the Trinity Church. During this period, its name changed from Bouwery to King Farm, then to Queen and finally Trinity Farm. In the early eighteenth century, at its watery western borders, indeed "at high Water Mark," Greenwich Street was established, as were the other neighborhood streets, such as Dey and Cortland. They began as piers stretched over areas exposed by low water marks, which were filled in with the refuse of the city. Manhattan had become a principal center for the slave trade (a market was located at the foot of Wall Street) and, by midcentury, the military headquarters of Britain in the American colonies. A port city had sprung into existence on all sides of the farm, so the church seized the opportunity by offering farmland up as leases for cheap housing. A working-class neighborhood quickly developed, complementing the rich one on the other side of Broadway around Wall Street. Between them emerged a brothel area that was soon named, and became widely known as, the Holy Ground.

The site achieved a different kind of notoriety during the American Revolution. Rebels lodging at one of its many hotels may have been the source of the great fire that swept the city on September 21, 1776. Coming a short time after General Washington and his troops had been driven from the city, and nearly destroyed, by the British army, the fire wiped out a quarter of the city's buildings, making it scarcely functional. Rebel arson was suspected; patriots were arrested and hung for the crime. The Trinity Church neighborhood, including of course the future site of the WTC, was reduced to ashes. The British marched away from the ruined city in 1783.

Yet in less than twenty years the city renewed itself, becoming by 1810 the most populous in the United States. Why? Because its leaders reshaped it for growth and turned it into a pivotal location for local, national, and international commerce. The word "Manhattan" is Algonquin for "Island of Hills." These were, mostly, leveled by De Witt Clinton in 1811, and a grid system created above 14th Street, consisting of 12 straight north-south avenues and 155 perpendicular east-west streets, or roughly 2,000 blocks of similar size, further divisible into lots. The aim was to encourage "the buying, selling and improving of real estate." This imposition of a singular geometry was extraordinary and went against the grain of the evolution of most European cities to that date. It was the local instance of the battle between the plan and the city that has driven urban modernization to this day. The Enlightenment ideals of rationality and perfectibility were imposed, literally (and not, as we shall see, for the last time), in the interests of making magical quantities of money. In the resultant boom, the Trinity area became a key point for ferry departures, an energetic commercial waterfront. This was reinforced by the opening of the Erie Canal in 1823, which had the effect of making Manhattan the port of preference for exports from the Midwest. The Trinity area became integrated into Manhattan, world capital of modernity, losing its residential character and becoming more and more a central business district, its workers commuting, each day, from elsewhere on the island and from throughout the region. The WTC was the culmination of exactly this development. The geography of the site, however, did not change much from the 1840s until 1966, when the building stock and all else in the vicinity was reduced to rubble, then interred within the massive landfill for a very 1970s form of farming: the upscale residential development of Battery Park City.

Like most other cities in the modern era, then, New York has a history of violent destruction of its pasts and of volatile transformation of itself from its insides in. This is essential to what makes such cities modern. Manhattan, as usual, just had more of it. It certainly drove New York City, which has been under constant attack—or stimulation, depending on your viewpoint—by ever more ambitious schemes to channel the energies of its citizens and its visitors into forms from which profits could be extracted. Robert Moses, planning czar of the city during the 1940s through to the 1960s, infamously said: "When you operate in an over-built metropolis, you have to hack your way with a meat axe."[13]

The Evacuators

The WTC project, in its earliest incarnation, was conceived by David Rockefeller, a vice-president but effectively in control of the then dominant Chase Manhattan Bank, that had just built a major skyscraper headquarters in Lower Manhattan. His unadorned motivation—inspired by the most powerful planner Manhattan has known, Robert Moses, and a now-forgotten real estate broker, William Zeckendorf—was to shore up the bank's real estate investments in the area, and to counter the tendency of the financial markets to gravitate toward Midtown, rather than Downtown, as their location for business and possible expansion.[14] In this, he was following the strategy pursued so successfully by his father, John D. Rockefeller, in the early 1930s. To build that much-boosted "city within a city," the Rockefeller Center, eight blocks of decaying townhouses were torn down and replaced with a business center that housed 50,000 occupants and 16,000 visitors a day. In ten years it grew to encompass a twelve-acre site, the core of a still-vibrant commercial and entertainment distinct. A generation later, in 1956, David Rockefeller formed the Downtown-Lower Manhattan Association (DLMA) to do the same thing for the now historic, and struggling, Wall Street area.

A 1958 *New York Times* article bubbles with excitement about the Downtown-Lower Manhattan Association's vision, redescribing the same neighborhoods in the language of "development":

A billion-dollar redevelopment scheme for lower Manhattan was presented in broad outline yesterday at City Hall. The proposals for public and private improvements would cause radical changes in the 564-acre district, where the tall towers of banking, shipping and insurance offices are fringed and outnumbered by low brick buildings that are more than 100 years old. The plan calls for the following improvements over a number of years:

Razing most of the outmoded structures to permit expansion of the financial district and other types of development;

Closing many of the narrow streets and crooked alleys through the assembling of housing and other industrial sites;

Widening the streets to create an interior traffic loop;

Replacing some East River piers with a heliport and small boat marina.

A few historic buildings would be preserved. The plan calls for the relocation of the Fulton Fish Market and the sprawling West Side wholesale produce market.[15]

The World Trade Center concept emerged as the landmark, linchpin building of this larger scheme. To see Manhattan from such a perspective, you need to picture

a New York without Soho, Tribeca, Chinatown, or Little Italy. There is no South Street Seaport, and the Southern end of Greenwich Village is gone. Imagine these communities are high-rise super-blocks and residential projects set amongst exit ramps for an expressway that bisects Manhattan at Broome Street. A broken wall of Corbusian slabs sprouts on pillars above the open cuts of vehicular flow. This east-west artery runs perpendicular to another massive thoroughfare obliterating Washington Square Park and running up Fifth Avenue, linking the business districts of Midtown and Wall Street.[16]

None of this erasive gigantism made its way unopposed, and it never succeeded, even in New York—not entirely, anyway. Moses, the Port Authority, and the expedient coalitions of businessmen such as the DLMA were confronted by a citizens' movement that celebrated the values of local communality, of street life and neighborhoods, of individual and collective distinctiveness within the melting pot. Their values were expressed in books such as Jane Jacobs's *The Death and Life of Great American Cities* (1961) and *The Economy of Cities* (1969). Such attitudes and protests helped stop most of Robert Moses's "urban renewals" during the 1960s, not least the cross-Manhattan freeway. Vociferous protest was raised in the streets and the shops against the evident fact that the Port Authority, in claiming a "public purpose" for its move into real estate, was exceeding its charter. For a time, Mayor Robert Wagner, elected on a behemoth-busting platform, pitched the power of the city against this abuse. So did his successor, John V. Lindsay. But nothing prevailed against the building of the WTC—the most visible, most extreme realization of developmentalism in the city's history. All thinking about New York seems structured around the dichotomy embodied in these struggles: the big, bold, epoch-defining idea and the multiplicitous, differentiated, ongoing flow of the everyday.

The city was the capital city of modernity just in that its warring against itself in this way was so pronounced, so up-front.

A side effect of this internal struggle is a city in a constant state of transformation, most visible in the excavations every few blocks, the road blockages and detours, the frameworks arising up from cosseted building sites, and the filigree of cranes along the skyline. Excavation is a long-running theme in New York art, from the Pictorialist photographs of Alfred Stieglitz through the vigorous cityscapes of George Bellows and the sharp-edged graphics of Louis Lozowick to the abstract unfoldings of Willem de Kooning, above all in his epic painting of 1950, *Excavation*. Experiencing this state of change on a daily basis as he grew up in the Bronx moved urbanist Marshall Berman to observe, "Among the many images and symbols that New York has contributed to modern culture, one of the most striking in recent years has been an image of modern ruin and devastation."[17]

"It's Hard to Be Down When You're Up!"

This slogan adorned the observation deck of the WTC during the 1970s. It captures the self-mockery that often accompanies the most blatant New Yorker hubris. In 1958, David Rockefeller's brother Nelson was elected governor of New York State and lent crucial support to the Downtown-Lower Manhattan Association's master plan. (An early nickname for the towers was "David and Nelson".) Plans for "a World Trade Center in the heart of the Port District" were announced in January 1960. As we have just seen, the DLMA initially concentrated its redevelopment plans on the East Side, first north, then south of the Brooklyn Bridge. But the urge to expand moved the planners' thoughts westward. By May 1960, their interests converged with those of the Port Authority of New York. This agency, established to oversight the health and growth of the ports of New York, had become a major player in the modernization of the city and the region. It had recently added a second deck to the George Washington Bridge, a third tube to the Lincoln Tunnel, and was involved in the Verrazano-Narrows Bridge, with its world-beating suspension span, then under construction. Its ambition was signaled by its taking control of the three regional airports. Clearly, at the Port Authority, "port" was as expandable a concept as "authority."[18]

The Port Authority had a crucial capacity, one that even the Rockefeller family lacked: it could take ownership of land by eminent domain for a public purpose within its charter. As well, it could avoid a multitude of regulations to which even private enterprise was subject. And, to sweeten any deal, it was a virtual tax haven. Yet it had a problem that, paradoxically, issued from its very success. The vast revenues earned from the tolls collected at its bridges and tunnels (approaching $200 million in 1960) made it a trusted issuer of bonds that could raise still more funds. It was therefore much sought after as a co-investor in activities that ranged far from the provision of port facilities and public transport through them—in real estate, for example. Yet the public expected these huge sums (especially surpluses, such as that of $79 million in 1960) to be turned to purposes for which the authority had been established: the supply of efficient and cheap public transit through the city and its environs. And local business expected the authority to provide cheap and efficient transit for the goods it imported and exported. But the leadership, notably executive director Austin Tobin, knew that mass transit was a financial sinkhole, one that would drain even its constantly replenished coffers. Nor did the authority have a plan to solve the most obvious problem in the transportation of goods to and from the city: that Manhattan remained an expensive and inefficient clearinghouse for goods that were being shipped to the New Jersey shores, and to other nearby ports, with increasing efficiency and at lower costs. At the time, both travelers and port users were turning away from Lower Manhattan, looking elsewhere for alternatives. Tobin saw the chance to avoid having to solve these problems, and to secure great revenues for the authority, by making it into a real estate player, on a gigantic scale. He saw the WTC as a "port without water."[19] Like an airport. It would be a virtual port, a node in a world wide web of economic exchange. Its ten million square feet of floor space was designed to entice foreign business organizations to take up office space in the complex, in order to trade with U.S. companies and agencies. In a curious predestination, its business plan was to invite otherness in—to the city, to the U.S., to do business.

The WTC proposal, especially when it was allied with the Battery Park development, seemed to solve all of these problems at a stroke. Or actually in two. In a bold repetition of the eighteenth-century device for creating new real estate out of thin air, director of the project for the Port Authority, Guy Tozzoli, came up with the idea of pouring the junk from demolished Radio Row and the dirt excavated from the building site into the Hudson right next door.[20] This move gave the project as much horizontal spread as its promoters wished it to have in the vertical dimension. At the level of organizational form, this was repeated in the creation of a new entity, the Port Authority of New York *and* New Jersey. By turning away from its primary public purposes, and reinventing itself as a real estate developer, the Port Authority seemed headed in a bold new direction. It could use its revenue millions to stoke up still more, in the form of profits ready for the taking.

In reality, as an economic adventure, the WTC became a monument to the lengths that various levels of government will go to in order to prop up the free market until it is ready to come in and reap profits. Governor Rockefeller paid top rental dollar to fill floor after floor with state office workers. The Port Authority, despite having to pay the city an annual fee miniscule in relation to what other developers pay in taxes, lost a fortune—between $10 and $15 million annually before it began, in 1981, to break even. Building costs blew out from the original $280 million estimate to close to $1 billion. A further $1.4 billion was spent over the following twenty-five years on construction and capital improvements. The WTC failed as a site on which the world came to trade with the U.S.; it paid its own way only in the 1980s and 1990s, when the burgeoning U.S. money market spread through the area, gobbling up available space. The WTC had gradually become the headquarters of more and more U.S. companies, above all banks, insurance companies, and those leading the money market. In pockets, there were a variety of minor usages, ranging from the New York headquarters of the CIA to a private collection of Rodin sculptures and two floors of resident artist studios. By 2000 it was 96 percent occupied, at increased rents. In July 2001, less than three months before the attacks, the Port Authority sold ninety-nine-year leases on the towers—for $3.5 billion—to developer Larry Silverstein and on the underground areas—for $127 million—to Westfield America, owned by Australian entrepreneur Frank Lowy, the Rupert Murdoch of malls. In what seems now an inevitable historical recursion, Silverstein hired David Childs, of Skidmore, Owings & Merrill, to upgrade the property, "to fix up the Trade Center's image and turn it into a kind of downtown Rockefeller Center."[21]

The WTC as Architecture

As a work of architecture, the WTC's two 110-story towers mixed a massiveness of size, so big that it went beyond scale into immeasurability, with a measure of formal invention so modest and a degree of social responsibility so small as to be scarcely discernable. This disjunction is at the heart of its failure as architecture and as urban planning. Nor, as a complex, did it succeed completely as destination architecture. It seemed to—it was so prominent, how could it not?—but it fell short in this dimension, too. Such a big and obtrusive failure, one that all could see, in such plain sight it was, that all we (those of us concerned with architecture) could do was look away. Yet, as an iconotype, as an image within the iconomy, it became one of the most prominent. Even unto the manner and the reproducibility of its disappearance.

The WTC was designed by Minoru Yamasaki & Associates with the support of Emery Roth & Sons, a New York firm very experienced in putting up supremely efficient, low-cost, and entirely forgettable office buildings. The Port Authority did not wish to have to deal with an outstanding architectural individualist, or with one of the then top corporate architects—Gordon Bunshaft, Wallace K. Harrison, and Edward Durrell Stone—each of whom had been retained in connection with earlier versions of the project. Nor did it turn to one of the leading partnerships, such as Skidmore, Owings & Merrill. Rather, it opted for a firm that had come to specialize in relatively small commercial projects, each of them International Modern in general style but modestly so. The chief architect, Minoru Yamasaki (1912–86), had served apprenticeships in the New York office of Harrison and Fouilhoux, prodigious producers of skyscrapers, and the office of famous industrial designer Raymond Loewy before designing many buildings in Detroit and establishing his own practice in Troy, Michigan, in 1949. Major office, university, and apartment buildings in U.S. cities became the chief work of the practice, although from 1978 it began a series of buildings for the Saudi royal family in Riyadh and Jeddah, including airport reception halls for the family and an Islamic women's center. This raises the prospect that Yamasaki's work and his company's presence in Saudi Arabia might figure somehow within the complex triangle of love-hate relationships obtaining between the Yemenite bin Laden family, builders of major architecture projects in Saudi Arabia, the ruling Fahd family, and Osama bin Laden's explicit hatred of both as betrayers of the Arab cause to the interests of the U.S.-led imperialists. But this is speculation, as likely to be no more relevant to the WTC bombing than the twenty years of deep investment by the bin Laden family in many U.S. businesses, including those of the Bush family.[22]

Minoru Yamasaki & Associates was hired in 1962. The site was cleared by 1969, tenants began entering the north tower in December 1970 (illus. 30), the main towers were up by 1974, and the project completed in 1977. The WTC consisted of seven buildings, all arranged in a semicircle around a five-acre plaza: the two towers, four low plaza buildings, and the Vista Hotel, a Skidmore, Owings & Merrill building of 1981. Below the plaza was a concourse, a sixty-shop mall, a 2,000-space parking lot, and entrances to a major city subway station serving the IRT, BMT, and IND lines. The WTC was also the downtown terminal for the PATH (Port Authority-Trans Hudson) rail system. Some 9.5 million square feet of office space housed more than 1,200 trading firms and other organizations. From 50,000 to 60,000 people worked each day in the building, and it attracted about 80,000 more as visitors to its businesses, its observation deck, or its other excitements (such as lightning-speed elevator rides in WTC 2). Commodity exchanges were open to the public to see on the ninth floor of WTC 4 (gold, silver, coffee, cotton, etc.) The WTC became one of the must-see stopovers for visitors to New York. It ranked, however, well behind other iconic buildings, such as the Empire State Building, and places, such as Central Park, in visitor numbers, frequency of representation, and public sentiment.

In a 1980 statement for *Contemporary Architects*, Yamasaki put forward his design philosophy in these terms:

> For me as an architect, my life has been a constant search for the best combination of aesthetics and function in the buildings I design . . . There is not a particle to spare in natural structures . . . and our art saves material by more skilful arrangement; and reaches its beauty by taking every superfluous ounce that can be spared from a wall and keeping its strength in the poetry of columns.

Recalling the inspiration of visits to traditional architecture in Japan—the bamboo wall around the Katsura Palace, Tokyo, was an acknowledged source—he goes on to object to "trendy" overimprovements (that is, the ornamental excesses of New Historicist Postmodernism), and stresses the basic sheltering purposes of architecture:

> We must provide protection from the normal elements of climate—wind, sun, rain, snow, cold and heat—as well as from the more violent aspects of nature, such as fire, earthquakes, hurricanes, etc. Beyond these basics, the architecture we build should give man an aesthetic and emotional fulfillment so that whenever he goes from home to work or to other activities in which he may be involved, he can anticipate the pleasure of his destination.[23]

This is the low-key, seemingly natural language of official modernism. Its modesty becomes unreal when one thinks of the extraordinary resources involved, of the violence of the powers necessary to their disposition. In the current context, the ordinary language of the concluding paragraph becomes strained. At the time, Yamasaki applied the standard logic of developmentalism. Surveying the site, all he could see was "a blighted section," readily relocatable, with "not a single building

30. G. E. Kidder Smith, World Trade Center Twin Towers under construction, 1970. 1970, photograph. © G. E. Kidder Smith/Corbis.

worth saving."[24] He wanted a cleared space, so his structure could be seen. He made a scale model, and began on the first of 150 possible configurations. One structure containing ten million square feet was, even if buildable, impossibly gargantuan. A long low slab would need a larger site, and anyway act as a wall, blockading the area. A multiplicity of towers recalled, painfully for Yamasaki, the Pruitt-Igoe housing project, and was too symbolically downmarket for a great Trade Center. He finally proposed two eighty- to ninety-floor towers, set at angles to provide maximal views for workers within them (echoing thereby Mies van der Rohe's siting of his 860–880 Lake Shore Drive Apartments, built in 1949–51, in Chicago), and surrounded by a cluster of smaller buildings. To Yamasaki, this met as many of his client's needs as possible, while maintaining a feasible aesthetic relation to the surrounding architecture and a defensible architectural relation to the famous Manhattan skyline. It was also at the upper limits of the practicalities and the economics of elevating people to their workstations in the sky.

This solution fell short of the Port Authority's desired rental goal by two million square feet. Tozzoli pressed Yamasaki to find a way, beyond current technology, to increase the height of the two towers, and to do so such that both buildings would be the tallest in the world. Echoing the battle between Midtown and Downtown business interests, this was consciously calculated as one hundred feet above the height of the Empire State Building. Such attitudes were a throwback to the strutting competitiveness of the 1920s. The secrecy surrounding the capping of an earlier icon, the Chrysler Building, with its famous Art Deco needle was the culmination of a continuous effort to outstrip rising rivals by surprise.[25] Philip Johnson's views on the deep roots of this kind of rivalry have been cited. In the literature on skyscrapers, every effort is made to link them to past high-rise edifices, such as the Mayan temples, to historically consecrated monuments, such as the Washington Monument, and to commercial, symbolic towers, such as the Eiffel Tower. But they all return to the persistent illogic of the race to cap the previous tallest building.[26] In the 9.11.01 aftermath, more people listened to David Childs, managing partner of Skidmore, Owings & Merrill repeat a point that he had often made before: "Above sixty-five to seventy stories, you lose the logic. The size of the core in relation to the floor plate, the amount of bracing you need to overcome the overturning loads, and all the other investments stop making sense after that. The rest is just ego."[27]

Yamasaki succumbed to this combination of commercial greed and masculinist competitiveness (illus. 31). Port Authority engineers applied the express stop and cross-town principles of the New York subway system to the problem of fitting 104 elevators into the structure, thus bypassing the need to fill the lower floors with entry doors and the upper ones with lifting equipment. Engineer Leslie Robertson, who had previously worked with Yamasaki on the Consolidated Gas Building in Detroit, adopted a design pioneered in 1965 in a Chicago apartment house by Fazlur Khan and Myron Goldsmith of Skidmore, Owings & Merrill. This involved supporting the structure with both an interior core and closely spaced, tubular exterior columns (the latter doing the wind-resistance work),

thus releasing the interior floor space from the need for many columns. When scaled up for Yamasaki's final twin 110-story tower design, the design created an acre of open space on each floor of the building, maximizing its rent potential, in all seven times that of the Empire State Building. The aluminum alloy-clad exterior columns constitute 70 percent of the building's surface, in stark contrast to the apparently all-glass facades of major International Style buildings. It was, technically, and programmatically, a brilliant solution.

31. Balthazar Korab, Minoru Yamasaki, and models of the WTC towers. 1962, photograph. Source: Balthazar Korab, Ltd.

But it was fragile. Despite its enormous size, its opaque stolidity, its much trumpeted the-future-is-now technology, and the seemingly all-powerful authority of its sponsors and purposes, the WTC projected a paradoxical sense of uncertainty, of provisionality. Some of this was due to its pastiche aesthetic: the filigreeing of the columns, especially their Venetian-style, mock-Arabic joined fluting near the base, seemed to spread a kind of nervous tension across the buildings' vast facades (illus. 32). Then there were the practical issues. It was,

32. Adam Woolfitt, World Trade Center Towers, Lower Manhattan. c. 1977, photograph. © Adam Woolfitt/Corbis.

from many reports, an unpleasant, alienating workplace. While most workers seemed to have made their peace with its limitations, a sense of uncertainty pervades their accounts of their experience of the building, both before and after 9.11.01. Much of the structural innovation had occurred at the limit of engineering knowledge: key aspects of it—for example, the ability of the upper floors to withstand high winds—were, in varying degrees, speculative. Inadequate fire proofing was a problem from the start; sprinklers had to be added, over time, at great costs, and the spray-on fireproof material was too thin, applied improperly and under constant repair. (A WTC subplot is that the contract for this task was leased to a supplier with Mafia connections: in 1990 his bullet-ridden body was found in one of the center's garages.)

These anxieties were often expressed by a fire department aware that the project was, as a Port Authority exercise, not subject to New York City fire standards. Contending capitalists lost no time in exploiting such fears. During the mid-1960s a coalition of midtown business people attacked the WTC on a number of grounds: it would overload the real estate market, it was economically unrealistic, its excessive size made it dangerous in the case of fire or explosion, and its height made it likely that an airplane might hit the towers. The Committee for a Reasonable World Trade Center took out full page advertisements featuring, in 1968, among other imagery of disaster, a montage of a large plane flying toward one of the towers (illus. 33).[28] A *Towering Inferno* scenario hovered around public perception of the building, especially after the film appeared in 1974. This fear was the spectacular face of an even more deeply rooted one: that a world increasingly dominated by the concerns of ruthless corporations, self-interested elites, and highly bureaucratized governments was symbolized by buildings such as the WTC. In a film of this period, *Three Days of the Condor*, the building has exactly this role, as the New York headquarters of the CIA, which turns against its agent, played by Robert Redford. The dense townhouses of the Lower East Side are, in contrast, pictured as his haven.[29]

In his initial proposal, Yamasaki had explained that he was setting out to create "a beautiful solution of form and silhouette which fits well into Lower Manhattan", and to find a balance between making it "inviting, friendly and humane." By the end of the process, his language had changed. "To be symbolic of its great purpose, of the working together in trade of the Nations of the World, it should have a sense of dignity and pride, and still stand for the humanity and democratic purposes in which we in the United States believe."[30]

That these goals proved, on the site and at that scale, both incompatible and impossible to fulfill is attested to by most commentary on the WTC. The response of other architects, critics, and art and architectural historians is telling. One might expect a project as prominent as this one to be fully documented in the professional, public, and educational publications of its time and since. It did, of course, attract copious professional and media attention during its years of planning and construction. Huxtable was one of the few to express misgivings straight away. Reviewing the basic proposal in 1966, she asked, "Who's afraid of the big, bad buildings? Everyone. Because there are so many things about giganticism that we just don't know." She concluded: "The Twin Towers could be the start of a new skyscraper age or the biggest tombstones in the world."[31]

The judgment of the profession as a whole has been a more measured matter. In *Icons of Architecture, The Twentieth Century*, for example, the WTC is there in a list that ranges from Gaudi's Sagrada Familia to Gehry's Guggenheim Museum at Bilbao. It qualifies under many of the editor's criteria:

New York Times (1857-Current file); May 2, 1968; ProQuest Historical Newspapers The New York Times (1851 - 2001)
pg. 38

GRANT AIDS LATINS IN THE SOUTHWEST

Ford Fund Gives $2-Million to New Legal Defense Unit

By KATHLEEN TELTSCH

An organization has been created to provide legal safeguards against discrimination for the country's five million Mexican-Americans.

Establishment of the Mexican American Legal Defense and Educational Fund was announced here yesterday by the Ford Foundation, which provided an initial grant of $2.2-million for the undertaking.

Ceremonies also were held in San Antonio, Tex., where the new organization will make its headquarters.

McGeorge Bundy, president of the Ford Foundation, in announcing the grant, also underscored the community's needs.

Bundy Stresses Needs

"In terms of legal enforcement of their civil rights," he said, "American citizens of Mexican descent are now where the Negro community was a quarter-century ago. There are not nearly enough Mexican-American lawyers, and most of them have neither the income nor experience to do civil rights work."

Another element, he declared, is the hesitancy of the Mexican-American community in seeking recourse to the courts.

"Because the law has often been used against Mexican-Americans, as well as other minority groups, they are suspicious of legal processes," he said.

Although he did not offer illustrations, advocates of the new organization in seeking Ford assistance had alleged police brutality, illegal arrests and exclusion from juries.

Studies Cited

The appeal for Ford assistance was buttressed by studies made in the Southwest showing that Mexican-Americans were recruited for lower-paying jobs, were discriminated against in employment in Government and private industry, and were often denied equal pay.

One-third of all Mexican-American families in the area, according to the studies, had an annual income below $3,000, the generally accepted poverty line. Many are farm or migrant workers living in California; large numbers also are in Texas, New Mexico, Colorado and Arizona.

The studies showed that Mexican-Americans as a group were the most poorly educated in the Southwest, with a school dropout rate of 50 per cent.

School segregation persists, it was charged, and Mexican-American youngsters often wind up in classes for the retarded because language and cultural differences led them to make a poor showing on aptitude tests that do not take these differences into account.

Lack of funds has kept lawyers from challenging segregation practices, it was said.

Patterned on NAACP Group

The establishment of the new legal defense fund was the outgrowth of discussions with community leaders and the NAACP Legal Defense and Educational Fund, Inc., and the National Office for the Rights of the Indigent. Jack Greenberg serves as director-counsel of both organizations.

The Mexican-American Fund will be modeled on the NAACP fund, set up nine years ago to defend Negroes' civil rights. The Field Foundation also assisted the Mexican-American fund in formulating its request for outside help.

Part of the Ford grant will go for scholarships to permit 55 Mexican-Americans to attend law schools. A separate $490,000 grant will be made to the Fund for Public Education, a unit of the American Bar Association, to support legal education of students from the Negro, Indian and Mexican-American communities.

Judge Carlos C. Cadena, associate justice of the state Civil Appeals Court at San Antonio, will be chairman of the new legal defense fund.

EISENHOWER RESTS; PROGRESS IS NOTED

Special to The New York Times

MARCH AIR FORCE BASE, Calif., May 1—Former President Dwight D. Eisenhower, who suffered what is described as a mild heart attack on Monday, spent a comfortable day in the hospital on this base today.

Doctors said that all evidence thus far indicated that General Eisenhower's heart attack was "not as severe" as his two previous ones. They said that a prognosis on the General's condition is very difficult to make at this time, but his progress has been "very encouraging."

The doctors explained that the most critical period for any patient with a heart attack was during the first three or four days.

General Eisenhower has seen no visitors other than his wife, who is living in a suite on the hospital. The General's son, John, has not come to this Air Force base, but he is being kept informed of the General's progress by telephone.

THE MOUNTAIN COMES TO MANHATTAN

We are a strange and mysterious people.

We build cars to cruise at 100 m.p.h., then try to make everybody keep them under 50.

We build airports that can handle gigantic jets but can't handle our luggage.

We undertake great projects with enthusiasm and never consider the consequences until we're choking on them.

Consider the case of the "Mountain" being built downtown.

New York's air traffic patterns are perilously overburdened. LIFE magazine reports this. So does THE NEW YORK TIMES. And the President of the Allied Pilots Assn., who speaks for 3500 commercial pilots, is "deeply concerned over the safety problems arising out of traffic congestion in this area." "Safe navigation," he says, "includes not only planned flight patterns, but also provisions for unforeseen and uncontrolled diversions."

Yet the Port of New York Authority is trying to build a trade center which, according to this pilot, "adds an additional risk to air navigation."

Its two towers are scheduled to be 1350 feet high. But at that height they will so thoroughly foul up TV reception that the Port Authority has agreed to top them out with new TV broadcasting facilities. By the time antennas are added, the North Tower, according to one TV expert, will be close to 1700 feet high...800 feet taller than anything else in the immediate area!

This means, according to the Federal Aviation Administration, that air traffic patterns will have to change, landing approaches will have to be altered, minimum altitudes in the area will be affected. The total potential hazard is staggering. No wonder airline pilots feel the risk is unjustified.

Unfortunately, we rarely recognize how serious these problems are until it's too late to do anything.

But in this case, there's still time.

The problem can be solved by keeping the height of the Trade Center at 900 feet.

The one problem that hasn't been solved is how to convince the Executive Director of the Port Authority to scale down his dream so it will coincide with the public interest.

Governor Rockefeller, the man he calls "my boss," is the one man in a position to say "900 feet" and make it stick.

If you're concerned about TV reception and safe air travel, write to the Governor today. Before it's too late.

Governor Nelson A. Rockefeller
22 West 55th Street, NY 10019.

He's the only man who has the power to keep the "Mountain" from coming to Manhattan.

Committee for a Reasonable World Trade Center
450 Seventh Avenue, NY 10001
(212) Judson 2-3931

Lawrence A. Wien, *Chairman*   Robert Kopple, *Executive Director*

33. Committee for a Reasonable World Trade Center, advertisement, *New York Times*, May 2, 1968. NYT Permissions: The New York Times.

Each of the buildings included here is spectacular in its own way: in the context of its time and its surroundings, by virtue of its structural achievements, its innovative use of materials, or its formal language, or perhaps because it represents the very first example of a new building type. Some of these buildings have become veritable places of pilgrimage for architectural enthusiasts, or have acquired a symbolic status as emblems of the cities or nations in which they stand. Others that were once considered revolutionary and were acclaimed by the critics of their times have been more or less forgotten today. Naturally, the opposite is also true: many buildings that were misunderstood and condemned in their day now serve as models for later generations of architects, and are regarded as icons of twentieth-century architecture.[32]

In contrast to, say, the Sydney Opera House—a building that the *Icons of Architecture* authors interpret sympathetically as architecturally innovative and praise because it "bears an iconic presence as a symbol of Australia"—the WTC towers are condemned in terms that will themselves become standard:

> Unfortunately, the most notable quality of the buildings is still their overbearing size. This is particularly apparent in the barren, windblown plaza, but also at a distance, where the tight columns of the curtain walls seem opaque; any intimacy is overwhelmed by the exterior walls' uninterrupted run through to their full height. These complaints are extreme versions of the indictments that have been leveled at many monuments of the era, but they seem particularly acute here.[33]

Elsewhere in the professional literature, the treatment is even more negative. The list of architectural history textbooks from which the WTC is absent is far longer than any list of those in which it appears.[34] A survey of standard histories, those most widely used in schools and universities between 1971 and now, uncovers six references, three in different editions of the same text. All are brief. For example, William Curtis characterized the towers in his first edition as "an extreme statement of the elegant, minimalist notion of the parallel-piped box standing in a plaza."[35] By the third, however, he takes the WTC as evidence that "the curtain wall/box formula for tall office building was revealing its limits," and his description of Yamasaki's slabs becomes "an extreme statement of the minimalist notion of a free-standing object standing in a plaza."[36]

A Professional Embarrassment

The WTC fares worse in the more critical histories. Kenneth Frampton mentions them, in passing, in a discussion of whether the grandiose projects of Boullée and Ledoux, and of Le Corbusier and Wright (in the case of the latter's 1956 One Mile High Skyscraper) were necessarily unrealizable, if sufficient resources and adequate technology were available. Perhaps, he feels, the WTC shows that they were feasible, but "such mega-buildings are too exceptional to serve as a model for general practice."[37] In their *Modern Architecture*, Manfredo Tarfuri and Francesco dal

Co treat the WTC project twice, as an instance of city planning, and as work of architecture. On both occasions, their language is marked by acute insight into how the fragility of the towers as a material edifice is indissolubly linked to the brutality of their effects on the humans touched by them. Pointing to the city's historic failure to address its substandard habitations, they canvass the various urban renewal projects of the 1960s, then observe that the WTC towers "did their part in modifying—traumatically—all possibilities for further development and progressive functional utilization of the area."[38] In their chapter reviewing the "architecture of bureaucracy" that settled everywhere in the 1950s and 1960s— "Symbols of efficiency and a willingness to bow to the imperative of organization, the steel and glass skyscrapers speak of an inescapable collective destiny"—the WTC comes in for a blast as typical of an architecture that appears to be "Neo-Rationalist" yet is, the authors argue, anything but that:

> Rather than proposing a rationalization of the urban structures, it accentuates their randomness and lack of overall purpose. Even the twin skyscrapers of the World Trade Center in New York, promoted by Governor Rockefeller for the tip of Manhattan and built between 1968 and 1973, were projected by Minoru Yamasaki as skeletal phantasms, theoretically transitory "happenings," superblocks unsure of what function they were meant to play. In this sense their excessive style encourages that ambiguity which is accentuated even more by their seamless facades. Yet the immediate exploitability of such edifices, called on as they are to change the entire appearance of the urban centers, realizes the dream of an architecture that uses a common and easily assimilable language and that is intimately connected with forms adaptable to commercial exploitation and with the laws of the real estate market.[39]

What of the standard histories of art, those that often lace into their chapters on painting, sculpture, and graphic art short accounts of contemporary architecture? It is the same story as with the specialist histories of architecture, although a little less restrained: bemused recognition turns into slamming condemnation, then a contemptuous turning away. The pattern is that there were some, mostly passing, mentions during the 1970s, a few of which persisted into the 1980s, but the WTC all but disappears from the architectural discourse during the 1990s.[40]

This declining incidence is matched by what is said by these experts. To Hunter and Jacobus, writing as the towers were being erected, the WTC was "a typical instance of the ruthlessness with which that city's skyline and ground-level appearance have been treated by builders ... the plaza zone in which these two towers are dropped again (like the Lincoln Center) seems to turn its back on the historic neighborhood, and the blunt height and graceless profile of the towers have nothing to do with the once characteristic, now overpowered cluster of tapered spires that for decades dominated lower Manhattan and the harbor."[41] By the mid-1970s, they were more negative. They characterize Yamasaki as "a prominent, fashionable designer, whose work is indicative of how easily this genre of building can become a matter of packaging and external design, even when a major new structural concept featuring a load-bearing wall is introduced." And they describe the towers thus: "These cracker-box forms have dwarfed the skyline of Manhattan in a way in which no other buildings have before, and seem more alien to the neighborhood and to the entire metropolis than any other imaginable forms. That they, along with many other recent urban towers, have provoked a surfeit of commercial office space and a depression in the building industry is only the least of the social problems generated by these colossi."[42]

Such savagery is scarcely typical of the bland generalizations that fill most textbooks. It seems that the WTC drove historians to such degrees of anger because they saw the towers as the most extreme instance of the betrayal of the contract between architecture and the people implicit in even the most top-down, indulgent, and expensive of modernist projects. Hunter and Jacobus put it this way:

> It is impossible, even when considering only formal and stylistic matters, to remain insensitive to the questionable social role played by the omnipresent towers, alienated objects in the midst of our contemporary metropolis, where they existed presumably as architectural demonstrations of contemporary society's power and efficacy. These sheer forms create a destructive visual tension between the old and the new. This vicious confrontation was not foreseen in the initial version of the Radiant City [as proposed by Le Corbusier], and it remains unclear whether the major flaw lies in the concept of the Cartesian skyscraper itself or in the superficial adaptation of a grand scheme in fragments rather than the entire plan.

They are quite clear, however, about the source of this debilitating reductiveness:

> One thing is certain: there has been too little large-scale, architecturally-determined planning and too much concern for short-term financial rewards, manipulation of private land values, speculation, and increases in the tax base. Predictably, there has been little concern for genuine social amenity and livability in nearly all gigantic building enterprises. One strains to find a convincing major exception to this rule.[43]

Even postmodernist historians of architecture find Yamasaki's work on the edge of conscionable architecture. The most prominent, Charles Jencks, used the planned implosion of the Pruitt-Igoe apartment complex in Saint Louis as the turning point between the modern and the postmodern, as the sign that the implicit social contract between modernist architecture and the people it set out to serve had become an admitted failure. Designed by Yamasaki, this public housing project seemed to successfully embody the highest principles of modernist urban planning. Yet, like many others, it was no match for the divisive contradictions of the 1960s in the U.S.: particularly those of race, class, crime, and corruption. Jencks had found his instant image of the Modern Movement in ruins, and (as he confessed subsequently) he milked it for all it was worth.[44] His deep antipathy to the architecture of Yamasaki did not stop there. In his *Modern Movements in Architecture*, Jencks includes Yamasaki within the category

"Bureaucratic School," and at other times mocks him as an exemplar of "High Camp."[45] Real venom was reserved for buildings such as the Consolidated Gas headquarters in Detroit. Yamasaki's crime, Jencks knew, was that he had found a way of using the formal and technical elements of modernism—those elements that had evolved, in the hands of the Modern Masters, as a symbolic language with its own abstract, general, distanced but commanding communicative tone—to convey brand-image banality, and to do so fussily, prettily, as big-scale kitsch. Yamasaki gave the bosses what they wanted: his was the architectural language of the corporate compromise. Guy Tozzoli visited the Michigan Consolidated Gas building, and saw this.

Taking all of these comments together, the consensus of architectural opinion before September 11, 2001, could be paraphrased thus. Lifting the whole precinct onto its own plaza created a ground-level domain that was both separated from its surrounds, repellent to pedestrians, and, given the labyrinthine traffic beneath it, an irresolute and ambiguous nonbase. The Twin Towers amounted to blandness extruded to gargantuan degrees, to the sheer fact of office-boxing extended upwards from nowhere to nothingness. In their provision of vast expanses of column-free interiors and their disproportionate vertical extension, the towers expressed the grasping logic of maximum rental space, that is, a raw economic fundamentalism, minimally adorned. Because they ignored the skyscraper language of Manhattan, especially the setback profiling and the symbolic finials to top off the building, they seemed foreign to the skyline of the island, disbalancing it.

This last effect may have been a result of their timing. Conceived at the high-point of U.S. capital expansiveness, the tower builders, in their most gung-ho moods, might have anticipated many companions of a similar kind. Yet the economic crisis of the early 1970s, precipitated by the oil producers of the Middle East, was bad for big business and for big building. It snap-froze the WTC in time, leaving it an isolated, off-the-chart peak in the seismic profile of Manhattan.

But the fault line on which the entire WTC project perched was not merely economic. It was a moral/aesthetic one. In her first response to 9.11.01, Huxtable pinpointed the aesthetic aspect:

> The Trade Center towers were never beautiful buildings; they achieved landmark status because of their size. There is nothing compelling about replacing them for their architectural distinction; they had none. The architect, Minoru Yamasaki, a Japanese-American, was a talented and gentle man best known for introducing an innovative kind of concrete construction, who did far better buildings elsewhere. His delicate, expressive style was essentially defeated by the enormous scale of the towers—perhaps there was a lesson about monumental civic architecture in their aesthetic failure, one that we failed to understand or acknowledge.[46]

The combination of massive size (the ten million square feet of rentable office space that was talismanic for the Port Authority, David Rockefeller, et al.) and lesser architectural invention (on the part of Yamasaki's team) is the root cause of a larger failure. This mismatch appears again and again in the story of the WTC. Guy

Tozzoli pressured Yamasaki into increasing the height of the towers so that they would be the biggest dick in the world (to the power of two): the implosive fissure of the whole project was triggered by Yamasaki's failure to take Tozzoli's demand back into the source of his design, to find a different yet still distinguished solution to the problems posed by the project. Instead, Yamasaki, working against the grain of his own architecture—and perhaps against his character—said yes, and simply projected upwards. This was one act of overreaching among many, and typical of "late capital" at the time. Now, it is evidence of a project pushed beyond the limits of both its technical and imaginative capacity, yet built nonetheless. An extraordinary risk was taken, and celebrated (by those close to it) as such.

In this, they were merely continuing what had, by the 1930s, become a tradition of boldness in the face of apparent adversity. Since the conception of the Rockefeller Center in defiance of the 1929 Crash, Manhattan's movers and shakers have believed that they could, by their sheer force and power, generate enough energy to turn an economy—the local economy, at least—around. Among the architects who worked for them, a kind of hubris by reflection was pervasive, and it proved catching to a wider public. Reflecting, in the early 1970s, on this phenomenon, which he called "Manhattanism," Dutch architect Rem Koolhaas observed: "Manhattan has generated a shameless architecture that has been loved in direct proportion to its defiant lack of self-hatred, has been respected exactly to the degree that it went too far."[47] He is right about this as a mood that attaches to Midtown, but it is hard to see it much in the air Downtown, at any time. It was brought to a halt, we have seen, by the nature of the overreaching at the WTC.

Habitus Drifts In

What of the broader affective dimension? Public perception of the towers as dauntingly inhuman monoliths gradually lessened in time, as they were integrated, however grudgingly or distantly, into everyday routines. This process was boosted by spectacular events such as Phillip Petit's 1974 high-wire walk between them, along with subsequent stunts, and a multiplicity of movie appearances. And by changes in the architectural context. The lower flats around the mountainous WTC were smoothed in 1981 by Cesar Pelli's World Finance Center buildings, each topped by an ur-form of architectural striving: the dome, the ziggurat, the pyramid, and the platform. This cap-tipping design implied, curiously, that architectural history itself should pay homage to a pair of buildings that most architectural historians regarded as scarcely worthy of the name "architecture." Perhaps Pelli was simply echoing, Downtown, the New York tradition of friendly rivalry between skyscraper finials that had animated earlier periods, especially in Midtown in the 1920s and 1930s. That he did so, in the 1980s, within new historicist stylistics, seems, when contrasted to the oversizing of the WTC, almost an exercise in tasteful (if schoolmasterish) restraint. Public acceptance of the WTC grew apace when the south tower observation deck was opened in 1975 (illus. 34). It attracted many visitors—towards the end, over one and half million each year.

34. Paul O. Colliton,
View north from WTC
2 observation deck.
c. 1980, photograph.
Source: Paul O. Colliton.

But the view was not as popular as that from the Empire State Building, which remained more central to tourism and to the symbolic heartland of New York.

The Empire State Building is not just a setting for key scenes in films such as *An Affair to Remember* and *Sleepless in Seattle*; it is a character in them. To date, it has appeared in no fewer than ninety films. In an amusing column in 1976, *New York Times* architecture critic Ada Louise Huxtable expressed her disappointment that the latest remake of the film *King Kong* showed, in its climactic scene, the great ape fending off attacking jets while he stood with one giant foot on each of the two towers of the World Trade Center. Compared to his earlier "perilously grabbing the famous Art Deco spire" of the ESB, this was, to Huxtable, a letdown. "The

Empire State Building, of course, is a star in its own right, with an enduring romantic charisma. Somehow it implies every cherished legend of New York glamour, from the glittering speakeasy era to the suave lux of the late seventies. It is genuinely immortal. By contrast, and as a symbol of the city, the World Trade Center towers are consummately uninspiring. (They still sell more Empire State Buildings in the five and ten.) . . . Today's tall buildings are not stars. They are impersonally impressive at best, giant nonentities at worst . . . *The Towering Inferno*, for example, was not about a building you could recognize or cherish. This was simply a large object to which catastrophe happened."[48] Action hero Bruce Willis and his various opponents—as they do their best to make skyscrapers into flaming battle zones—seem to agree.

Terrible Twins

What of the *two* towers? What are we to make of the doubling of a building that already exceeded all previous size, all current technology, yet fell aesthetically and architecturally short of its appropriate form? The discomfort at oddity—indeed, the alarm traditionally felt around twins, provoked by their rare, even unnatural doubling of human singularity—never seemed to attach itself to the towers. More broadly, this superstition has been in retreat in many cultures during this century. Indeed, to some, the pairing of the buildings raised warm and fuzzy feelings toward their coupling, twinning, sharing—senses that permitted human identification with them. For some architects and critics, the two towers seemed to mitigate the shortcomings that would have been condemned in a single building of this design. Yet for others, the two amounted to an even greater arrogance of high capital in boasting to the world of its works. They seemed to say: "Look, we can do this, and do it twice!" More: "We can do this again, endlessly, all over the world, wherever and whenever we wish!" This impulse has been obscured by the fact that the economic downturn of the early 1970s, precipitated by the oil crisis of 1973, called a halt to huge-scale building in Western capitals. Given the history of exponential growth in the height of modern buildings, the constructors of the WTC may have thought that even their gigantism would be matched in the years ahead, that their towers—instead of awkwardly disbalancing one end of the island—would eventually subside into a higher but more even skyline. In his book *The Practice of Everyday Life*, Michel de Certeau sets the beginning of a chapter on the observation platform of the WTC in the early 1970s. Looking out, he grasped the fundamental difference between the walked-around city of modernity and the overlooked plan of the future. A city, that is, with the potential to repeat the stripped structure of the WTC ad infinitum.[49]

Jean Baudrillard has a more speculative reading of this impulse:

> The fact that there were two of them signifies the end of any original reference. If there were only one, monopoly would not have been perfectly embodied. Only the doubling of a sign truly puts an end to what it designates. There is a peculiar

fascination in this reduplication. However tall they may have been the two towers signified, none the less, a halt to verticality. They were not of the same breed
as other buildings. They culminated in the exact reflection of each other. The
glass and steel façades of the Rockefeller Center buildings still mirrored each
other in an endless specularity. But the Twin Towers no longer had any façades,
any faces. With the rhetoric of verticality disappears also the rhetoric of the mirror. There remains only a kind of black box, a series closed on the figure two, as
though architecture, like the system, was now merely a product of cloning, and
of a changeless genetic code.[50]

We cannot say that these qualities were, in some sense, a cause of the attacks. Too
many other motivators exist. We can, however, say that the countless acts of overreaching that created the WTC also drew opprobrium, hatred, and eventually ter-
roristic violence toward it. Its overreaching also shaped the effects of the attacks,
both on the day and throughout the aftermath. The overreachers could not have
anticipated a world political and economic order spinning out of control so fast
that its peripheries would strike out against its power centers. Could they have
guessed that their overreaching would materialize at some point, in a failure that
would match the energies of its origins? Perhaps so, but that was a risk they were
prepared to take, as representatives of a can-do culture whose leading lights
(which they were) believed that no problem was insoluble. But if their gamble was
to fail, what form would it take? A dematerialization? A fiery inferno? A collapse?
We cannot say. Now, we can never say.

  Because it has already happened.

Daydreams of Domination: A Trade-off in Terror

In this chapter we have traced the birth of an icon: a building that, while it fell
short of becoming an icon of twentieth-century architecture, became nevertheless
an iconotype of the skyscraper form in its American, metropolitan, specifically
New York incarnation. Its image was recognized all over the world as the biggest,
the most blatant, and the most brutal of the skyscraper clusters that created the
bristling skyline of the capital city of Western modernity. Yet it was, as we have
seen, the product of a series of acts of bad faith, the outcome of a number of
decisions made as compromises, the result of second-best solutions to core problems that remained unsolved, unresolved. David Rockefeller's urge to shore up his
isolated Chase headquarters. Austin Tobin's evasion of the core responsibilities of
the Port Authority to mass transit and a twentieth-if not twenty-first-century
port. Nelson Rockefeller's investment of state funds and people in a private project. The rampant experimentalism of the usually conservative structural engineers. And Minori Yamasaki's sacrifice of aesthetic judgment in his submission to
the illogic of the tallest. When faced forward into the test of time, the WTC did
not stand a chance—or, better, it stood only because of chance, and stayed up due
to the inertia of habit.

In anthropological explanations of why some symbols induce ritual behavior aimed at them, a distinction is often made between those whose power derives from their summative force and those that invite devotees to add to, or elaborate, the symbol itself.[51] With this distinction in mind, we can characterize the Rockefellers, Tobin, Tozzoli, Yamasaki, Robertson, et al. as having produced a summative symbol par excellence, one that, from day one, repelled human-scale association, blocked everydayness, turned an unyielding face to its users and visitors, and thus prevented the rise of familiarity, of acceptance leading to occasional tender feelings, perhaps, even to fondness. These warmer responses were a long time coming. Yamasaki's critics attacked the WTC precisely because they saw it as impervious to elaboration, to the differencing processes essential to life as lived. Some were driven to fury by what they saw as its colossal indifference to heterogeneity.

Joseph B. Juhasz, author of the commentary on Yamasaki in the 1994 edition of *Contemporary Architects*, argued that the bombing of the WTC the previous year had instantly come to frame the architect's reputation:

> The WTC had been our Ivory Gates to the White City . . . Though, at least when viewed from a distance, the WTC still shimmers—it is at the moment thoroughly besmirched by its unfortunate role as a target for Middle-East terrorism. When the WTC was nearly blown to smithereens from a bomb placed in its underground parking garage, a new chapter in the story of Cold War architecture began—and perforce a new chapter in our appreciation of the work of Yamasaki—for the WTC can be best understood as the premier work of mercantile Cold War architecture on the Western side.[52]

The Cold War reference conjures the thirty years during which a style of frozen concrete classicism characterized U.S. embassies, offices, and hotels around the world, particularly in states bordering the USSR, and including many in the Middle East.[53] Juhasz sees the WTC as a triumphalist symbol of "the victory of the West over the East"; he adds, "The choice of the WTC as the first salvo of a terrorist hot war of the Shia against the infidel money-changers of Wall Street is emblematic of the status of the Cold War architecture of which the WTC was the primary resource-trader emblem." Far from accepting Yamasaki's modest modernism, he rails against him as "the Architect of Cold War mercantilism" and the WTC as a building that "deceives in its very whiteness—with its shimmering spirituality," inducing the sense that "appearance is more important than substance" and that "all conflict—whether between form and function, or whether between history and the present, or the future—must be suppressed." Thus its form: "its twin towers literally attempt to contain the City within the four walls of the building—a final Tower of Babel." Modernism's long, and productive, warring between the city and plan culminates in the ultimate, freeze-framed defeat of both. Juhasz concludes his comments by conjuring—in eerily jihad language—a scene that, I can only presume, now haunts him with the nightmares of a prophecy too exactly fulfilled:

Of course, any "stability" based on the suppression of open systems becomes an element in a drama which in its own terms *must* terminate in cataclysm. In an allegorical sense, the vast, twinned doubled ghostly presence of WTC presents a sepulchre from which ghosts will not rise as on the day of cataclysm as the resurrected dead: rather as a tombstone it prophecies the raising of Golems and Zombies . . . Finally, its fortress-like separation in lieu of union, like the worst of the foods and drugs on which New York thrives, caters to addictions only. We are left with a white city that is dirty; a city in which cracks spew pollution rather than resurrect new life.[54]

In the war waged by iconoclasm against idolatry, W. J. T. Mitchell has shown us that iconophobia and iconophilia are closely linked. Logics of repression are the key. Although the iconoclast "prefers to think that he worships no images of any sort . . . one might argue that iconoclasm is simply the obverse of idolatry, that it is nothing more than idolatry turned outwards to the image of a rival, threatening tribe."[55] An idolatry in reverse, then. In reverse action, even. Urbanist Eric Darton is one of the few to confront this issue in its specificity and to see both of its sides—indeed, to see each as the mirror image of the other. In a book on the WTC published in 1999, *Divided We Stand*, he underscored the "the abstract nature of the planners' and architects' thinking, their willingness to reduce lived actuality to a set of disembodied qualities." Seeing in this abstraction a parallel to the strategies involved in the 1993 bombing, he wrote:

> You need only to stand for a moment in Austin Tobin plaza to become immediately and keenly aware of how Yamasaki's abstract sculptural ethos achieved a kind of chilling perfection in his World Trade Center design. Here you find yourself in the presence of two monumental structures whose formal relationship gives us no indication of their purpose or intent. You know they are office buildings, yet their design makes it nearly impossible to imagine that they are full of people. It is at this point that—even without invoking the optical trick of standing at a tower's corner and looking upward—you realize the trade towers disappear as sites of human habitation and reassert their power at the level of an aesthetic relationship. And it is through recognizing this process that you may become uncomfortably aware of a kindred spirit linking the apparently polar realms of skyscraper terrorist and skyscraper builder.
>
> This analogy between those who seek to destroy the structures the latter thought it rational and desirable to build becomes possible by shifting focus momentarily to the shared, underlying predicate of their acts. To attempt creation or destruction on such an immense scale requires both bombers and master-builders to view living processes in general, and social life in particular, with a high degree of abstraction. Both must undertake a radical distancing of themselves from the flesh and blood of mundane experience "on the ground" . . . For the terrorist and the skyscraper builder alike, day-to-day existence shrinks to insignificance—reality distills itself to the instrumental use of physical forces in service of an abstract goal.[56]

These remarks point us right at the attractor qualities of extreme forms of anti-humanism, that is, their mesmeric drag upon humans and their insatiable urge to unite with each other. We have seen these dark forces at work throughout our discussion of the WTC design process. The mutual attraction, in this case, proved fatal: its antilife character took a literally murderous turn—as it is destined to do. (Which is why those romancing the WTC are naïve; it would eventually have caused its own destruction.)

In an essay written after the attacks, Darton went on to note the parallels between the careers of Yamasaki and Atta, urban planning graduate and pilot of American Airlines Flight 11 that was first to strike, that these two "members of the same highly disciplined profession" exercised, under powerful direction, "their skills at the highest level," albeit "to opposing purpose." These skills went into calculating how to exercise, in actuality, the theoretical extremes necessary to enact completely opposite, but in this case convergent, "daydreams of domination."[57]

Four Trajectories, One Trail

At the end of the twentieth century, there were four main trajectories within advanced architecture in the West. Personified by the work of Gehry, Meier, Calatrava, and Libeskind, they may be shorthanded as, in turn, open-form spectacle, past-modern quotation, engineering featurism, and grounding the contradictions. Meanwhile, the tall building artistically reconsidered by Late Modernism continued to make its mark in the capital cities of the world, as it had done throughout the century. This happened, mostly, at a slower pace. Except, of course, in Asia, where local capitalists and ambitious politicians became eager to demonstrate that economic modernity had been achieved, and that the place of each "tiger economy" in the globalizing world order was well deserved. More modest but, in local terms, flauntingly ambitious projects also appeared throughout the Middle East, not least in oil-rich states such as Saudi Arabia, Bahrain, and Qatar. Architecture everywhere was subject to the conditions of contemporaneity. And, as we might expect, in each situation these conditions shaped architecture differently. We have been reviewing the strengths and limitations of these developments. What happened to them as they were swept up into the maelstrom of yet another aftermath, that of 9.11.01?

Architecture's Unconscious: *Trauma and the Contemporary Sublime at Ground Zero*

Architecture and Violence

In 1975 New York architect Bernard Tschumi released a set of posters entitled *Advertisements for Architecture*. One featured the headline "To really appreciate architecture, you may even need to commit a murder," next to which is an image of a body being pushed from a window high in a tall building (illus. 35). The enterprise here is akin to Andy Warhol's *Suicide* paintings of 1962, all of which reworked news photos of human figures falling through blank space alongside tall buildings. Tschumi's posters were part of contemporary architecture's project to examine itself in relation to the question of political freedom. As posters, they applied what was then the most effective form of public art to dramatize the underlying political currents of architecture itself. At that time, these currents were invisible to most people, and most architects were oblivious to them.

But not to Michel Foucault, who theorized modernity as defined by certain kinds of violence inherent in social spaces, in forms of social organization, and in practices of thought. Architectural forms, such as the Panopticon prison promoted by the Bentham brothers during the later eighteenth century, literalized the operations of the "eye of power." In modern "surveillance states," Foucault argued, spatial organization became the primary medium through which power was both imposed and internalized. Riots, insurrections, and wars were obvious instances of violent struggles in space, about space. Architecture was subject to these larger currents, as well as being their instrument. For this reason, the socially ameliorative intentions of the Modern Master architects, it seemed to many (although not Foucault himself), had been realized in too few of their buildings, projects, or city plans. Nor were they to be found in the vast majority of public structures built during the past two centuries. Critical architects and theorists asked why and how this was so, and whether these larger currents of modernity could be designed against.[1]

Some years later, Tschumi developed the idea behind his poster imagery into a more general theory of deconstructive architecture. In his 1981 essay, "Violence of Architecture," he spoke of the violence that everyone who enters an architectural space perpetrates upon it and of the kinds of violence that architectural space enacts upon its users. He saw formal violence, "the violence of form versus form," and of forms pitted against their settings, as "contextual," as, by and large, harmless experimentation. At its best, it should lead to "turning points" (Foucault) and heterogeneity (Derrida), to new "pleasures" (such as, presumably, the play sculptures and

35. Bernard Tschumi, *Advertisements for Architecture*. 1975, poster. Source: Bernard Tschumi.

fanciful service structures that dot the park at La Villette, Paris, designed by him)—this being, to Tschumi, the point of thinking of architecture in terms of events. He drew a sharp distinction between this suggestive and metaphoric use of the concept of violence and what he called "programmatic violence." By this he meant those "uses, actions, events, and programs that, by accident or design, are specifically evil and destructive. Among them are killing, internment, and torture, which become slaughterhouses, concentration camps, or torture chambers." Tschumi's program called for "a new heterotopia," and for architects to help achieve this goal by "intensifying the rich collision of events and spaces." He concluded:

"Tokyo and New York only appear chaotic. Instead, they mark the appearance of a new urban structure, a new urbanity. Their confrontations and combinations of elements may provide us with the event, the shock, that I hope will make the architecture of our cities a turning point in culture and society."[2]

Everything written or imagined along these lines before 9.11.01 will forever seem both prescient and off the mark. Excited talk about signature, brand, symbolic, and even destination architecture is now a disrupted discourse: it can only mix bad faith with false comfort. In contrast, much of the language enveloping the WTC before and after 9.11.01 has been cast in psychoanalytic terms, specifically those that describe traumatic episodes or the states of trauma. This is an obvious effect of shock. But does this indicate that the WTC was, had become, or is now and forever will be, a traumatized architecture? In such an extreme situation, when the psychic management of a building is so drastically disrupted, fears surface. Will traumatic effects always mark anything raised on this site? Will all building, from now on, be architecture of aftermath? These are exaggerated questions, themselves the product of trauma. But they were asked in the months following 9.11.01, and continue to be resonant. In this chapter I will excavate the conditions of their asking. I will test a number of hypotheses—particularly those advanced by contemporary theorists—against the realities of aftermath.

Hindsights

There were, as always, and especially in hindsight, warning signs. Most obviously, the chaos caused by the partially successful attempt to blow up the World Trade Center by explosives placed in its underground parking garage on February 26, 1993. Six people were killed, over a thousand injured, and $500 million in damage was caused. The anti-Western, anticapitalist attestations of Sheik Omar Abdul Rahman and others charged and convicted are clear enough evidence of motivation. While en route to prison by helicopter, one of the attackers responded to a taunt that the buildings were still standing, by stating that this time they had not had sufficient explosives, but next time they would. From jail, Rahman issued a fatwa against the U.S.: "Destroy them thoroughly and erase them from the face of the earth. Ruin their economies, set their companies on fire, turn their conspiracies into powder and dust. Sink their ships, bring their planes down. Slay them in air, on land, on water..."[3]

On the morning of September 11, 2001, in one of the residential studios in the WTC towers administered by the Lower Manhattan Cultural Council, Jamaican American sculptor Michael Richards was working on his series honoring the Tuskegee airmen, the belatedly recognized African American pilots who flew in World War II. Richards often cast these life-size figurative sculptures from his own body, and to indicate the sacrifice and the subsequent shabby treatment of these men, he frequently used a Saint Sebastian motif. In lieu of the arrows suffered by that saint, he would show the twisted figure, its eyes turned heavenward, lacerated and pierced by airplanes. He was the only professional artist known to be among the victims of 9.11.01.[4]

36. José Clemente Orozco, *New York: The Dead*. 1931, oil on canvas. Source: Museo de Arte Carillo Gil, Mexico City. © Clemente Orozco V.

The history of art is replete with anticipations of its own later developments, and, to a lesser but nonetheless noticeable extent, offers up imagery that, in hindsight, seems to prevision actual events. Mexican painter José Clemente Orozco is just one among many artists who have imagined the modern city as hell-bent on its own destruction. When he arrived in New York in 1928, it was its soaring architecture, rather than contemporary U.S. art, that challenged him. In his 1929 manifesto "New World, New Races, New Art," he wrote: "Already, the architecture of Manhattan is a new value . . . [it] is the first step. Painting and sculpture must certainly follow as inevitable second steps."[5] His excitement abated when he understood the economic forces that drove their excessive verticality, their schematic bodies and their often superficial ornamentation—in Lewis Mumford's words: "a desire for central administration, a desire to increase ground rents, a desire for advertisements."[6]

Orozco explored this insight in a series of apocalyptic images that culminated in the 1931 painting *New York: The Dead* (illus. 36).[7] Architectural forms are its only visible elements. Typical New York skyscrapers crash into each other, a number broken like so many bones; others suggest rent, twisted limbs, still others trunks chopped in half. They crash down upon each other and lie in ghastly attitudes; a funeral pyre of destroyed bodies. One structure, perhaps the tallest, is seen from above: at the base of the image, it protrudes out from the architectural corpses stacked on top of it. No human figures are shown; rather, the red lines that course through each form, which we might expect to read as electrical fires, in fact suggest blood spurting from truncated veins. The anthropomorphic nature of buildings, their character as frames for our bodies, and their affinity to trees as the basic, natural elements of shelter—all this is strikingly conveyed. And thrown into terminal chaos. There is nothing here of the concept of Resurrection, nor of the generalized sense of redemption that colors much Mexican art, for example, the mural cycles of Diego Rivera.

Connotations such as these take Orozco's painting beneath its face value: an "I told you so" commentary on the Wall Street Crash of 1929, a literalization of market collapse and an embodiment of stockbrokers and financiers jumping to their deaths. In his autobiography Orozco recalls the Crash as a moment of surreal economics: "A morning in 1929, something grave was happening in New York. People were rushing more than usual... You could hear the sirens of firemen and the Red Cross sounding furiously... Wall Street and its surrounding area was an infernal sea. Many speculators had thrown themselves from their windows onto the street... This was the crash, the disaster."[8] Spanish poet Gabriel García Lorca turned his direct experience of that day into a lower Manhattan destroyed by "hurricanes of gold" and "tumults of windows," contrasting these metaphors of spectacle with others, deeper and more chilling: the "merciless silence of money," that led him to feel "the sensation of real death, death without hope, death that is nothing but rottenness."[9] Neither Lorca nor Orozco was a literalizing Communist—indeed, hatred of all ideologies was the driving force of the latter's art. There are many parallels between this painting and the imagery of dismembered bodies in his political lithographs, and his raging against the self-destructiveness of mechanized modernity in his murals of the early 1930s, including those at the New School for Social Research, New York, and at Dartmouth College, Hanover, New Hampshire.

Now, in the tailings of another aftermath, something seems different about *New York: The Dead*. Orozco had used a Cubist composition, but less as the understructure of his painting, more as a sign for modernity in general, taking Cubism as the quintessential art of the modern city. Cubism, then, does not undergird his subject, it is part of the depicted subject matter itself. The painting's aesthetic baseline—we can now see—is a figuration that hovers over the abyss of its own absence, over the black unrepresentable beneath. The tower-body shapes are, as painting, a slashing, an overlaying of broad brushstrokes that are detailed to suggest buildings. The forces outside that which is shown, forces that brought about the destruction before us, are, like the black void beneath, implied, not shown. *New York: The Dead* is not, therefore, simply a picturing of implosion, or of self-destruction.

It is an image of collapse, of hopeless surrender, abandonment, brought out by unseeable powers. In this strange, untimely sense, it prefigures aspects of 9.11.01. The immediate incomprehensibility of its causality: not so much who did it, or even why. More, this question: how could they? And this: from which death-dealing, suicidal darkness did they come?

> As the airships sailed along they smashed up the city as a child will shatter its cities of brick and card. Below they left ruins and blazing conflagrations and heaped and scattered dead: men, women and children mixed together as though they had been no more than Moors, or Zulus, or Chinese . . . Lower Manhattan was soon a furnace of crimson flames, from which there was no escape. Cars, railways, ferries, all had ceased, and never a light lit the way of distracted fugitives in that dusky confusion than the light of burning . . . Dust and black smoke came pouring into the street, and were presently shot with red flame.

This is from the American edition of H. G. Wells's 1907 novel, *The War in the Air*, in which he imagines a Wilhelmine Germany launching its zeppelins against primary targets around the world.[10] It is the opening scene of Mike Davis's brilliant description and interpretation of 9.11.01.[11] The city brought to its knees is a prospect imagined by many writers—of novels, sci-fi, and screenplays—during Manhattan's reign as Gotham, the capital of modernity. Usually, an alien force threatens the city, above all by bringing out something other in the character of the city itself that seems ready to conspire with, or accede to, the external force. The city is saved, usually, by a person or an event that embodies its innocence. This is, in turn, a personification of the presumption that the city's destruction is imaginable only as an aberration, as an apocalypse that will fail to occur precisely because the city is impregnable.

Even more specifically prefigurative was the film *Independence Day*, which rehearsed the violent destruction, by aliens, of the most familiar U.S. icons, including those targeted on 9.11.01. Yet it was, of course, framed by a narrative that, every viewer knew, would deliver salvation via American heroism. In the larger political sphere, however, no savior has emerged since 9.11.01, despite President Bush's enormous efforts to put himself forward in this role. The conclusion to Stanley Kubrick's last film *AI: Artificial Intelligence*, released in June 2001, was closer to the mark. Returning to a theme of his *2001: A Space Odyssey*, Kubrick imagines a future world in which robots and humans live, perpetually discomforted, in settings ominously influenced by monoliths. In *AI*'s climax, a robot child returns to the Forbidden Zone to confront his replicants. Set in Lower Manhattan (where else?) post-World War III, the remains of the city include, half-sunken beneath the waters, the WTC towers.

The Spectacle Imagines Its Own Deconstruction

Hindsight also allows us to see some architectural phenomena as premonitory. Most obvious is the fate of the Pruitt-Igoe apartments in Saint Louis, designed by

Yamasaki. They were demolished in 1972—by a planned implosion—after the failure of many efforts over nearly twenty years to make them viable as low-cost housing (illus. 43). These apartments do not appear on the list of works provided by Yamasaki's firm to *Contemporary Architects*.[12] More suggestive prefigurations may be found in the rendering of Manhattan skyscrapers produced by architectural draftsman Hugh Ferriss from the 1930s through the 1950s. Favored by leading architects and developers as ways of envisaging proposals for a variety of projects that now dot the island, Ferris's drawings were frequently cast in solemn tones, darkly shadowed, showing buildings as forms stripped of ornament, as if they were memorials to themselves, set in spaces filled with smoke and, mostly, devoid of all but a few scattered people and blurred vehicles. Ferriss's hellish vision exercised a great hold on the architectural imagination of the city. He revealed the ponderous vacuity of its spectral essence—the spare gravestones that appear when the flounces and the flourishes of the roof profiles, and the popular address of the lower façades, are spirited away. It is a deep compliment to the early and midcentury developers of the city that such dark secrets were their images of choice when it came to showing each other their core intentions.[13]

In 1968 American artist Claes Oldenburg proposed a monument for downtown Chicago. It was one of his many amusing, often discomforting, propositions for a kind of public art that would replace official efforts at image control with icons from the world of advertising, everyday life, the movies, or fantasy. This displacement from one arena of visual culture to another was typical of the work of Pop artists everywhere and has become a standard strategy for all the visual arts all over the world. Oldenburg's projects often entail another popular strategy: the use of a radical shift in scale, usually upwards, a kind of gigantism at odds with the trivial goofiness of his shapes—Mickey Mouse ears, clothes pegs, soft typewriters, cigarette butts. *Proposal for a Skyscraper for Michigan Avenue, Chicago in the Form of Lorado Taft's Sculpture "Death"* adds an element of the foreboding: right across the street from the John Hancock Building he posits the erection of a huge hooded figure, an apparition of death (illus. 37). Oldenburg read the shape of the Hancock Building as an enlarged echo of an Art Deco mausoleum. In a well-known grave design, Taft had indeed used the form for this purpose and staged his cloaked figure in front of it, as if emergent from the tomb's darkness. Oldenburg projects the revenant as appearing out of the fissure of Otherness, as a force that comes from the past to claim the present.[14] In hindsight, this image is uncannily prescient. The Hancock Building was, for a period, in direct competition with the World Trade Center towers for the title of tallest building in the world: both were eclipsed by the Sears Tower on its completion in 1974. The Sears building was, according to some evidence, on the list of targets for 9.11.01. Oldenburg, in 1968, intuited something of pivotal relevance to our inquiry: that the outward-going, dazzling, over-the-top qualities of the spectacular are accompanied, always, by the closed, internalizing, unknowable shadows of the spectral.

A more obtuse irony now flavors a joint project submitted by Frank Gehry and Richard Serra in 1981 to an exhibition *Collaboration: Artists and Architects* held at

37. Claes Oldenburg,
Proposal for a
Skyscraper for Michigan
Avenue, Chicago in the
Form of Lorado Taft's
Sculpture "Death."
1968, photographs
and pencil. Artist's
collection. Courtesy the
artist.

the Architectural League of New York. Their theme was a bridge for New York. Serra conceived a massive steel slab, wedged into the East River and tilted away from Manhattan, while Gehry came up with a gigantic fish emerging from the Hudson River, also leaning away from the island. Serra's steel was to anchor great cables that passed through the apex of the Chrysler Building (or perhaps the Empire State Building; the drawing is unclear), Gehry's fish to anchor cables that pierced the World Trade Center buildings at about three-quarters of their height.[15] Established icons are tied to forms that their creators presumably hoped would emerge as new icons. But 1981 was the year that Serra's *Tilted Arc* was installed in the Federal Plaza, New York. Its challenge to public space attracted such public and official hostility that it would not survive the decade.[16] Gehry's leaping sea bass fared better: he subsumed it into his design processes, abstracting it as a flavor of generic organicism, with the result that his subsequent architecture became infused with a subliminal, paleoichthyic attractiveness.

In chapter 3 I detailed my reading of Gehry's proposed Guggenheim Museum on the East River, New York, and cited the Museum's publicity that boosted the design's "deconstructive" daring: "The rigid forms characteristic of a skyscraper—the quintessence of New York architecture—are fractured and recombined with a curvilinear body suggestive of the water's fluid movement and the energy of the city" (illus. 19 and 38).[17] Yet deconstruction is not a negative force; it is about the reconstitutive and inventive energies released by its processes.[18] There is no doubt, however, that the publicist's hyperbole expresses a definitive current of Gehry's design thinking: the conjuring of buildings, such as the WTC, as collapsing under the weight of their redundancy, a forest of structures fallen out of fashion. Modernist figments submitting to history, fading in order to allow a new kind of architecture to be born. The idea of built-in de/reconstruction is a typical Gehry theme, one that has persisted in his work since he renovated a pink Dutch Colonial bungalow in Santa Monica in 1978 as his own house. It symbolizes architecture as the product of the construction site, as a place of constant self-renovation (indeed, Gehry remodeled again in 1993, along more accommodating lines). As many commentators have noted, the Gehry House was, and remains, the House That Built Gehry. This may change when his design for a family compound on a clear lot at Venice, California, is realized in the near future.

The economic and psychic fallout from 9.11.01 led the museum, in February 2003, to announce that it was shelving the New York project.[19] Yet the coincidence of Gehry's central mass and the imploding WTC does raise an interesting conundrum for architecture that, by instinct, attempts to propel us into a future that is unknowable but presumed to be positive. Critique of current form is, within modernism and its postmodernist echo, the primary method of this propulsion. This has been the driver behind many of Gehry's innovations, including the Guggenheim Museum, Bilbao. It also incites powerful critiques of Gehry's work, such as that offered by artist Allan Sekula in parts of his photo-text work *Titanic's Wake* (illus. 7).[20] Naïve futurism is a luxury the avant-garde has not been able to afford for decades: what is to come may be not be an as yet unimaginable but nonetheless positive extension of the best of the present. It may be unimaginable horror, or it may be all too imaginable recursion to dark premodernities. Architectural fast-forwarding, from now on, is certain to face many constraints. This will make the task of forging a new kind of social contract even harder.

Ruin Value

The prefigurations we have been discussing tend to become visible in retrospect; they have no evident determinative significance, nor did they cause the event with

38. Frank Gehry, site
with current design
model, proposed
Guggenheim Museum
New York, 1998–
2001. Photo by David
Heald, 2001. Source:
Guggenheim Museum.

which we have associated them to come to pass. In most monotheistic religions, the doctrine of predestination has the specific sense of God having already chosen or foreordained those on whom he will bestow the grace of salvation and the afterlife. For St. Augustine, St. Thomas Aquinas, Leibniz, Calvin, and many others, including orthodox Islam in general, predestination has the sense of God foreordaining what-soever comes to pass. The language of predestination suffused the inspirational text that the 9.11.01 hijackers used as a framework for their actions.[21] Martyrdom in the name of Islam and for a perceived political advantage for one's people is seen by many in the Arab world at the moment as hastening grace for the martyr, and as helping to bring about God's will, that is, as doubly predestined.[22]

Can we say of a building, or a structure or set of buildings, that it was architecture of the kind that would occasion, or at least be the site of, predestination in the more general sense? We can certainly say this of most significant religious architecture. The sense that it was, is, and forever will be the setting for predestined election or events is surely precisely what major religious architecture strives to stimulate—in mosques as much as in the worship centers of the eschatological current that is rising in the great Western-based religions. Yet this is the opposite of what happens when fundamentalist elements of a belief system built around predestination uncoil from within the quiet settings of its normally peaceful preordination and reaches across a cultural divide to strike at a destination monument in another, secular culture, reducing it to rubble, and all that it symbolizes to shaky equivocality.

Can we say of any architecture that it invited its own obliteration, that it prefigured it, even foretold it? "Beautiful ruins" was part of the Nazi aesthetic developed by Albert Speer for Hitler, but the desire for buildings that anticipate their own pastness as a kind of elegant afterlife, is a wide and deep current in European architecture, especially in Romantic and post-Romantic memorials: Mies van der Rohe's youthful proposal for the Bismarck Memorial (Bingen on the Rhine 1912), for example, in contrast to his Memorial to Karl Liebkneckt and Rosa Luxemburg (Berlin 1926). It elaborates the ready-made ruin of the eighteenth century, and its fondness for imagining the present as ruined—in the work of Hubert Robert, "the Rembrandt of Ruins," in Gandy's paintings of Soane's new Bank of England as already ancient, and in the more subtle allusions to the past in the modern times of J. M. W. Turner. Romantics loved the double message that they saw inscribed in surviving antique ruins: human life was short, but greatness would leave awe-inspiring legacies.

Modern Master architecture set itself against double standards, both classical and Romantic. It boldly rejected historicism, banished time in favor of space, made transparent its interior purposes, declared its methods of construction, all in a spirit of utopic idealism. The hope was to step outside of, above, the ravages of history—especially that of a Europe embroiled in one disastrous war after another. By and large, it failed to do so—even though it prolonged the dream by emigrating to America.

Larger forces were unfolding. Within them, there was a distinction to be made between a building that crumbles slowly into ruin and one devastated by an act of war. As Jonathan Jones puts it, "the difference between the richly rotting fruits of time, and a building destroyed in a moment: the difference between dying of old age and murder."[23] There is a further distinction to be made if we are to recognize the calculated usage, by a conquering people, or by a subsequent regime, of the material of a major monument of the conquered or the displacement. For example, the attrition worked upon pagan monuments, such as the Coliseum, by the succession of popes who leased this and other pre-Christian sites as stone quarries to the builders of their churches.[24]

In contrast, Juhasz clearly believed that the WTC, because it was emblematic of U.S. Cold War policy and actions in the Middle East, had brought its (at that time attempted) destruction upon itself. His metaphorical leap to architectural form is to see that the suppressions at the heart of the WTC's design called in their own implosion, like ranks of the devil's angels destroying each other through their perverse version of "friendly fire." This would be the opposite of Speer's eager anticipation of eventual, eternal ruined beauty; to Juhasz, Yamasaki was defying the contingency that is our mortal lot by insisting that the current solution, his solution, was itself eternal. However long we draw the bow of cause and effect, this connection makes sense only as itself a metaphor for ethical restraint in architecture, as a call for the observance of architecture's social contract. The 1993 bombers, and those of 2001, were motivated, according to their own testimony, more by fury over U.S. policy in the Middle East than anger at the WTC builders' abuse of their obligations to their community. It required no great metaphorical stretch by the 9.11.01 attackers for them to see the towers, along with the Pentagon and the White House, as embodiments of the same kind of arrogance. The attackers were hardly alone in seeing this kind of attitude as informing the entirety of American polity, both abroad and at home. Their strike was aimed at the most obvious pinnacles of this continuum, and was intended to shake the entire edifice. As it did.

Ruin value hovered around the WTC site for a time, and affected many who spent any time in or near Ground Zero. For the general public, however, the site became iconic when it was stilled by the survival of a section of the lower levels of the exterior wall. This elegant lattice made a striking silhouette. That it recalled the Venetian "Arabic" decorative motif of the fusing columns was a significant, if unspoken, subtextual element. Much talk was heard of leaving it, just where it lay, as the centerpiece of a monument. In a rush of emotion, Metropolitan Museum of Art director Philippe de Montebello declared it a "masterpiece" to be cherished and preserved. But it was destroyed, as the program of clearance made its relentless, violent progress towards total erasure of all signs of the violence that had occurred.

Disable, Dismember, Destroy

Events have two irreducible, but dichotomous, qualities: they happen, definitively, in time and space, in the lives of people and in the existence of things, but their shape is never entirely predictable and their outcomes go quickly beyond the anticipated to the unfathomable. An event, its impact and its interpretation (including the mourning necessary to absorb trauma-inducing events) are all subject to this double logic of actuality and excess. This realization is at the heart of Jacques Derrida's response to 9.11.01:

> Is, then, what was touched, wounded, or traumatized by this double *crash* only some particular thing or other, a "what" or a "who," buildings, strategic urban structures, symbols of political, military or capitalist power, or a considerable number of people of many different origins living in a national territory that

had remained untouched for so long? No, it was not *only* all that but perhaps especially, through all that, the conceptual, semantic, and one could even say hermeneutic apparatus that might have allowed one to see coming, to comprehend, interpret, describe, speak of, and name "September 11"—and in so doing to neutralize the traumatism and come to terms with it through a "work of mourning."[25]

One step towards this work is to try to imagine the imagoes that animated, perhaps even haunted, the attackers as they devised this event and precipitated it. Derrida's first stab at it is this: "Archaic and forever puerile, terribly childish, these masculine phantasms were in fact fed by an entire technocinematographic culture, and not only the genre of science fiction."[26] Let us begin from this point: the scenario of a small band of enraged but calculating people, armed with prosthetic machines, pitting themselves against buildings. How might we imagine these space warriors to imagine their targets?

No building, no matter how simple, or "rude," is without its sense of standing in some relation of distinctness and relatedness to human being, itself embodied. Even those buildings that house secret functions address us by turning their backs to the street or hiding behind a misleading façade. We can observe them doing this. No public building is faceless, certainly not the Pentagon, in whose name, and from whose briefing rooms, may be regularly heard the voice of the U.S. military. Certainly not the WTC, as we have noted in the discourse that surrounds it. The White House is not only the home of the president of the United States, but becomes the personification of the office by direct cutaway during the opening titles of a presidential address to the nation, or as the stage of a White House lawn press conference. To those who conspired so long and carefully to destroy them (bin Laden's hatred went back to 1982), these buildings were the bodies of the enemy (illus. 39).[27] They set out to dismember these false idols, and to disfigure these false ideals, to tear down their façades so as to expose the emptiness behind them. As targets, these symbol-buildings were readily prefigurable: the attackers could bring to mind countless images of them from within the iconomy, and match them with countless other images of intentional, effective destruction. Not only had they seen such images in the mass and entertainment print media, and perhaps in the cinema, they had been on the receiving end of attacks in their own countries, attacks planned and authorized from within some of these very buildings.

To grasp the phantasms, and to set some space around the event itself, we need to reach back behind it, to the possibilities that were open before it occurred. While more and more details as to the plans and hopes of the attackers emerged during the inquiries of the National Commission on Terrorist Attacks on the United States, conducted by the U.S. Congress, the precise nature of their intentions may never be known, or reliably known. It is not certain that the quality of completeness embodied in the deadly finality of the WTC implosions can be imported to the entire event—although the imagery of the attack and collapse of

39. Al-Jazeera, logo
for television talk
show *The First of
the Century's Wars*,
September 2001.
[public domain]

the towers eclipsed all other representation of 9.11.01 and has indubitably dominated its interpretation. While destroying utterly every vestige of the enemy target
might be the dream of the attacker, while eradicating the icon from existence and
memory might be the fantasy of the iconoclast, every professional demolisher
knows that this happens rarely. Disabling the enemy's functionality is a more
limited goal and a more commonly achieved objective. This is what happened,
concretely at the Pentagon, and more generally throughout the economy and the
public sphere of the United States and elsewhere. Dismembering is most likely
what the attackers hoped to do to the WTC towers: to impale their giant spears
through the bodies of the enemy, creating thereby a symbol of martyrdom and
a sign of the West's vulnerability. That would have met the goals Al Qaeda typically sets for its spectacular terrorism, and frequently achieves. The fact that, in
the event, a host of factors, many of which were unpredictable and unknowable to
the planners of the attack, converged to bring down the towers meant that the
attack turned into one of all-out destruction. Assuming that the third airplane
had the White House as its target, destruction may well have been the goal there
too. If the Capitol was a target, then probably dismemberment was the hope. As
it may have been if the Hancock Building was on the hit list.[28]

Disable, dismember, destroy. These possibilities attend every event of this kind.
None of them is predestined. But if the event occurs, one of them will be its shape,
and the structure of its misshaping. The fact that the towers, after standing
dismembered for a time, then imploded, gave the attackers and their sympathizers
the added frisson of seeing their enemy self-destruct through an unknown but
always suspected weakness. The collapse of the towers demonstrated unequivocally

that the action had been brought to its maximal conclusion, that the event had achieved closure—at least from the viewpoint of the planners and attackers. Fallout would resonate in ways still to be seen, and a new iconotype was released into the iconomy. As an attack, however, the job was done, and done to the full.

Disembody

"A very tall building absorbs a plane and collapses after 105 defiant minutes, having watched its twin suffer the same fate. Everyone sees it. Again and again. It captures every eye and ear in stunned amazement. When the towers fell, the world shook." Body language is preeminent here, in these opening words to perhaps the most insightful of the more considered responses to the event by a member of the architectural community, Mark Wigley's essay "Insecurity by Design."[29] The Twin Towers are personified: wounded, empathetic siblings, they see each other and live (then die) in the sight of every other sentient being, all of whom are affected. Wigley explains that these relationships are fundamental. Buildings protect their fragile occupants, they last longer than humans, they are witnesses to our lives, they are the continuity between our shared experience, they sustain our shared sense of time. To act as our witness, to protect our bodies, buildings "must be themselves a kind of body; a surrogate body, a superbody with a face, a façade, that watches us."[30] Everything opposite to this is abhorrent: being hurt by a building part, or by its collapsing on us, removing a building prematurely from the culture, or disfiguring it—all these are offensive, painful acts. Terrorists know what every general knows: that damaging the buildings of the enemy is to damage their bodies, and to spread the threat of more damage. "The terrorist mobilizes the whole psychopathology of fears buried beneath the architect's obsession with efficiency, comfort and pleasure."[31] The towers became victims, over which people grieved, and in doing so grieved for themselves.

On 9.11.01 these metaphorical relations became literal for the people of Lower Manhattan: for days, those who survived lived in the dust of the collapsed structures, literally breathing in the bodies of their neighbors and of the destroyed buildings. A common experience in war zones, not so common in modern cities outside of such situations, although Downtown Manhattan had been razed by fire in both 1776 and 1835, and the 1906 San Francisco earthquake produced scenes uncannily like those of 9.11.01.[32] Furthermore, the deaths of nearly three thousand meant, in this implosion, almost no visible human bodies. Just those few who waited, appealed, then fell or jumped (illus. 40). And whose images disappeared from at least American television screens very fast. Most victims were pulverized, and those whose parts were identified were not shown to the public. The absence of damaged people meant more investment in the remains of the mangled buildings.

Wigley offers a subtle twist on the mostly negative readings of the WTC that we have seen to be almost unanimous among architects and related professionals. Speaking of the general attitude of the public in Manhattan towards the WTC

he remarks: "At some level, an extraordinary identification with the buildings took place that exceeded the expectations of both the boosters of the project (whose only real interest was real estate speculation) and the architectural critics (whose only real interest was to promote an alternative aesthetic model that would be used in subsequent real estate speculations)."[33] He suggests that the awkwardness of the buildings suited them to "a city of refugees and misfits of every kind," one that mixed the local with the international in unpredictable ways. They were the neighborhood sign for otherness, for connectedness to the rest of the world, for the fact that this connection was pursued by other, faceless, unknowable people, and that that was fine by me. Wigley is saying that the people understood that the towers, like international capital itself, were meant to exist at some remove from everyone else's everyday life, like any multinational corporation. "The key symbolic role of the World Trade Center, the rationale for both its design and its destruction, was to represent the global market-place. In a strange way, [these] supersolid, supervisible, superlocated buildings stood as a figure for the dematerialized, invisible, placeless market."[34]

Here is a paradox. A bland, featureless structure—two of them, in fact, side by side, each of the eight sides being the same as the others—opaque to the external gaze, so basic in shape that they could be any other equally basic shape, so generic in form that anything could occur within them, they could serve any function, all functions being equally abstracted, removed from the life-flows around them. In this sense, they seemed to lack any interior, a common experience of those who

40. David Surowiecki, people jump from World Trade Center tower. photograph, 2001. David Surowiecki/Getty Images.

worked in them. Images of their interiors are rare to the point of being extraordinary exceptions. In sum, their featurelessness led them to become two million square feet of "vast, uncannily duplicated" screen for whatever may be projected onto them. Mostly, Wigley believes, nothing in particular was projected. Just the mild warmth of familiarity. Until 9.11.01, when "the façades came down, the faces of the invisible occupants who were lost came up, filling the vertical surfaces of the city in pasted photocopies and covering the surfaces of televisions, computers and newspapers all around the world. They formed a new kind of façade, a dispersed image of diversity in place of the singular monolithic screen—each face, each personality, each story, suddenly in focus."[35] Architecture itself evaporated. It had failed to protect its inhabitants against forces greater than what it usually has to provide for in the way of security.

This is an astute analysis, adding much to our understanding of the paradoxical nature of the buildings and their reception. Wigley does not, however, acknowledge that the WTC was, as we have shown, designed over and above, indeed, *against* the principles of body metaphor that he, rightly, adumbrates as fundamental to architecture for humans. The Twin Towers did violence to these principles from the beginning, as most independent professional commentators saw. Whether *most people* did so is, like Wigley's guesses about how warmly the towers were regarded by broader publics, a matter of speculation. As is the idea that most who turn their emotional intelligence to the matter might sense that there is a relation, however strange, attenuated, and subterranean, between the nature of the towers and their fate.

Media as Missile

The 9.11.01 attacks were designed as a media event, one that involved at least four planes, and at least four targets, all to be hit roughly simultaneously, or in close sequence, and in ways that would command maximal attention, that would create the most spectacular effect within a spectacle-saturated world. The cinematic quality of the staging of the attacks has caused much comment. A typical example is this comment by the editors of *Der Spiegel*:

> The theatre of destruction offered to the world on September 11 was larger than structural engineer bin Laden could ever have dreamed. Shock is of course the one goal of terrorism: the greater number of people in shock, the better. That is why the attacks of September 11 are to date the most perfect act of terror in history. First you attract the media to a place like the World Trade Center with the crash of the first plane, and then you deliver unforgettable images of terror twenty minutes later with a second plane. It was an idea that almost could have been thought up by the Hollywood screenwriters from whom the Bush administration sought advice about potential terrorist scenarios after September 11.[36]

Among those invited to "brainstorm about Terrorist targets and schemes in America and offer solutions to those threats" were Spike Jonze (*Being John*

Malkovich) and Steven De Souza (*Die Hard*), both of them members of the Institute for Creative Technology, a U.S. Army joint venture with the University of Southern California. One of their inventions, Real War, trains military to battle "insurgents in the Middle East."[37] The handcuff between the virtual and the real that is so typical of the times was confirmed by this aspect of 9.11.01: newspaper reports frequently cited viewers, seeing the television images of the planes hitting the towers for the first time, claiming that they assumed that some kind of action movie was playing. It took repeated viewing, on a number of channels, to convince them that they were seeing an event that has actually occurred, was still occurring. For many, perhaps all of us, 9.11.01 remains, in varying degrees, phantasmic.

These patterns of thought resonate, in reverse echo, throughout much Al Qaeda activity. The use of the media, and of the implicit violence of everyday communication, in order to do something that is both an actual political intervention and a symbolic act of great significance is evident, for example, in the assassination of anti-Taliban leader Ahmed Shah Massoud. This occurred two days before 9.11.01. Few in the intelligence community doubt that the two events are connected. They were certainly similar in their structure.[38] In the era of mass media and communications, the Middle East is not exempt from the structural iconophilia and the staging of spectacle events that is the rule elsewhere. Al Qaeda has made extensive use of the quasi-independent television station Al-Jazeera, based in Qatar, and widely watched throughout the Middle East and by Arab exile and immigrant communities throughout the world.[39] Media presence is as crucial to the effectiveness of Islamist spectacular terrorism as it is to the war against it.[40] I have already posed the possibility that the attackers previsualized the uncanny effect, glimpsed in slow-motion film of the planes hitting the towers: the gradual erasure of two key words emblazoned on the sides of the airplane bodies, "American" and "United." This is, however, more likely to be an excess, an unanticipated effect of an event that flew beyond its staging (as, we have seen, such events tend to do). In his outstanding analysis of the impacts and implications of 9.11.01, Slavoj Žižek notes that "we can perceive the collapse of the WTC towers as the cinematic conclusion of twentieth century art's 'passion for the Real'—the 'terrorists' themselves did not do it primarily to provoke real material damage, but for *the spectacular effect of it*."[41] While accepting Žižek's point, it is important not to lose sight of the claim made in my introduction, and repeated since, that it was the *double* value of each of the targets, their combination of symbolic prominence and real time and place operation, that was crucial to their being chosen, and to the resonance of the effect of their destruction.

Some argue, against Žižek's claim that events such as 9.11.01 re-release the Real into the largely fictive nature of everyday life, that spectacle has saturated us with so many images that their point is blunted. Excess is normal in advertising and fashion imagery, pushing those spheres to ever more outrageous, attention-grabbing extremes. The same effect debilitates imagery that might have a potent, and positive, political effect. If so, were not the 9.11.01 attackers out of date? Is not the imagery of deadly visitation repellent, and its circulation, therefore,

counterproductive? These questions have only to be put in the context of the
9.11.01 aftermath to be seen to be puerile. During the heyday of the mass circulation of images through magazines and newspapers, from the 1930s through the
1980s, this enervating effect was palpable. But so too was the constant occurrence
of visceral imagery. Susan Sontag evokes this interplay:

> Imagine a spread of loose photographs extracted from an envelope that arrived
> in the morning mail. They show the mangled bodies of adults and children. They
> show how war evacuates, shatters, breaks apart, levels the built world. A bomb
> has torn open the side of a house. To be sure, a cityscape is not made of flesh.
> Still, sheared-off buildings are almost as eloquent as body parts (Kabul; Sarajevo;
> East Mostar; Grozny; sixteen acres of Lower Manhattan after September 11,
> 2001; the refugee camp in Jenin). Look, the photographs say, *this* is what it's like.
> This is what war *does*. And *that*, that is what it does. War tears, rends. War rips
> open, eviscerates. War scorches. War dismembers. War *ruins*.[42]

Since then, as she goes on to demonstrate, the imagery of violent destruction has
gained a currency that can be read in a variety of ways. It can lead some to paci-
fism, while others take it as evidence that their enemy is capable of monstrous
acts and must be opposed by all possible means, including the committing of
monstrous acts. We have inherited from the twentieth century the expectation
that scenes such as these will occur, almost as a normality, in many parts of the
world. On the civilizational "fault lines," mostly, and most likely . . . but not in
Manhattan, surely, not on a sunny day in September . . .

The Return of the Iconoclast?

What should we make of the dark prophecy, forwarded by Salman Rushdie among
others, that iconoclasm has returned to the world as a new antivisual regime? This
is true only if you generalize what is, in Islamic societies, a widespread but not universal prohibition of images of God into an all-out iconophobia. Bin Laden is not
the only Muslim to despise tall buildings, apart from minarets, especially secular
buildings that might seem to tower over religious structures, to proclaim worldly
vanity. Nervous (or fear-mongering) commentators frequently note that fifty of
the world's one hundred tallest buildings are in the U.S. Opposing the radical
Islamists whom he sees as responsible for the attacks, Rushdie drew attention to
an Al Qaeda warning: "there will be rain of aircraft from the skies, Muslims in the
West are warned not to live in tall buildings."[43]

Iconophobia is certainly not universal in the Arab world, or among Muslims
anywhere. There are rich traditions of figurative imagery in most Arab countries.
The philosophy and science of optics has among its founders medieval Islamic
thinkers such as Al-Kindi and Alhazen.[44] Images of holy cities, great palaces and
points of pilgrimage abound: what are these, if not iconotypes? Is not the fabled
Temple of Solomon, that on some accounts included a wonderzone of glass in its
entrance hall, a template of Islamic aesthetics?[45]

But this level of generalization is not particularly helpful at the point of understanding specific acts of destruction: it implies a trenchant hatred of all landmark structures, all destination architecture except that with a sanctioned religious purpose. Not that this latter quality saves powerful images; consider the destruction of the Buddha statues at Bamiyan in March 2001, an action that some saw as prefiguring the attack on the WTC (illus. 41). But the elimination of the Bamiyan colossi was, it seems, the action of a Pashtun group of Wahhabi who wished to remove a powerful embodiment of the cultural and religious patrimony of the Hazari, a local people. It was a historically specific act, an iconoclastic moment in Islamic history to be sure but not necessarily an instance of a generalized Islamic iconoclasm. Since the actions and statements of Muhammad himself distinctions have been drawn between the distinct settings in which different kinds of imagery are appropriate: for centuries figurative imagery has been unobjectionable in secular situations, less so in sacred ones. Iconoclasm has often meant the erasure of the face in a representation (as in the case of the Bamiyan Buddhas since, probably, medieval times), or the "cutting" of the depicted figure by a literal incision or by marking a line across its throat. Decapitation of a statue can be quite literal, as is the act of removing its carved eyeballs, or its weapons of power, symbols of authority, or marks of identification. Iconoclastic acts of this kind are not uncommon across all cultures and civilizations. To highlight Islamic iconoclasm to the exclusion of Islam's more complex range of attitudes toward imagery is Orientalist. It is the equivalent of imagining that "the destruction of pagan

41. Amir Shah, Taliban soldiers wave to journalists while standing in front of the empty shell where a statue of the Buddha once stood, March 26, 2001, Bamiyan, Afghanistan. 2001, photograph. Associated Press.

images by Christians in late antiquity, the mutilation of icons in ninth-century Byzantium, the iconoclastic depredations of the Reformation, and the events of the French Revolution" could be described under the rubric of "Christian iconoclasm," and taken to be definitive of the main attitude to visual imagery in the West since the first century.[46]

Obviously, iconoclasts have an intense awareness of the power of images, including their power to distract believers from their spiritual path. Yet this is true, in degrees, of all organized religions and of many secular authorities. Iconoclasm is a resort of authority that feels itself profoundly threatened by difference: in the words of novelist Barry Unsworth, it is "a final resource that illustrates one of the most terrible lessons of our time: if the images cannot be controlled, destroy them, obliterate the traces, leave only the evidence of power."[47] So it is important to keep in mind that the recent attacks on visual imagery as such in Afghanistan and elsewhere have been led by an extremist group of Wahhabi Muslims who condemn every depiction of living beings as an offense against Allah.[48] Nor was this a new thing for Afghanistan. Much of the destruction of cultural monuments occurred during the mujahadeen period (1993-96). Indeed, for some time after assuming power, the Taliban acted in ways that contradicted Western expectations as to their fundamentalism.[49] By early 2001, however, much had changed. Under pressure from hard-liners within the government, and from the Al Qaeda representatives on which his government had increasingly come to rely, he issued, on February 26, 2001, a further decree: "In view of the *fatwa* of prominent Afghan scholars and the verdict of the Afghan Supreme Court, it has been decided to break down all statues/idols present in different parts of the country. This is because those idols have been gods of the infidels, who worshipped them, and these are respected even now and perhaps may be turned into gods again. The only real god is Allah, and all other false gods should be removed."[50]

Nicholas Mirzoeff astutely notes the paradoxical use of primarily visual media by groups and regimes that actively pursue the restoration of aniconic feudalism:

> Since their takeover of power, the Taliban in Afghanistan held public destructions of artworks, televisions and videotapes, while forcibly constraining women in the home and making them literally invisible in public behind the veil. The anti-modernity of the Taliban and their allies relied on the global media to disseminate their actions and to discipline their subjects, even as it disavowed visual culture. For it was an open secret, reported in the Western media, that many Afghans continued to watch television and videos and these were of course the people least convinced by the Taliban. The destruction of the Buddhist statues at Bamiyan was one example of this televised iconoclasm and September 11 was its apogee.[51]

The continuing tragedy in all this is that governments—which in practice represent very temporary configurations of power, with very specific and limited value profiles—nevertheless have the capacity to remove forever the material being of a cultural monument with the same lack of concern that it might have for the lives of its opponents. The Taliban's impermanence became apparent in the aftermath of 9.11.01 as it fell victim to an angry U.S. war machine. Yet its outlook was millennial, indeed, eternal: it was striving to institute a permanent Islamist order. Evidence for this may be found not only in its own statements but its actions in enforcing its strict regime. Video film and photographs smuggled out of Afghanistan by the Revolutionary Association of Women of Afghanistan record the execution—in the most public places: markets, sports stadiums, shopping streets, and popular cafes—of women who had broken Islamic law.[52] These videos and photographs are not intended as objective documentaries of Afghan life; they concentrate on showing the dismembered bodies of regime opponents strewn around the streets and constant scenes of hanging. They record the acts of a state terrorizing its citizens into conformity with its values and behaviors. The Taliban's message was unmistakable: they were irrecoverably committed to the reintroduction of feudal practices of social control to Afghanistan.

So, in a significant sense, were the 9.11.01 attackers, although their target audience was wider. 9.11.01 was an object lesson to the infidel, and to those tempted by the infidel ways of the West. The technological know-how of the attackers, their management skills, and their conceptual sophistication in their choice of weapons is acknowledged. As is their spectacular use of the international media. But their goal was retroactive in intent and deliberately feudal in the style of its execution. This kind of disjunction is exactly what we have come to expect of the condition of contemporaneity. 9.11.01 was a public execution, not only of those who happened to be in the buildings, and of those leaders who the attackers hoped would be in the buildings, but the buildings themselves as prideful personifications of American unbelief, materialism, and corruption. Within the iconomy, stereotyping can be fatal. It desires the obliteration of particularity, of too much difference, of uncontainable complexity, of heterogeneity. It wipes out things and people and threatens whole classes and categories of peoples. Islamic fundamentalists live in the memory of their religion in its insurgent phase and in the aftermath of the decline and fall of the great Muslim empires. Their fantastical campaign attempts to evaporate the shameful fact of aftermath altogether. It imagines the world without those who have brought about their shame. In its targeting of "Americans" it slides towards the specter of symbolic genocide. On a smaller scale, the profiling by the U.S. government of MEAs ("men of Middle Eastern appearance") follows the same logic. In the forces that converged in 9.11.01, and that have played out, powerfully, ever since, Paul Virilio recognizes an aspiration to bring about a millenarian transformation of the world: "that 'beyond Good and Evil' that has for centuries been the dream of the high priests of iconoclastic progress."[53] It is an aspiration that drives fundamentalism of all kinds, and is active on both sides of the "War on Terror."

Artists of Death: The Contemporary Sublime

Composer Karlheinz Stockhausen shocked many, and attracted extraordinary opprobrium, when he speculated that 9.11.01 was "like the greatest work of art that is possible in the whole cosmos," that the attackers had achieved "in one act . . . something we couldn't even dream of in music . . . Just imagine, you have people who are dispatched to eternity, in a single moment. I couldn't do that. In comparison to that, we are nothing as composers." He stressed the dedication of the perpetrators, comparing them to the most committed of artists, and described 9.11.01 as a performance for which "people practice like crazy for ten years, totally frantically, for a concert, and then die."[54] However aberrant, however abhorrent, his comments surprise from its hiding place a natural secret: shocked admiration for such a spectacular outcome, the result of what seemed to be extraordinarily precise planning (Norman Mailer: "We had to recognize that the people that did this were brilliant"), and exquisite aesthetic preconception (Jonathan Franzen labeled them "death artists").[55] There was also, for many, the further shame—trivializing, sacrilegious even—of seeing beauty in the burning, collapsing towers. Many children did the latter immediately, without shame.

Generations of viewers have been induced to admire the conflagration of images of authority in action films and novels, a training also undergone by the attackers. We have already noted the filmic plotting in the hijacking, and that the attack was staged as a sequenced, camera-ready event, with very telegenic climaxes and a suspenseful aftermath. Ideal televisual fodder. Yet the sublimity effect has both an ancient and a recent history. It was, for example, a well-known element in responses to images of the atomic and especially the hydrogen bomb and was, therefore, a problem for image-making activists in the antinuclear movement in the 1970s. Awe before icons may be nothing more complex than an acculturated conflation of the sense of beauty with any powerful, moving, spectacular visual image—the iconomy is, after all, the aesthetic regime now shared by more people than any other. Or such reactions may be a hardwired neural response to any image that combines clarity of meaning with detail of effect, to any narrative that follows its telegraphed form to its end, to any event that arrives at what seems to be its natural closure.

In many instances, however, powerful responses are elicited by the ways in which the images have been made. After all, many pictures of 9.11.01 were taken by photographers who were not only outstanding, experienced photojournalists but also fine artists: Gilles Peress, Steve McCurry, Joel Meyerowitz, and Susan Meiselas among them (illus. 42).[56] Others, such as Jeff Marmelstein, a self-described "whimsical New York Street photographer," was drawn into this aesthetic in his memorable shots of sections of parks, buildings, and people stained a warm ash brown.[57] We respond to the framing power that such artists carry in their perceptual makeup, an apparatus of perception that works to organize whatever chaos is unfolding before them. We respond to their skill in transforming inchoate particulars into a configuration that seems to have achieved a kind of resolution, to have "caught" something that will stop the flow, that will hold even the most incoherent event in an image suitable for memory. The WTC site happened to be within easy walking distance of an area that contains the homes and studios of perhaps the largest concentration of photographers in any city. Most of them grabbed cameras

42. Steve McCurry, World Trade Center attack. photograph, 2001. Magnum photographers.

and rushed towards the site within minutes of the first strike. In one case, that of political photojournalist Bill Biggart, veteran of Wounded Knee, Belfast, the West Bank, and the Berlin Wall, it proved his last assignment. At 10:28.24 A.M. he stepped out from under an overpass to shoot a slightly closer picture of what later became the iconic remnants of the collapsed South Tower, at which moment the North Tower fell, burying him and the firemen sheltering with him.[58]

Television journalism has developed a parallel aesthetic: it is on an unceasing search for the logo image, one that will attach so firmly to a subject that it is

43. Implosion of
Pruitt-Igoe apartments
(designed by Yamasaki
1952-55), St. Louis,
1972. From Charles
Jencks, *The Language
of Postmodern
Architecture* (New York:
Rizzoli, 1977), 9.

obliged to cover again and again, one that will stop, for a moment, its own cease-less flow. Televisual imagery combines shock and cliché in equal proportions, attracting our distracted attention while at the same time confirming a relatively reduced understanding of the current slice of information. And then it goes on, via its endless chatter, to the next mix. Television broadcasters all over the world reacted to 9.11.01 with shock and found themselves scrambling to fit the infotain-ment formats that had come, especially in the U.S., to dominate news broadcast-ing, to an event that exceeded, for a time, its stunted grasp.[59]

It was common, in the first moments of 9.11.01, to describe the images of the planes hitting the towers, of the imploding buildings, the escaping crowds, the converging firemen, the ashen streets, as "surreal." As Sontag has noted, this was "a hectic euphemism behind which the disgraced notion of beauty cowered."[60] "Surreal" is itself a term in common currency for the kind of effect much used in movies and music video: the familiar exaggerated, made weird, dreamlike, even nightmarish. There is accuracy here, too, when we recall André Breton's character-ization of Surrealist poetry and art as committed to a kind of beauty that he called "convulsive." This is beauty as an effect of the uncontrollable, as the thrill of the unexpected, the spontaneous, that which wells up from the world and from the human unconscious at once, the combustion that threatens to consume us all. It is an intuition that something portentous is not only happening, but is being revealed. Revelation often takes the form of the funeral pyre, of the dazzling conflagration of the outer, material body at the moment that the spirit is released to transcendence.[61]

Heinz Schütz recognized this effect at work in the success of Charles Jencks's use of images of the imploding Pruitt-Igoe housing complex as a metaphor for the end of the Modern Movement in architecture and the beginning of Postmodernism (illus. 43). Explosion as such, he noted, had connotations of the avant-gardes of the early twentieth century, such as the Futurists' love of violence and war, whereas the image of an imploding architecture fascinates because it shows "the ruin at the moment of its creation." This is why the ruin becomes a central topos of Postmodernism; it conjures "the overcoming of history as the ruin of history, in a hall of fame in which time has come to a standstill." Postmodern instant classics such Charles Moore and William Hersey's Piazza d'Italia, New Orleans, 1978-79, stand as illustrations of this idea. Relating this impulse to the global threats of 2000—in his view these were "ecological collapse, an arms build-up and forced economies"–Schütz concluded, presciently, "On a symbolic level a type of apocalyptic bliss has developed, a yearning for solemnity and exiting from history. In a compensatory manner, both levels find their symbolically transfigured expression in the image of the frozen implosion."[62] Is it a coincidence that frozen implosion is a fair metaphorical characterization of the Guggenheim Museum, Bilbao, and even more accurate of the proposed New York Guggenheim? Against their rhetorical grain, of course, but quite descriptive of their eruptive ground plans.

On 9.11.01, the exploding, fiery husk of the collapsing towers consumed those who died within them and around them. For religious believers, the site became sacred at that moment, and will continue to be so in contemplation of that moment and its meanings. For families of the victims, Ground Zero remains an even more intense focal point, as it is the location of the remains of loved ones. However much the authorities might insist that the site is cleared, these people know that it was not, could never be. For the rest of us, the collapsing towers became sacral in ways they may not have been during their actual existence. What truths did their burning reveal? For one thing, we have learned much about the details of the daily lives of those who worked in them: this is the common material of the mountains of close reporting that has followed in their wake. Michael Taussig offers another possible answer: "When the human body, a nation's flag, money, or a public statue is defaced, a strange surplus of negative energy is likely to be aroused within the defaced thing itself."[63]

These are the opening words of his book *Defacement: Public Secrets and the Labor of the Negative*. They are counterintuitive. Is not the work of sacralization, of taking something to be sacral and behaving in a sacred/secular way towards it, precisely a passaging from something evidently negative into a positive state? So that desecration would be, crudely, the reverse of the psychic movement highlighted by Taussig. Yet the negative energy, for him, is not confined to subjectivity, to subject-to-subject relations, to how individuals experience these processes personally. It is the "public secret" released by the act of destruction that is the negative force. The secret is the structural necessity of shared silence, the repression required by most social contracts, that is the real work of the negative. These protocols coach us in knowing when not to speak, indeed, of "knowing what not to know." We bow to the somehow tolerable, at times even comforting, pressure of conformity, of being confined by the code of secrecy to one's subjectivization, to the mode of individuality set out for one by one's society. In acts of defacement, Taussig argues, it is the fragile sham of this situation that is suddenly struck away or goes up in flames. None of the examples he deals with in his book, however, approaches the destruction of the WTC in scale and scope. The public secret that the bombers set out to reveal was quickly out in the open: it is the fragility of capitalism, both as a system and as the occasion and design spirit of this particular building.[64]

Zero Sum Ground

During the last months of 2001 and up to May 2002, images of the painstaking clearance of Ground Zero permeated nightly news reports (illus. 44). As the televisual media, especially, fostered a climate of always-alert anxiety, a daily narrative of traumatic aftermath took shape. Incidents occurred with unsurprising frequency. In late October 2001, for example, New York firefighters fought police— comrades alongside whom they had risked their lives for weeks—in protest against cutbacks in the number of those turning over the vast rubble in search of bodies. This reminds us that, while the impact of the planes led to the spectacular and horrific collapse of the Twin Towers and related buildings, the site itself was systematically razed, by those who wished it well, in the hunt for remains and in preparation for rebuilding. None of the forces involved in this process were simple, or singular. They created their own metaphorical architecture of trauma: traumatic in the precise sense that, like the 9.11.01 attacks themselves, they produced a set of effects the nature of which few have frameworks to encompass, and the causes of which keep changing, evading the grasp of understanding.

This trauma does not constitute a solid structure: on the contrary, the effects create, metonymically, a mobile anti-architecture, an *unbuilding*, one in which destruction searches for a shadow identity, an otherworldly parallelism, for life as a kind of impossible construction.[65] Many elements of 9.11.01 have this characteristic. The landscape of Ground Zero itself: how evocative of a war zone in the desert regions of the world! Expanses of rubble, caked in dust, sudden movements, trucks passing, people searching for the dead, the missing. The recent experience of Afghanistan, for example, occurred, uncannily, in the heart of Manhattan. Meanwhile, on the other side of Empire's mirror, during the same months: the relentless bombing of Tora Bora, the demolition of the caves—those underground cities, with their houses, markets, storage depots, and offices, that were the fantastical products of the U.S. military imaginary. The terrorists who brought down "our" proudest towers have obliged "us" to hunt them down, forced "us" underground, drawn "us" into attacking the spaces beneath, to join "them" in the catacombs of nullity.

Was the excavation of the Ground Zero site a deconstruction? Not to the Lower Manhattan Development Corporation, who wants to see the site economically active again. Nor for the legal teams who battled over the size of the insurance payout to Larry Silverstein (who asked—against common sense, and ultimately without success—for $7 billion on the basis that the attacks were "two events"): they accumulated an unparalleled quantity of expert analysis that

44. Associated Press,
Ground Zero. 2001,
photograph. Source:
AP/Wide World Photos.

simulates the attacks, their actuality, and their ramifications, even their virtual outcomes. Although conducted largely away from the public eye, the massive effort to document the situation before, during, and after the attacks gradually amounted to a mammoth Babel of aftermath. Consider the time, energy, and money devoted to the preparation of legal cases by the victims and those they are litigating against: the WTC, the lessees, the Port Authority, the City of New York, the airline companies, the airports from which the planes departed, New York State, the federal government—to name only the most obvious. The scientific and engineering information and expertise assembled around the Silverstein insurance claim has been described thus: "Taken in aggregate, it represents a milestone in the forensic engineering of a disaster . . . I have never seen this level of technical knowledge and experience brought to bear on a single problem."[66] Again, a kind of self-simulating gigantism, one that seems to have attended not only the ambitions for the WTC but also those of 9.11.01, and of much of its aftermath.

Then there is the repeat trauma of rehearsing experience in forms that will be readable to the operations of the law. Over three days in late September 2001, Congress drafted, passed, and received the president's signature on a bill to establish a Victim Compensation Fund. Intended primarily to defend the already shaky airlines from suits that would bring them down (potential damages were estimated at $40 billion), the issue of compensation to families of victims turned into a roiling ethical quagmire, with distinctions being made between the net worth of victims, confusion over whether the families of victims of related disasters should also be compensated (those of the African embassy bombings are, those of the *U.S.S. Cole* and the Oklahoma bombing not), and questions asked about whether the government should be involved in such activity at all. Because the fund was uncapped, payouts could have been infinite. Nor were victim families obliged to apply, so some pursued litigation anyway. Trauma spread, elaborating itself. To reduce any suffering to fixed amounts is yet another instance of generality stifling particularity. As journalist Lisa Belkin puts it: "Tragedy, particularly American tragedy, is always and inevitably about money. As much as we rail against this and insist that it is not true, as much as we would prefer to talk about love and honor and legacy, in the end we find our talk turning to dollars. We do this in part because we need to eat, and pay the rent, and to continue on with our lives in the face of death. We also do this because cash is the only tangible way to measure infinite loss."[67]

Examples such as these suggest that 9.11.01 may have drawn all of us to the uncontainable, that is, to the reality that the drive to structure, to the taking of shape, to its making, is one that occurs only at the cusp of dissembling itself again. And yet, within this unbuilding there emerge, hopefully and unpredictably, new kinds of making, creating, building, kinds that no longer depend on the models of progress and developmentalism that went into the construction of the targeted architecture of 9.11.01. Homi Bhabha saw this straight away: "Neither construction or deconstruction, the Unbuilt is the creation of a form whose virtual absence raises the question of what it would mean to start again, in the same place, as if it were elsewhere, adjacent to the site of a historic disaster or a personal trauma."[68] The heroism of the firemen and police rushing into the towers was, to him, one element of this Unbuilding.

These ideas are concretized by William Langewiesche in his *Atlantic Monthly* essays "American Ground: Unbuilding the World Trade Center."[69] An engrossing and subtle journey through the "unconscious" of the site is told through profiles of those involved in its clearing, and through vivid word picturing of its spaces and settings. The profiles celebrate, from the inside out, those can-do middle managers (mostly from the little-known Department of Design and Construction within the city government) who took command of a chaos that was beyond the comprehension and way beneath the flexibility of the great agencies charged with dealing with such disasters. At astonishing speed, and with no further loss of life on a dangerous site, these "doers" succeeded in demolishing the ruins of the WTC and identifying thousands of human remains. Their activity went a long way towards unbuilding the explosive event architecture of 9.11.01, perhaps because it substituted, for a time and mostly in the media, the drama of the clearing for that of the destruction.

The material sublimity of Langewiesche's account lies in its pedestrian pace, its measured movement through an underground pictured in Piranesi-like fashion. The account demonstrates a sensitivity that enriches, albeit only in our imaginations, the actual paucity at which the relentless "clearing" eventually arrived. The author adopts a cool, "just the facts" sensibility, one that pits the compressed ingenuity of the engineers against the high-pitched emotionalism that attended most public activity at and around the site.[70] In the days before Thanksgiving 2002, Langewiesche came under siege by mobs of firemen, who spurned his heroizing of many of their number because he mentions, in passing, the discovery of a fire truck full of neatly stacked, brand-new jeans, looted from a store in WTC 1, a crime frozen in time by the truck and its occupants falling victim to the collapse of the second tower. In these protests, stereotypicality rules again, the messily specific is sacrificed for the comforting reduction.[71]

For many architectural critics the WTC has occasioned trauma from its very conception. An analysis of the Pentagon and trauma, a study of that long history—the history of the U.S. at war—would be an interesting parallel to this one. The summative character of the Twin Towers, their exclusion of elaborative connections, has been already noted, as has the design shortfall, from which—in a strange misalliance with an imposed phallocentrism—the towers arose. Psych 101 will teach us that the repressed always returns, often violently, as a pathology. This was Juhasz's apocryphal message, after the 1993 attempt. The 9.11.01 attackers also traded in trauma, portraying their struggle as a battle within an array of stereotypes, including iconotypes. Thus bin Laden in 1998, objecting to American influence in Saudi Arabia: "The call to wage war against America was made because America has spearheaded the crusade against the Islamic nation, sending tens of thousands of its troops to the land of the two holy mosques over and above its meddling in its affairs and its politics and its support of the oppressive, corrupt and tyrannical regime that is in control."[72] The logic here moves from a just and reasonable critique of bad foreign policy to an unrealistic, perhaps paranoid refusal to see anything but U.S. influence as a cause of Islam's decline, and to an even more unrealistic, desperate course of reaction. In response to the besmirching of the iconic homeland of Islam itself, this is a call for the removal of what is seen as trauma's causes, for their eradication. Rhetorically, there is an uncanny echo between "the two holy mosques" and "the Twin Towers."

But something more drastic happens when the object is abruptly removed, when it collapses in incandescence. Does this erase the symptom, the pathology itself, even its psychic framework, its body, everything? Such a clearing is, of course, impossible, but it is nonetheless desired by the perpetrator and feared by the victim. For the victims, the figure of total erasure, the black hole of utter obliteration, gapes suddenly before you. And then there are the infinite reverberations of aftermath, when, as we can see in the unfolding saga of compensation for victim families, and the protracted indecision over the right kind of memorial for Ground Zero, mourning turns into melancholia, and for some, mania. The other side of this coin is that perpetrators and their allies have now, as I have suggested, to deal with the rebound of being entangled in the world of imagery—the hated, flashy spectacle—the most prominent icons of which they sought so assiduously to eradicate.

The Chimera

Four distinct yet entangled chimeras have taken their peculiar shapes. First, the negative energy of the WTC's public secret, its work of containment, repression, and exclusion, has been released. The stale breath of all those hells of the twentieth century in which the limits of economic efficiency, the shortfalls of standardization, the cold succor of the commodity, and the evils of bureaucratic banality gasp out their last, largest exhalation. In a bizarre coincidence, the ways in which the towers collapsed in on themselves replayed, in speeded-up reverse, the relentless exclusions of its origins. It remains to be seen to what degree this release becomes banishment, and how readily—trailing what diminishment—the constraints will return to their positions of power.

The second chimera is the shape of the unconscious itself, its layered spatiality. The ground level of the WTC was, as we have noted, an inhospitable raised plaza perforated with exits, an invitation to ambiguity. This made it difficult to read the painstaking excavation of the site as it went on. Clearly, it was done in a search for bodies, to shore up the site against further collapse and to prepare it for rebuilding. Psychically, however, the clearing could be read as a matching of one kind of obsession against another (against two, in fact, that of the tower builders and that of the destroyers). Was it not also a collective therapy, with the mourners, the comrades, the city, perhaps even the nation, raking over the details of what was there, taking each compacted particle and imagining it whole? It was an effort to match the 9.11.01 destroyers with an equally dogged destruction, here performed in the name of recovery. Mourning, the psychoanalysts tell us, should give way to a sense of recovery, of sadness yes, but not the manic self-aggression of melancholia. Yet, given the ambiguity of the now-obliterated entry point, given the violence of the implosion, and given the fissures of difference that it opened up between incommensurable cultures, 9.11.01 might be a nightmare of ambivalence that could continue for some unknowable time to come. Small wonder that the term "ground zero"–that is, the posited space on the earth's surface exactly beneath the point of a bomb's explosion in the air just above it—was used immediately and has stuck as a descriptor of that zone. How long before it fades? Will it outlast the memory of its previous major usage: Hiroshima and Nagasaki? Will it survive the building over of the actual site? I fear not. It will become a historical point, a moment of time past, framed by an architectural and economic solution that will museumize part of it, explain the rest through adjacent panels that will themselves become historical artifacts, and build over most of it.

Langewiesche closes *American Ground* with an account of the preparation of the WTC steel girders for shipping to the blast furnaces of China, now consuming much of the world's available scrap steel. On a pier in Newark Bay, the support structure of the Twin Towers was cut into three-foot lengths and loaded onto freighters, by crews utterly indifferent to the prehistory of their task. A reviewer draws the conclusion: "No bagpipes, no speeches, no CNN, just a pile of steel and a dirty ship on a grimy bay; this is how the story ends, the bones of the World Trade Center becoming a commodity in world trade."[73]

But these stories do not end so neatly. In the event, the bringing down of the WTC towers generated a countersymbol, an anti-iconotype that paradoxically took the form of an image that showed in starkly graphic form the perishability of all worldly symbols. And did so in a way that invited its constant repetition within the iconomy. This is the third chimera that remains with us, and is unlikely to go away. Depressed, during the moment of 9.11.01 after-shock, by the futility of his task, architectural critic Herbert Muschamp noted that "since the toppling of the Berlin Wall in 1989, no new building has so fully captured the public imagination as the growing list of wrecked, demolished or exploding structures around the globe . . . the city of Sarajevo, the 1993 World Trade Center bombing, the Branch Davidian Compound in Waco, Tex., the federal office building in Oklahoma City, and Afghanistan's Buddhist sculptures. This destruction has communicated powerfully to people around the world. It symbolizes, more than any new building, the challenges of global complexity in the post–cold war era."[74]

It was the first attack on the WTC that precipitated this insight. In a 1993 essay, while trying to define the mood that emanated from exploded buildings, like the smoke clouds that erupted, hovered then drifted away, Muschamp hit on this: "Chaos. Turbulence on a global scale. A feeling Virginia Woolf once described in her diary as 'things generally wrong in the universe.' That is part of the message that came out of the World Trade Center's basement."[75] Against such all-pervasive disorder, he drew attention to architecture's historic role of boundary setting, walling up, enclosing, its long-term service to military purposes, to the controlling of public and private space, from town squares to gated communities. He defended the validity of open, democratic self-regulating communities, those made famous in Jane Jacobs's account of the lively, beneficent heterogeneity of New York City streets during the early 1960s. At that time, America's enemy was known, distant, and largely containable (this story ignores the demonization of black Americans as the enemy within). Since the collapse of Communism, however, symbolized by the fall of the Berlin Wall, a kind of "community of chaos" has emerged, one in which isolated individuals, groups, even nations can no longer look out and see themselves and others located at specific places within a decipherable landscape. Instead:

> Exploding buildings are this community's landmarks—its inverted arches of triumph, its sinister Taj Mahals. They provide images of a collective experience that is otherwise elusive. Traditionally, we look to buildings to provide symbols of social cohesion. Exploding buildings now perform a similar symbolic role. People may build in different styles, but explosions are universal. Though each may have a different cause, they become linked in our perception to some fearful grand design. They focus public attention. They fill up TV screens. The World Trade Center bombing spawned a new style of disaster T-shirt.[76]

Muschamp's remarks alert us to a visual stereotype in formation, to the coming into being of a negative iconography, one that draws its force from an imagery of devastation, attack, of razing to rubble actual buildings, structures, or statues. It combines the graphic energies of one or more of three kinds of visualization: the structure under attack, collapsing, succumbing to the physical erasure that will end its material life; the structure crippled, blasted, as ruin and remnant, or as a gaping void; and the still, yet constantly dating record image of the no longer extant structure. Among Muschamp's examples are those that were created to serve as icons, those that became iconic over time, and those that became iconic only in their destruction. An important element in the power of this iconography is its antivisuality, its incorporation of the prospect of the erasure of imagery as such. It is to this that the 9.11.01 attackers were so irresistibly drawn. Welcome to the image architecture of trauma. Welcome to the conditions of contemporaneity.

Looked at from both sides of the actual flashpoint, 9.11.01 was, at base, an instantaneous exchange of forces that snuffed out the lives of nearly 3,000 people, decimated two buildings, and wounded another while at the same time filling the communicative screens that hover between all of us. On the one side, the meticulous planning and category-reversing imaginative inventiveness of the attackers (the rational architecture of their enterprise) was transformed, at a hit, into an actual image-event the elements of which exploded through the spaces of the iconomy (its anti-architecture, if you will). On the other, the ultra-rational planning of the WTC itself, its excessive conformity, its inhuman emptiness was transformed, in a hit, into a yawning absence, a memory void that millions of words and images (including these) are rushing to fill, desperately seeking to restructure an iconomy in turmoil. Photographs of missing loved ones appeared all over the city, and many shrines were improvised around them. Images of the WTC towers were mourned with some fervor. Every conceivable form of visual culture was put to service, along with a myriad of other responses. In all of these, the deep doubles of the iconomy stood out, suddenly, in blunt relief. They do so, still, splintering it with the shards of aftermath.

Bursting out against these apparently overwhelming labors of the negative, there appeared, amid the ashen aftermath, a fourth chimera: all those elaborative

45. Ruby Washington, impromptu memorial at the Brooklyn Promenade, September 16, 2001. 2001, photograph. Ruby Washington/The New York Times.

energies banished at the towers' birth, and held mostly at bay ever since, came rushing in to try to fill the void with constructive positivity. An extraordinary community spirit emerged among famously self-involved New Yorkers. The hands-on assistance to an oft-maligned city from the national heartland was immediate and colossal. Human regeneration swung into fast-forward mode (figured in imagery such as the oft-reproduced photograph of the young mother on a Brooklyn Heights rooftop feeding her baby as the towers burn across the river beyond). An alternative imagery of impact and renewal began to take shape, the work of both agency and amateur photographers and filmmakers, in instant exhibitions near the site. On walls all over the city, pasteboards of appeal and memorials sprung up. In parks and along sidewalks, people built installations of witness (illus. 45). The imagery of community spread through the City, over the net, and into books and exhibitions all over the world—for example, *here is new york, a democracy of photographs*.[77] This was no museum without walls; it was an open iconomy of mourning and filiation. Its characteristics were determinedly in opposition to those of the new media, especially television, and of official communicative systems.

And a great debate started up, immediately, as New Yorkers talked to each other about how to rebuild their community. Mike Wallace's *A New Deal for New York* both describes this spirit and captures its best qualities.[78] Within this storm of talk there emerged, among many other pressing issues, this question: what would a post-9.11.01 architecture of survival be, an architecture of trauma passing into

46. Lebbeus Woods, *The Ascent*, from *World Trade Center Project*. 2002, pencil and crayon on illustration board. Courtesy Lebbeus Woods.

persistence and growth? In the throes of shock, "community" became the watchword for effectively pursuing the work of mourning. It became, for some, the mooring for a new, posttraumatic architecture. Lebbeus Woods strove to symbolize it in his World Trade Center project 2002, specifically the drawing *The Ascent* (illus. 46).[79] But there were, as well, many other powers in play. They came into titanic struggle over the fate of Ground Zero. And, in the aftermath of 9.11.01, much of their convoluted wrestling had to happen in plain sight, in the glare of publicity. Rare it is that we catch a glimpse of the spectral apparatus that is the true machinery of the spectacle. Let's look at it now.

Shock.Build.Mourn.Hope: *Architects Confront Contemporaneity*

Fallout: The Professions React

> A very tall building absorbs a plane and collapses after 105 defiant minutes, having watched its twin suffer the same fate. Everyone sees it. Again and again. It captures every eye and ear in stunned amazement. When the towers fell, the world shook. Nobody could accept what they saw. Such a vertical drop seemed impossible. And no amount of analysis of the mechanics of the collapse, the simple way the attack was carried out, or the strategic mission of the attackers can ease the incredulity. The event remains unbelievable, surprising even those who initiated it. People turned to architects for answers.[1]

The natural questions were asked first. All events elicit them. What had happened? Why? Are there more threats coming—now, soon, in the not too distant future? Perhaps this event is still happening. What else might appear? From where? Then, as explanations began to take shape, more questions. How was it done? Why did it happen this way? How should we respond? Can we prevent such attacks? How might we prepare for the next one? What kind of architecture can be built now?

The media swarmed for answers to all of these questions at once. The responses they got provide us with a profile of the 9.11.01 aftermath as it was experienced by professionals of the built environment: the engineers, planners, architects, designers, developers, commissioners, as well as reporters, critics, and other monitors and users of architecture. And as it was manifest overtly, as public statements, in contrast to the unconscious passageways that we surveyed in the previous chapter. I will begin by tracing reactions as they moved from shock to a period of mourning—for the victims, yes, for the city, that too, but also for the evident end of an era in which their professions (or at least the fabled heart of them) could, by and large, function without addressing the most pressing problems of contemporaneity. Mark Wigley, whose words opened this chapter, observed that the sudden rush of professional chatter post-9.11.01 seemed like "a kind of disciplinary therapy, a reassertion of the traditional figure of the architect as the generator of culturally reassuring objects, an ongoing denial of the fact that architects are just as confused as the traumatized people they serve."[2] Although by and large true, this is a harsh and ultimately simplistic judgment on the architects, critics, and urban planners who have been active in the aftermath. While no little grandstanding did occur, I will show in this chapter that the ground was cleared for a collective professional response to the question of what to build next, in an aftershock world, now that contemporaneity has come home, late and with a bang, to the capital city of modernity.

Differences surfaced before the day was out. Some applauded the capacity of the towers to withstand the attack and its effects long enough to allow thousands to escape—the south tower for fifty-six minutes, the north for one hour and forty-six minutes. Others, perhaps recalling that the engineering of the building was pitched at the extremity of possibility for its time, that the whole project prided itself on being a gargantuan High Capitalist gamble, asked whether the design of the buildings might have, in some way, contributed to the loss of life. Both responses arise naturally from our psychic need for buildings to offer protection. Yet, in crises, humans also reach for generality, for the stunted language of "objectivity." For many, the terms of the debate became, quickly and entirely, functional.

One day after the attacks the American Institute of Steel Construction moved to bring together leading structural engineering associations to investigate the structural collapses of the WTC buildings.[3] On the same day the *New York Times* devoted a lead story to "A Day of Terror: The Buildings," citing representatives of the WTC design and engineering firms, as well as other experts, to the effect that no building could withstand the impact of such heavy planes, nor such intense heat. Yamasaki Associates, a firm that continued the traditions of its deceased founder, offered sympathy for the victims and their families, but declined to comment on any other matter.[4] The material causes of collapse became a preoccupation, and have remained so, as one sign that the period of aftermath is still not over. Public reporting followed this issue closely, and stories about the attacks featured interviews with engineers and designers associated with the building, especially Leslie E. Robertson.[5] The structural sustainability of the building is the concrete issue at the heart of such questions as, do buildings have a moral responsibility to their inhabitants, even when they are destroyed by acts of God, nature, or man? In law, this can only mean, do those who build them have such a responsibility? Determining the facts of such a matter is something that citizens expect of their national agencies, and that those of us who use the products of professionals expect professionals (who are after all their own primary regulators) to do. These two expectations came together in the Federal Emergency Management Agency report *World Trade Center Building Performance Study: Data Collection, Preliminary Observations, and Recommendations*, issued in May 2002.[6] The sober conclusions reached some months later—that the fire cladding was too thin to act as an effective retardant once a fire of any size had begun, that the sprinklers failed utterly, that the millions spent on upgrading these two systems over the years were wasted, that the shear connections between floors and core were vulnerable, that gyprock instead of concrete had been used to encase the elevators, that the open floors were open to fires engulfing them, that the external support structure, once breached, was fatally unstable—differ hardly at all from the guesses advanced by expert engineers in the days after the attacks. These same conclusions became current in the media, and have remained in place ever since. Meanwhile, the engineering profession moved carefully to a position at which blame could be dispersed, and future tall buildings more cautiously conceived.[7]

No More Big Donalds?

Within hours of the attack, former mayor Ed Koch was on television defiantly insisting that the Twin Towers be re-created exactly as they had been built, and from the original plans. Team Twin Towers was formed, and eventually came up with a design that replicated the towers, but with added security features. Sculptor James Turrell, creator of light spaces and the long-term skyview earthwork at Roden Crater, Arizona, was even more reactive: "I am interested in seeing the working culture of New York continue. People want a memorial now because they're feeling emotional, but emotions pass, all emotion passes, and then the memorial has no meaning. The new buildings should be higher than the old ones, and there should be three of them."[8] Yet doubts about the viability of such tall buildings quickly surfaced. Two "urbanists" at the Brookings Institution, James Howard Kunstler and Nikos A. Salingaros, posted an article stating, "We are convinced that the age of skyscrapers is at an end. It must now be considered an experimental building typology that has failed. We predict that no new megatowers will be built, and existing ones are destined to be dismantled."[9] They offered few arguments, rather a list of antimodernist clichés, ranging from a tedious recycling of Prince Charles's attack on Cesar Pelli's design for Canary Wharf, London, to the chilling thought that "every would-be terrorist who is now a child will grow up and be instructed by those surreal, riveting images of the two airplanes crashing into the World Trade Towers."[10] One week after 9.11.01, Pelli was asked whether the attacks meant an end to chart-topping skyscrapers. His reply registers the contradictory impulses of the moment: "The desire to reach for the sky runs deep in our human psyche. Since the Tower of Babel there is this desire to put a marker up in the sky. I imagine that there will be a slowdown in the pursuit of tall buildings for a while. In some ways it was an attack on architecture. But the worst thing would be to stop building tall buildings. It would be like New York knuckling under."[11] In a similar vein, Robert Stern, dean of the Yale School of Architecture, asserted, "We should not lose confidence in this great building type. The sky has always been the limit for us."[12] A. Eugene Kohn, of prominent New York firm Kohn Pedersen Fox, pointed out that the towers recently built and under construction in Asia were following much more rigid disaster standards than any in the U.S., citing provisions made in his own firm's Shanghai World Financial Center, which will be the tallest building in the world when completed in 2007.[13] A tower with a twisting sheath torsioning up its shaft, and revealing an eighty-meter hole at its top, this huge edifice was halted in midconstruction in 2003 to accommodate the redesigning necessary to increase its height from 450 to 492 meters, that is, to make it higher than its competitors.[14] After 9.11.01, this dick measuring stands out, red-knobbed in all its childishness.

The economic heart of the matter led David M. Childs of Skidmore, Owings & Merrill, designers of major high-rises in the U.S. and Asia (the Sears Tower in Chicago, the Jin Mao Building in Shanghai) into doubt: "I don't think tenants are immediately going to be at the top of a tall building, especially one that's an icon."[15] Childs is the architect of choice of Larry Silverstein, developer and lessee of the WTC site, and was even then at work on a development plan for the site commissioned by Silverstein, a project ultimately subsumed within the process being overseen by the Lower Manhattan Development Corporation.[16] Childs elaborated: "I think many of our clients would not want to build such a visible symbol, that they would want to build not so iconic and not so tall, the way the wealthy in Mexico started driving around in Volkswagens instead of Jaguars."[17] Corporate architects and their clients, it seemed, wanted out of the iconomy of conspicuous consumption they had done so much to drive to dominance.

During modernity, building high meant flaunting in-your-face power. Building long, low, and wide, taking up vast acreage of much-competed-for space, was a way of expressing power more subtly, in the manner of older money. Skyscrapers stacked up the power of their commissioners for all to see: from afar as a landmark, from close up in mouth-dropping awe. While the powerful in Chicago found ways of doing this with some subtlety, the squeeze on space and the higher competitive volume of New York meant that vertical striving became the distinctive language of its architecture, and "an intimate connection was forged between the tallest tower in the city and the biggest corporation, the richest bank, or whatever financial entity wanted to be seen as running the place."[18] By the 1980s, the developer himself became the prime example. Has this impulse ever outed itself more unabashedly than in the bold letters spelling out the owner's name on the Trump Towers sprouting from every landmark crossing in New York city?

The Critics Talk

That the WTC towers were so prominent within the global iconomy that they had become targets was a fact that came home, to many Americans, as a shock. For architects and critics—most of whom, as we have seen, had come to dismiss the buildings from their internal histories of what counted as modern architecture— the attacks caused an instant confusion of emotions. Robert Stern, for example, allowed that he had enjoyed the "small sliver of sky" discernable between the towers when seen from afar, but felt, as did many others, that they lacked intimacy (to put it at its mildest) when experienced close up: "It's the Building everybody loved to hate and hated to love . . . Nevertheless, they are powerful symbols of America and modern life. If architecture functions in the realm of symbols, they were tremendously successful, as successful as the pyramids. And, boy, do we miss them."[19] From within their shock and mourning, a number of commentators offered acute insights. For example, Nicolai Ouroussoff of the *Los Angeles Times* sat down on 9.11.01 and confronted his belief in the fundamentally optimistic nature of architecture: that it is, whatever else it is, and no matter how modestly, always a matter of building for the future.

> No event in recent memory exposes the limits of such optimism like Tuesday's catastrophic attack on the World Trade Center, which resulted in the collapse of two of the world's tallest towers and the presumed death of thousands. What, after all, is the point of symbols in the face of such real horror? Even the stunning image of the tower's collapse will soon be overshadowed by the mounting body count. In such a context, issues such as a building's symbolic potency or aesthetic beauty seem of negligible importance.
>
> Yet the targeting of the World Trade Center revealed a keen understanding on the part of the terrorists of the symbolic importance such buildings play in the collective consciousness of a people. Like the Pentagon, which was also attacked Tuesday, the twin towers embody an essential element of American identity: an unshakable faith in the future. Like the disaster site itself, that faith has been severely damaged. Both will have to be carefully reconstructed. And once that process begins, architecture will become a critical tool in reshaping that symbolic landscape.

This recognizes that architecture is irretrievably tied to its societal setting, not only through the functional services it provides, but also as the out-there generator of symbols through which a society defines itself to itself. Bravely, Ouroussoff described the just destroyed WTC in terms that did not resile from his profession's distaste for it.

> The World Trade Center towers were the offspring of such monuments to the country's emerging global power. Completed in 1973, they were seen as the final testament to New York's position at the center of the financial world. As architecture, they were not particularly stylish. With its repetitive rows of steel columns and slot-like windows, the towers lacked the dignity of the Empire State Building's limestone facades, for example, or the element of fantasy that made the Chrysler Building such a beloved monument. Yet despite its mediocrity as a work of architecture, the Trade Center's psychological impact on the city's collective identity was indisputable. Visually, it was more than a blunt symbol of a capitalist society. Its massive forms provided a reassuring image of stability amid New York's congested, sometimes chaotic urban landscape. Set at Manhattan's southern tip, it was the city's emotional anchor.[20]

So far, these comments reprise the phases of his profession's hate-tolerate relationship with the towers. Very few of his colleagues repeated their earlier dismissals of the towers—exceptions include Herbert Muschamp.[21] Others, such as Paul Goldberger, swung around nearly 180 degrees.[22] Ouroussoff went on, however, to make a point that is especially telling for an architecture that has become embedded in the symbolic iconomy, and accordingly has accumulated considerable depths and ranges of emotional association: "The horrific image of Tuesday's events will deal a permanent blow to that sense of shared identity. When the second tower fell, 103 minutes after being hit by a hijacked jet, the implosion demonstrated that even the most enduring images from our collective identity can disappear instantly."[23]

How can a building less than thirty years old be thought of as being among the "most enduring"? Ouroussoff is slipping here from the WTC to skyscraper architecture in general as expressive of American technological know-how and determined entrepreneurship. But this too is only a few hundred years old, even less in its association with the tallest building in town. But his sense is clear: powerful iconotypes such as the WTC can seem permanent, a part of the givenness of human experience, to be stuff that will exist so far beyond any individual's life span that it comes to seem "enduring." Raising a new symbol, proposing a building, any image, for candidature in the iconomy, is to affirm this process. Violently extracting an icon from it—it would seem—is to strike a blow against it. But this is to evoke the crude coupling of Islamist fundamentalism and "the West," of darkness visible directed against the Enlightenment. It is to position the attackers as beyond the compass of humanity, or as hopelessly misguided, even mad. In contrast, our analysis has repeatedly shown that such attacks reveal the unpalatable truth that an internal warring between creation and destruction energizes the entire iconomic process. Every icon is won from a concentration that, however affirmative, has exclusion, narrowing, suffering among its side effects. It invites devotion, primarily, but also courts defacement. The enemy's self-defining icons are always potential targets. The point is not to be surprised that it happens. The challenge is to create a public imagery that absorbs negativity and celebrates openness. To his credit, Ouroussoff arrived at this conclusion quickly. Rather than succumb to the security fears that have crippled federal building since the 1995 Oklahoma City bombing, producing a kind of bunker architecture, he urged that the most truly democratic response would be to create "an urban landscape shaped by qualities of openness and empathy, not paranoia."[24]

Two weeks after the attacks, which he witnessed from his Cooper Union office on Astor Place, Anthony Vidler took up the urban landscape theme. Noting that 9.11.01 had propelled debate about whether "to change the way Americans experience and ultimately build urban public spaces," he posed two questions: "Are a city's assets—density, concentration, monumental structures—still alluring? Will a desire for 'defensible space' radically transform the city as Americans know it?"[25] These questions are international in scope and have been tackled in parts of Europe and Asia for some years, even centuries. 9.11.01 brings them home to Americans with emphatic urgency. Vidler sketched the historical interplay between the city's assets and the opposite model: "Dispersal rather than concentration is being talked about as the viable pattern of life and work, where monumental buildings will give way to camouflaged sheds, or entirely scattered to home offices." On September 11, decentralization became very attractive to many large businesses headquartered in Manhattan and other capitals—although, in truth, this had been happening to the city, like others all over the world, for two decades and is, many argue, an irreversible trend of globalization. Responding to the mood in the city after the attacks, Vidler argued strongly that "real community, as evident over the last week, is bred in cities more strongly than suburbs. The street as a site of interaction, encounter and support of strangers for each other; the square as a place of gathering and vigil; the corner store a communicator of information and interchange. These places, without romanticism or nostalgia, still define an urban culture, one that resists all efforts to 'secure' it out of existence."[26] His conclusion follows from this sudden, forced, yet fulsome experience of Manhattan as a community rather than as a city that held community as a state that it was close to, could achieve, indeed would achieve but had to get this deal done, this personal gain wrapped up, this event on, this piece of work done *first*. Planners, Vidler urges, should "learn from the difficulties of past utopias as well as avoid the nostalgia of anticity programs. We should search for design alternatives that retain the dense and vital mix of uses critical to urban life, rethinking the exclusions resulting from outdated zoning, real estate values and private ownership, to provide vital incentives for building public spaces equal to our present needs for community."[27]

The concept of community gives content to the realization by many that the challenge was not to replicate the WTC, either exactly or in type. Architect Bernard Tschumi, retreating from his earlier celebration of symbolic violence, put it this way: "One should not be sentimental, one should not be nostalgic. The tip of the island has to be reinvented. You have to arrive at a concept for the whole area, [but not turn it into a] theme park. You have to rebuild . . . in such a way that says that cities are good."[28]

Broad views of this kind were widespread in the early days, yet they struggled to counter the prevailing anxiety about filling the physical void of the site itself. Debate about what should be built was instant and, to many, urgent. Against this rush, wiser voices urged caution, a pause for reflection, before any commitments were made. These included Frank Gehry, who responded to a suggestion that he be invited to design a "world arts center" on the site with the comment: "There are 6,000 families to be considered. I think it's in bad taste for a bunch of developers and architects to be saying things now. We have to give it time."[29] Some—most notably New York mayor Guiliani, "hero" of the recovery effort—insisted that nothing should be raised on such "hallowed ground" save, perhaps, a modest memorial. The idea of a public park, with a memorial to the 9.11.01 dead as its centerpiece, gained rapid ground in all walks of life. Others offered a number of virtual solutions, such as tall buildings clad with electrochromatic glass or phantom towers projected by light— an idea quickly realized in the popular projections that shone from the site from March to May 2002. The loudest voices, however, were all for building soon, to show that the City and the Nation were unbowed by terrorism. Some wanted to seize the opportunity to build the same kind of prodigious office space structure even bigger and—they implied—better. Developer Larry Silverstein, to whom the Port Authority had leased the WTC three months earlier, had the same idea at first. But the strength of the popular lobby—especially that of the families of victims— pushed him toward compromise. By October he was asking: why not divide the two hundred-and-ten-stories of the Twin Towers by half and build four fifty-story towers? Ideas of such aching banality attracted, rightly, a storm of abuse: what sort of memorial would that be? and what architectural dreariness it would invite!

Contemporary Architects Respond Too Soon

Many in the architectural community went into fast-forward invention mode. Charles Gwathmey: "There's a great opportunity to rethink what the possibilities are...The really interesting thing is about memory—those two towers were indelible. The replacement has to be incredibly spiritual and dynamic architecture. Whatever is built there is going to be visited forever."[30] The first major, concentrated showing of responses by international architects, from the "starchitects" to the up-and-coming, was a very mixed bag. New York gallery owner Max Protech leaped boldly into an emotionally charged breech, fearful that "business as usual" would produce the usual Manhattan compromise: good buildings but no great ones. For a month from January 17, 2002, he showed "design proposals from leading architects worldwide" under the title "A New World Trade Center."[31] Ranging from the daft to the disappointing, the proposals showed that many of the most inventive designers in the world were rendered as confused by the turn of events as everyone else. A representative example is that submitted by conceptual artist Vito Acconci's studio, recently much concerned with rethinking living space: "A Building Full of Holes," a WTC-sized chunk of blue cheese. The felt obligation to echo the dimensions of the WTC crimped many proposals, such as those by Asymptote, NOX, and Foreign Office Architects. Many entrants favored multicolored, perpetually changing cladding to express a more upbeat outlook, while CAD-based, techno-organic blobs were predictably popular. Symbolic imagery attracted few architects. A surprising exception was Daniel Libeskind, whose design clustered five different forms that, together, managed to suggest a bunch of sticks and the tracery of an explosion. It is a measure of the impact of 9.11.01 that, in this proposal, the architect's record of subtlety was thrown into disarray.

The most suggestive proposals abandoned the idea of replacing the towers in however displaced a fashion. They took the site as part of a continuum, as an opening in an urban environment that already, well before the attacks, had demanded radical rethinking. Archi-Tectonics proposed "Flex-City," a running set of interactive electronic environments, readily changeable as needs shifted, with users able to determine their own living and work spaces according to eighty-one variants of what Winka Dubbeldam terms "Flex Space" and "Green Flex." Mel Chin strung a "social platform" through the area, seventy-two feet above the street, and carrying all necessary living spaces and services. Urbanist Michael Sorkin was for leaving Ground Zero as a gigantic urn of rubble while dispersing all of the office and other usages that had been lost to the many unused spaces readily available on Manhattan and in the nearby suburbs.[32] None of the proposed designs matched the potential quality of thinking that existed in the architectural and planning community. It was, simply, too soon.

Business as Usual

The tangled web that is 9.11.01 was also evident in the complex politics that quickly emerged around who would get to propose the commission and choose the solution as to what to build on Ground Zero.[33] In the event, key parties were obliged by the state and the city to join into a Lower Manhattan Development Corporation, which undertook the management of the rebuilding on December 3, 2001. Its board members were overwhelmingly those with a financial and political stake in the area. Victim representatives and community members soon dropped away or were diverted onto the groups advising the memorial committee.[34]

Immediately after the attacks, Ada Louise Huxtable had sounded a timely warning against the inevitable return of "New York's hubris," fearing that "if the usual scenario is followed, the debate will lead to a 'solution' in which principle is lost and an epic opportunity squandered."[35] As if on cue, after intense public interest and the appearance of widespread consultation, on July 16, 2002 the LMDC unveiled six different "concept plans," prepared under the direction of the New York firm Beyer Blinder Belle. Plans they were, concepts hardly, different they were not. Was it surprising that the proposals were essentially the same, and that inspiration evaporated, when architects and designers were faced with, and accepted, a set of constraints that mixed pre-9/11 greed and arrogance with post-9/11 shock and traumatic retreat? Silverstein's compromise had become the template. Paul Goldberger's comment summed it up: "Never underestimate the power of banality—at least, not in the world of New York real estate."[36]

Ways to Go

At stake in all this see-sawing between alarmed inventiveness and the relentless pursuit of the bottom line is the question that has exercised us throughout: in the aftermath of modernity, what is the architecture appropriate to contemporaneity? The materials given to us by the twentieth century—landscapes horizoned by trauma, yet still sparking with hopes for liberation, like electrical wire loose across a floor—are as intractable as they are unavoidable. In the immediate aftermath of 9.11.01, the question could be put this way: how might we build up from out of Ground Zero, given that it is by the very terms of its creation, its double erasure, a fleeting state? That is also to say, how might "we" be built—out and up from groundlessness, from the grounds now taken away, from those now shown (to those who had not seen this) to have never been there?

The folks at the Pentagon had a ready answer to such questions: don't ask. At the headquarters of the U.S. Department of Defense, restoration to the status quo was the immediate, self-evident, priority. How to do it most efficiently, cost-effectively, and quickly were the only matters discussed. The planning and procedures were military in their character, and in their reporting. Near total media silence was maintained until, in June 2002, the Pentagon announced with casual pride that the "Phoenix Project" was on track to complete what would normally be three years' work in one. Repairs to the Pentagon were done in time for a memorial service on September 11, 2002. They replaced its former fabric and functions, and rehoused the 2,600 displaced personnel in their previous positions. Increased security has been built in: a direct entry from the Metrorail station has been removed, an adjacent bus station relocated further away.[37] A memorial competition has been held and a design commissioned: designed by Julie Beckman and Keith Kaseman, it features 184 illuminated benches, each engraved with the name of a victim, arranged in rows and set into grassland just across from the building, at the angle of the attacking airplane's flight path.

The WTC site remains a greater challenge. As a physical setting, it is bound around with powerful, but not impossible, constraints. Yet its relentless erasure returned it to an in-between space so lacking in character that it appeared to offer the invitation to start ab initio. Ground Zero was, however, anything but a tabula rasa: it was quickly piled high with many competing memories, littered with the machinery of historical forgetting, and already staked out by the chalk marks of an intense competition between differing paradigms for going on. In this sense, it became the ideal site for constructing—prefiguratively—the architectural forms of the twenty-first century. Having been cleared, messily, incompletely—by both the attackers and the unbuilders—it became, for a time, in the eyes of the world's media, the new century's site of ambiguity, its metaphorical ground.

In his early reaction to 9.11.01 Rafael Viñoly described the void that had been so suddenly opened out by the imploding towers as "charged with the weight of emotion, the fears of risk and the expectation we can overcome." Such a place, he noted, is "the common territory of art . . . the place where the unexpected power of invention can reach beyond the limits of logic to set a new direction." Convention, both social and cultural, was destroyed by 9.11.01. This psychosocial void would be filled in many ways. Of the physical void at Ground Zero, Viñoly said: "We cannot leave it empty, yet we cannot fill it with the simplistic notions of commerce wrapped in the thin skin of symbolism. We must fill it with an architecture that assumes its full potential as public art. It should be filled by a place that can reinstate the values of innovation, pragmatism and beauty."[38]

As if in response to Viñoly's plea, in June 2002 Herbert Muschamp wrote an enthusiastic review of Zaha Hadid's architecture and design retrospective at the National Center for Contemporary Arts, Rome (illus. 47). "I came away persuaded that it would be an injustice if Hadid weren't invited to submit a design for the transportation terminal under discussion for Lower Manhattan. As a pure virtuoso of design, she has no living rival."[39] This bears on the WTC question, as of course the site is the transport hub for the region. The design featured in the article is that for the Rome Center itself, renamed "Maaxi" by the architect. It consists of "a campus with separate structures for contemporary art galleries, an architecture museum, an auditorium and offices. These are connected to one another by five curving, elevated slabs equipped with glass roofs. The pieces slide over and beneath one another, as at a highway intersection or an express stop for

47. Zaha Hadid,
National Center for
Contemporary Arts,
Rome, project design,
2002. Source: Zaha
Hadid Architects/Centro
Nazionale per le Arti
Contemporane, Rome.

converging subway lines. Sun screens and lighting baffles, running parallel to the curves, accentuate the infrastructural image. Viewed from above, as it will be in this city of hills, the roofs also evoke electronic circuitry." So replete are these references to past and modern experiences of space that Muschamp characterized Hadid's design as "an excavation into the field of contemporaneity."[40] When I look at this design I see one more image surfacing, allusively, subversively: a word, or phrase, articulating itself from within an intricate tracery. This is a Muslim template—the most basic one, the name of Allah. This was, as we saw, an element in Libeskind's imagining of the ground plan for the Jewish Museum.

Other signs that the contemporary architectural imagination was being pushed beyond the brilliant boxes of Late Modern spectacle appeared. Dismayed at the low-grade thinking being promoted by the LMDC, a number of groups of architects, planners, engineers, and writers formed and devoted countless hours to developing more interesting approaches. Most prominent was the group of outstanding architects, including Richard Meier, Peter Eisenman, Charles Gwathmey, Rem Koolhaas, Steven Holl, Zaha Hadid, Rafael Viñoly, and many exceptional teams, such as TEN Arquitectos, gathered by critic Muschamp. Their project began from the assumption that the required office, commercial, housing, and cultural space could be generated by covering the section of West Street that goes by the WTC site, turning it into a tunnel, and allowing the riverside parkland to flow over it. The resultant new space could be interspersed with a series of extraordinary structures, a veritable instant museum of the most imaginative architecture![41] While most of these designs were dedicated to building community, serving memory, and providing sites for reflection that might lead to reconciliation, rather than the violence that visited on 9.11.01, they did so as intentions on the part of the starchitects involved, not as the outcome of any community process. Consequently, they soon faded from view.

Fresh Ideas for the Empty Site

By August 2002, after receiving a resoundingly negative response at a "Listening to the City" meeting held at the Javits Center the previous month, the LMDC recognized that the "Six Concepts" were puce compromises that pleased nobody.[42] On August 14, 2002, in an uncharacteristically bold step, it announced a "Design Study for the World Trade Center Site and Surrounding Areas." An open invitation to "the most innovative architects and planners around the world," it was moderated by New York New Visions, a coalition of twenty architecture, engineering, planning, landscape architecture, and design organizations that had formed the previous November. This group had put out a series of planning documents devoted to the rebuilding of Lower Manhattan.[43] It had advised the LMDC to stage an open competition calling for fresh ideas. Innovative architects and planners were asked to propose bold and creative solutions. Yet they were required to incorporate the following ideas into their designs: a distinctive skyline, recognition of the tower footprints, commercial and retail space, a grand promenade on West Street, a new street grid, a transit center, residential housing, cultural elements, and a sequence of public open spaces of different sizes. This sounded uncannily like the constraints of the six concept plans, and did not inspire confidence that they might force a brilliant solution into the light. Neither the LMDC nor many members of the public were ready to hand over the WTC site to an architect without constraints, whatever his or her track record at producing spectacularly successful built solutions. *This* was different: this was, after all, Ground Zero, post-9.11.01. Lower Manhattan itself was at stake, perhaps even the future viability of the city. Accordingly, the LMDC insisted that it was seeking only "innovative design proposals" for "a land-use plan" for the area. It did not want "the detailed architecture of individual structures," rather, "building forms to help the public imagine how the site could look if the Plan was fully realized."[44]

The LMDC received 406 responses from "every continent except Antarctica," six chosen (Daniel Libeskind having been given a special prompt), and the local firm of Petersen/Littenberg added. The seven finalists—all well-known architectural firms, or consortiums of well-known architects—had six weeks to shape their initial ideas into a proposal.[45] During this period Port Authority officials unveiled early designs for the permanent transportation hub and commenced building subway track casings across sections of the site.[46] Internecine warring between the authority and the LMDC, and between these and the host of other agencies involved in the planning, was constantly on the verge of public eruption.[47] In mid-December, Mayor Bloomberg weighed in against tall office buildings as the key to the future of Lower Manhattan. He saw, instead, a rebirth based on many more residents in the area, with museums, smaller companies, and some financial services. The Twin Towers, he believed, had retarded this kind of development. The same mistake should not be made now.[48] Meanwhile, designing the memorial had been siphoned off to a separate process: an LMDC committee covered the country, visiting different kinds of memorials, working at guidelines that were released late December.[49] Their efforts were eclipsed by the exhibition of the seven designs for the site at the Winter Garden, World Financial Center, New York, on December 18, 2002.

Spectorama

The nine proposals put forward by the seven groups of architects received much comment, from critics, the profession, and the public.[50] Few, however, asked of the proposals that they posit a form of life with resonance across the deadly divisions that precipitated the brief in the first place. The Holocaust, the Vietnam War, the bombing of Sarajevo, 9.11.01 itself: these were instances of inhumanity brought about by cultural disjunction so extreme that they seem to repeat and reinforce Adorno's dire admonition. Yet some architects, as I have shown, are capable of embracing these contradictions and then building out from them, responsibly, creatively, convincingly. What more might we expect from the artistic process, from sculpture, public art, or architecture? This is surely the apogee of any kind of art. That it transcend its ordinary associations, and its utility, even its place in the history of its art. That it is the result of an act of independent critical insight. That it embodies its most profoundly human content in its actual form. And that it does all this in a way that moves human experience—that of individuals and of social collectivities—beyond the impasse between the reconciled and the irreconcilable.

A successful solution to the WTC site, then, would be one with the widest resonance. It was not a question of erecting a building so striking (in the target architecture context, this term becomes more concrete than ever) that it would be "worth destroying."[51] In the spotlight of world attention, it had to be a solution that went beyond even the most defiant negativity, a solution that both enacted and symbolized worlding practices of the most ordinary and exceptional kind. These were extraordinary demands. How well were they met?

In the event, all of the December 18 designs were shaped by each of the themes discussed in this book. At the Winter Garden, adjacent to the WTC site, each entrant presented his or her proposal in a diorama: wooden models, plastic assemblages, a hologram in one case, diagrams, explanatory texts, enlarged photographs, and virtual tours by video. Serious statements of intent elicited from the principals by television-style interviews provided voice-over. Small wonder that pictorial attractiveness, instant legibility, and speed-reading prevailed over the challenges of spatial, functional, and symbolic integration that we ask for from architecture. On this showing, 9.11.01 did not banish spectacle. Rather, it called more spectacle out, competitively.

The four currents of contemporary spectacle architecture identified in the first part of this book were very much in evidence. Extraordinary technology dominated

48. United Architects, *Innovative Design Study for World Trade Center Site*, 2002, detail of sky lobby. Photo courtesy Lower Manhattan Development Corporation.

most submissions. Gehry-style complexity infused the United Architects proposal, perhaps due to the input of Greg Lynn FORM (illus. 48), and it pervaded the organic, staged "vertical city" of the group led by Skidmore, Owings & Merrill (illus. 49). The assertive geometry of the Meier group's design would have imposed on New York a modernism more implacable than it has ever absorbed (illus. 50). The thought of its gridded gates marching through the rest of Manhattan is a neo-Corbusian nightmare. Foster's Late Modern twinned towers were more subdued (illus. 51). Recycling the past was the main point in Petersen/Littenberg's Garden for New York, a quiet place of recreation surrounded by buildings that repeat the comforting ordinariness of Deco period

49. Skidmore, Owings &
Merrill, SANAA, Michael
Maltzan Architecture,
Field Operations, Tom
Leader Studio,
Neutelings Riedijk,
Inigo Manglano-Ovalle,
Rita McBride, Jessica
Stockholder, Elyn
Zimmerman, *Innovative
Design Study for World
Trade Center Site*, 2002.
Photo courtesy Lower
Manhattan
Development
Corporation.

Manhattan (illus. 52). The three proposals by the group Think had qualities of all
of these tendencies (illus. 53). Studio Daniel Libeskind, building on the Jewish
Museum experience, began from a set of antispectacular premises, and yet did not
avoid spectacle in its proposed design, however much it dispersed and diverted its
elements (illus. 54).

   Without exception, each design attempted to generate an instant iconotype.
Foster and Meier did so through a huge, stand-out, defiant form, Skidmore,

50. Richard Meier and Partners Architects, Eisenman Architects, Gwathmey Siegel & Associates, Steven Holl Architects, *Innovative Design Study for World Trade Center Site*, 2002. Photo courtesy Lower Manhattan Development Corporation.

Owings & Merrill and United Architects by clustered complexity, while Think resorted to bets-each-way variants: a park plus high tower, a glass shed plus tower, and twin towers. Petersen/Littenberg replayed, through a time warp, a generalized but unmistakably Manhattan setting. Libeskind worked against iconotypy for most of his design, but succumbed to the pull of height by inserting a "vertical world garden" that would jut from the skyline, a swordlike echo of the Statue of Liberty.

None of the proposals prioritized the economistic demand to provide the maximum commercial and retail space in the most compact, cheapest possible form. The core values of the World Trade Center were banished from sight (for the positive PR of this occasion, at least). Almost. Libeskind parked them at the peripheries of his design, in irregular polyhedrons that encroached on space around the eastern edges of the site. And said, during an interview following his "win" in the "competition," that, watching the WTC being built while an architecture student at Cooper Union, was "such an inspiring and controversial and wonderful moment."[52] That WTC values would be met by Meier et al. was an unspoken premise. As it was in the Foster offering: two criss-crossed, "kissing" parallelepipeds—the Twin Towers imagined as benign, gently related forms, as extruded glass Brancusis, as the towers so fondly misremembered by so many after their disappearance. Yet their economic efficiency was well disguised with ecological inclusions. Small wonder that this design received by far the most votes

51. Norman Foster and
Partners, *Innovative
Design Study for
World Trade Center
Site*, 2002. Photo
courtesy Lower
Manhattan
Development
Corporation.

in public polling. Yet the computer graphic of this building pasted in to the existing skyline shows it, instantly, to be a ghost of the original WTC, albeit crystal-
prismed for the New Age, and to be as out of place as its predecessor.[53]

Twin towers appeared in most of the proposals. Each high-rise in the
Skidmore, Owings & Merrill village of towers connected at the top, while United
Architects' five towers leaned against each other like a well-advanced encounter
group. One of the two "gates" in the Meier model was a pair of towers (an egre-
gious 1,111 feet high) joined at four places. And its basic shape repeated, albeit at
gargantuan scale, the remnant of the original tower that sat so long amid the
wreckage at Ground Zero that it has become iconic. Among the three ideas
advanced by Think was a pair of open steel frame towers, with various functions
strung within them, such as a World Cultural Center, a performing arts space,
a conference center, and a 9.11.01 museum. The last took the form of a white shape
twisted against itself. Inserted into the towers, and strung between them, it
looked for all the world like the wreckage of an airplane: indeed, it was positioned
in the skeletons at the points and angles of impact of the attacking planes. It is as
if the team had invited Lebbeus Woods in as a consultant and taken him at his
first word. The net result was a curious picturing of 9.11.01 partway through its

52. Petersen/Littenberg Architecture and Urban Design, *Innovative Design Study for World Trade Center Site*, 2002. Photo courtesy Lower Manhattan Development Corporation.

cinematic unfolding, as if the event were freeze-framed at a moment when the antimodernist attackers could be seen to have dashed themselves fruitlessly against the might of modernist structure and flexibility, that impossible moment—so deeply desired ever since by the attacked—before time resumed its rush and drew the towers down into the self-destruction that now seems natural to them.

This was, however, only the most literal instance of the huge impact that spectacular terrorism made on each of the designs. LMDC chairman John C. Whitehead pinpointed this effect in his introductory remarks: "The architects have responded with great depth to the question, 'What does September 11 represent?' Their responses vary, just as our own reactions to the trauma, the aftermath and the recovery were so very personal and so very different."[54] Despite the fact that the LMDC had separated off the design of the memorial from this part of the process, asking only that the design provide an opportunity to incorporate a memorial into it, each team sought to include the memorializing function within its basic concept. This is least obvious in the Petersen/Littenberg plan, yet their unalloyed nostalgia is a reversion to a pretraumatic imaginary. It is most

53. Think Design, *Innovative Design Study for World Trade Center Site*, 2002. Photo courtesy Lower Manhattan Development Corporation.

54. Studio Daniel Libeskind, *Innovative Design Study for World Trade Center Site*, 2002. Source: Lower Manhattan Development Corporation. Credit: Studio Daniel Libeskind.

obvious in the Libeskind concept, which builds up from and around the slurry wall that held back the Hudson while the WTC was built and Ground Zero was excavated. Libeskind began his statement to the LMDC with a recollection:

> I arrived by ship to New York as a teenager, an immigrant, and like millions of others before me, my first sight was the Statue of Liberty and the amazing skyline of Manhattan. I have never forgotten that sight or what it stands for. This is what this project is all about.[55]

An expert spruiker is at work. Libeskind knew that stealing the show meant coming up with an architectural form that would be immediately seen to work as an instant icon and had the potential to become what I have named an iconotype—a form that would cluster associations and affections to it for the foreseeable future. He led his presentations and anchored his entire design with a "Vertical World Garden," shaping it like a flagpole wrapped with an unfurled flag, and presenting it insistently from a viewpoint that included the raised arm and torch of the Statue of Liberty. His statement continued:

> When I first began this project, New Yorkers were divided as to whether to keep the site of the World Trade Center empty or to fill the site completely and build upon it. I meditated many days on this seemingly impossible dichotomy. To acknowledge the terrible deaths which occurred on this site, while looking to the future with hope, seemed like two moments which could not be joined. I sought to find a solution which would bring these seemingly contradictory viewpoints into an unexpected unity. So, I went to look at the site, to stand within it, to see people walking around it, to feel its power and to listen to its voices. And this is what I heard, felt and saw.
>
> The great slurry walls are the most dramatic elements which survived the attack, an engineering wonder constructed on bedrock foundations and designed to hold back the Hudson River. The foundations withstood the unimaginable trauma of the destruction and stand as eloquent as the Constitution itself asserting the durability of Democracy and the value of individual life.

As at the Jewish Museum, he then built up his design from this deep, underground negativity, reaching for hope and redemption, against the odds, and in full recognition of difference: "We have to be able to enter this hallowed, sacred ground while creating a quiet, meditative and spiritual space. We need to journey down, some 70 feet into Ground Zero, onto the bedrock foundation, a procession with deliberation into the deep indelible footprints of Tower One and Tower Two."

This conception replays the descending/ascending pathway so effectively established as a template for enacted mourning in America by Lin's Vietnam Veterans Memorial. It also follows a theme I raised in the chapters on Gehry, Meier, and the Jewish Museum, the application of a Minimalist aesthetic to broad public symbolization. Yet Libeskind's design adds—or perhaps has been obliged, by the event-site itself, to recognize—its Real in the most literal way: the "great slurry walls" that so moved him. What he saw, I suggest, was an opportunity for an intense moment of history to reenact itself *as an architectural element*. Indeed, the intensity is itself literalized in the most material sense: the slurry wall is the exact meeting of an architectural (engineering) element with the natural forces it is called on to modify. Any visitor can see this, instantly, once it is pointed out (as it will be, prominently). And can feel its force, imaginatively. History and architecture, nature and engineering, hold each other at arm's length, in dramatic interdependence. This solution to the grounding of architecture in a foundation of memorialization is arguably so powerful that it obviates the need for a separate memorial competition.[56]

Visitors would enter Ground Zero through "a museum of the event, of memory and hope." Reliving 9.11.01 occurs in orienting the public places as a "Park of Heroes" and a "Wedge of Light," such that "each year on September 11th between the hours of 8:46 a.m., when the first airplane hit and 10:28 a.m., when the second tower collapsed, the sun will shine without shadow, in perpetual tribute to altruism and courage." Beneath this, a concourse would link to the PATH trains, the subways would be connected, and the required plethora of New York culture and community would be fitted in: hotels, a performing arts center, office towers, underground malls, street-level shops, restaurants, cafes—the usual. Libeskind's emotional literalism culminates in "a towering spire of 1776 feet high"—1776, get it? Instead of the colors of the American flag, it would project the greens and yellows of a Gardens of the World. Why gardens? Libeskind answered himself: "Because gardens are a constant affirmation of life. A skyscraper rises above its predecessors, reasserting the preeminence of freedom and beauty, restoring the spiritual peak to the city, creating an icon that speaks of our vitality in the face of danger and our optimism in the aftermath of tragedy." He ended his highly emotive statement with the call: "Life victorious."[57]

I have cited these words at length because of what they show of the design thinking and public relations smarts of the architect who produced what most of his fellows, and most critics and commentators, thought was the subtlest response in the circumstances. Libeskind's statement also attests to the pervasiveness of 9.11.01, to the fact that the event, the shock, and the traumatic aftermath, as LMDC chairman Whitehead said, touched every aspect of these architects' designs, every point of decision making.

The power of 9.11.01 is evident in every proposal. Much of this followed from the brief. Unlike the recent norm for museum design (set by Gehry, but evident in less spectacular ways in the museum architecture of Ando and others), no entrant sought to override the indecision and imprecision of the client's catchall list of conditions by a concept that knocked them—or, at least, some of them—for six. All preserved the "footprints" of the Twin Towers, exactly. This had the effect of quarantining two large blocks of the site, leaving their arbitrary shapes as eternal absences, uncitylike vacancies at the heart of anything that may grow around and over them. It also meant that the only buildable areas of the site are on the north and eastern edges, guaranteeing very tall, thin towers. The spectral shapes of the Twin Towers appeared in some form in the vertical elements of most of the designs (Libeskind excepted). Furthermore, all the proposals reenacted the event itself by deriving a major design element from its architecture, its occurrence or its effects. Even the high modernism of the Meier team's "geometric clarity in glowing glass" was, in their terms, a "quiet abstraction," that, in the placement of the two sets of buildings "nearly touching," symbolized "the interlaced fingers of protective hands."

The past, pre-9.11.01, was reintroduced in key elements of each scheme, notably at ground level, where reestablishing the streets obliterated by the WTC collapse became sine qua non. The built icons of New York City echoed throughout:

the paired archways of the Brooklyn Bridge were a favorite, as were the profile of the Empire State Building and the aspiring form of the Statue of Liberty. The healing, growing power of open, green spaces was central to all schemes: as a park, a promenade, or a forest in the skies. Cultural exchange, human interaction, community building: these needs rose to the surface of most designs, peripheralizing the commercial—for that moment, at least.

It is this last aspiration that finally produced the scattered positive outcomes of this exercise. Although the illustrations of the parks and shopping areas in each proposal were mired in 1980s happy consumerville, some of the actual designs suggested lively communal spaces. Think's Sky Park was one of these. Ecology in the sky was an idea common to most. And horizontal, sky-level "living spaces," that staple of modernist futurism, now seems to be so instinctive to these urbanists that its time may well be at hand. In this vein, the Skidmore, Owings & Merrill team put forward a "trans-horizon for the resurrected global city," and United Architects proposed a "City in the Sky." These were efforts to rethink the forms of community.[58]

Yet while every design was an effort to apply the best thinking each team could muster on urban renewal, and while many of them strove to reconceptualize urban renewal itself, the marks of 9.11.01 were so pervasive that, in the end, they— as much as the constraints laid down by the Port Authority, the LMDC, the lessees—amounted to a distorting presence. The drive to memorialize, it turned out, has deadened the creativity of some of the world's most inventive and subtle designers. It drew Libeskind, for example, to a literalism that confused his normally freewheeling form splintering: only the Ground Zero memorial section of his proposal was fully convincing, only it was new architecture at his normal standard. And, it has to be said, in his normal vein: it was a holocaust space. This prompted the uncomfortable question: why "a large piece of Manhattan should be permanently dedicated to an artistic representation of an enemy assault?"[59]

What irony! The event architecture of 9.11.01 unfolds still, and crimps actual architecture's capacity to generate an architecture that is not only equal to the event that precipitated this set of architectural acts but that points pathways beyond it. The designs as they stood were signs of shortfall.

There was, in the weeks during which the proposals were on display, no consensus within the architectural community that any one design was so good that the profession and its supporters should go to the wall for it.[60] None of the designs seemed powerful enough to hold out against entrenched interests. Philip Nobel's skepticism was a tonic:

> This is still business as usual, remember, even if writ large and strangely burdened. The odds-on future of the site remains a queasy trains-below, cubicles-above, memorial-in-the-footprints, shopping-everywhere dollop of old-normal Manhattan. And as in every other local real estate venture, the architect will be brought in to dress up the developers' numbers. No one should be surprised; that is the bone we are always thrown.[61]

The Winter Garden dioramas ranged from Libeskind's emotional pyrotechnics to the upbeat lattices of Think's twin towers with all the elements required by the brief suspended in and between them. The latter proposal was, in itself, a striking display of the state of unresolved good intentions that seemed characteristic of the process itself (if you banish, for a moment, specters of the bean-counters hovering in the wings). The elements appeared to float, right out there for all to see, but with nowhere to go. It was no surprise that, in February 2003, these two firms were invited by the LMDC to remain in consultation about taking the process forward. It *was* a surprise to many that, in March, the Studio Libeskind design was chosen—after heavy pressure from Governor Pataki and Mayor Bloomberg—as the basis on which to build. It has become clear since that Pataki was driven above all by the role that a speedy start to rebuilding, pushed by him, would play in his impending reelection, and that Bloomberg saw the pragmatics of a scheme that had delay and deferral built into it.[62] Yet Libeskind, in Berlin, had achieved an extraordinary result against seemingly insuperable odds. Had the politicians invited into their parlor a spider wilier than even they could conceive?

After Auschwitz in Manhattan?

Much was at stake in the decision to choose the Libeskind design as it stood in March 2003 and to banish all others from consideration. At base, it was to elect to tie whatever is built on this site into the black hole of human incompatibility that gaped open on September 11, 2001, right here, at this place in Manhattan. It was to restore something of Ground Zero, to work back against the relentless erasure, the zero-sum game of clearing the space for commerce. In the decision, as in Libeskind's initial design, a *foreign* consciousness appears, spectrally. It had been steeped in aftermath, in the Jewish sense of being as interrogation. European societies have staged their own self- or mutual destruction so thoroughly over so many centuries that their cities may be said to be built, in part, of these immaterial remains, their structures to be cemented by trauma, their spaces shaded by fearful memory. New York's incessant excavation of itself, however unthinkingly destructive, has been a precondition of its seemingly irrepressible futurism. The relentless unbuilding at Ground Zero was driven, as we have seen, by many forces. Simply clearing a hazard, for starters. Erasing a clear sign of the Islamic Other's newly troubling potency was another. Or maybe it was a more general, instinctive reaction: to cover a weakness, to deny vulnerability. Perhaps it was an instinctive healing of a wound or, conversely, a leaping at an opportunity to rebuild bigger and better—both of which went, awkwardly, too far. But a deeply embedded reflex may have also driven it, in part: to confine war to foreign lands, to keep it offshore. No quarter was given to the possibility of a ruin emerging. Nor any chance for a plant to grow, a few rats to scurry. This destruction was to have no natural history, only that of the heritage industry, something suitable for presentation in an on-site museum.[63]

Instead, events turned out unpredictably again, as events will. In the competition to remember and rebuild, an architect whose design instincts are most deeply embedded in the consciousness of Europe's most experienced, and persistent, victims was given the task of supervising the transformation and stasis of what is, at least at this time, the city's most sacred space. If the European imaginary cannot escape constant return to its most shattering moments, to the horrors that it has so often wreaked upon itself, the U.S. is habitually characterized—especially in Europe, but now globally—as a culture consumed with forgetting, one in which social amnesia is the norm. Both characterizations are, of course, stereotypes. These forces operate throughout the world, in an infinite variety of contexts. They can be accepted as irresistible, or they can be fought against. In seeking and accepting the Ground Zero commission, Libeskind embarked on a daily struggle with the local moneymen, the efficiency experts, and, less evidently but more fundamentally, with the developers and their architects, mandarins of the pragmatic compromise. It is through these agents that the great tides of repression and simplification that have built Homeland America would insist on having their ways. Would Libeskind have his?

The History of Banality

One year after the attacks, Ground Zero became a silent, empty memorial to its own relentless unbuilding. The excavation of Downtown's unconscious, so compellingly chronicled by Langewiesche, completed its journey through the social imaginary and arrived at a state of otherworldly suspension. Physically, the clearing resulted in a domain that was almost empty, a void delimited by a mix of concrete walls, compacted earth, steel frames, and an encasement over a subway passage. This was not the site prior to the beginning of work on the original WTC, not exactly: the landfill, the compacted refuse used then makes what remains now not precisely what one would have seen in 1969. Yet the place eerily re-created the zone that Yamasaki et al. built upon: a place without constraint, without the earth's givenness insisting that it be taken as given. By repeating, or returning to, its own birthing in an initiating act of obliteration, the WTC fulfilled the other half of its bargain with destiny, its dicing with fragility, with the risks of its near impossibility. No physical vestiges of the WTC remained: it is as if the heritage, the material culture of WTC, could exist, after this firestorm of hatred and hurt, only in virtual states, as visual imagery detached from its first place in the world, as an iconotype in mourning. The Twin Towers site became a seemingly untouchable space, around which the rebuilding proposals hovered, twisting and turning, like specters over an empty grave. Yet, like many graveyards, this one was visited—indeed, visited constantly by New Yorkers, tourists, critics, architects, government officials, security officers, the press. Inhabited, that is, despite every effort to expunge it.

Around the edges of the site, above the milling spectators, there appeared a rolling horizon of older high- and middle-rise buildings. They evoked the scenario of Downtown before the WTC. They signaled that randomness, compromise, individualism, and greed would amount to a recipe for failure, if the same forces, however disguised and distractive, prevail during the current rebuilding process. There was also the basic hard economics: in 1995 Eric Darton asked the question that even now, as boosters try to lift the country out of its 9.11.01 aftermath, has the potential to bring all this discussion to its knees: "Would the city that weathered a horrifying terrorist attack, and before that, the loss of much of its port and manufacturing base, be capable of surviving abandonment by its financial service industries?"[64] This was a good question to ask at the end of the recession of the late 1980s and early 1990s, after the remaining companies had extracted over $2 billion in tax breaks and grants from the city to stay downtown, yet still departed in droves, for midtown, New Jersey, and points upstate or out of the state altogether. Not least the Chase Manhattan Bank, whose headquartering in the area David and Nelson Rockefeller had done so much to shore up, including, as we saw, building the World Trade Center. The stock exchange took its $1.1 billion and is still there, in principle at least.[65] Darton's question needed to be asked again, and has been, by the LMDC. The answers it received were not promising, and it has remained quiet about them. Nonetheless, they were hot topics among potential clients and users: "Without a huge, coordinated strategy, taking in high-speed rail links to Kennedy and Newark airports, rapid replacement of the office space, and new infrastructure to lure business back, the economic viability of the area is doomed."[66] From this perspective, the pragmatics often cited for the viability of skyscrapers—their saving of land and their concentration of energy use in one easy-to-service place, preferably a transport hub—return to prominence. The developers keep pushing for the maximum profitable space: meanwhile, seventeen million square feet of office space stands idle in the downtown area.

The planners had a $20 billion disaster-relief cushion from the federal government. That was never likely to go far in New York without considerable leverage. Insiders claimed that at least four or five major global companies would have to commit to whatever is built, a sufficient number of world-oriented "creative transformers" would have to decide that this is the place to be, and a displaced community would need to return or a new one emerge (no bets that it would be led by the efforts of the area's latest wave of immigrants, mostly Spanish speaking). Away from the headliner rhetoric of how the site will present itself to the spectacle, how it will reappear in the iconomy (if it does), there was the quiet murmur of the pragmatists. Frank Lowy, chairman of the Westfield Corporation (which managed, without fanfare, to have the amount of "respectful" retail space required under the new guidelines upped from the sixty-shop mall under the WTC to between 600,000 and 1 million square feet): "The challenge for us is to get where we want to be, but to avoid the perception that we just want to create a big shopping mall. This is New York and it's the most sophisticated city in the world, and we want to create the most sophisticated shopping precinct in the world. We want to make it commercially successful, but we are also extremely cognizant of our reputation."[67] Malls work when there is uninterrupted pedestrian space, readily accessible at its peripheries by cars. Not eighteenth-century streets cutting through the site, nor huge, blank, no-profit zones of sacred space. Despite Lowy's blandishments, New York is not in any general sense the most sophisticated of cities. But it is perhaps the hardest city—as so many of its chroniclers, such as Paul Auster and Martin Scorcese, continue to attest. Its hardness comes, in part, from the war of attrition conducted with relentless mutuality between its powerful and its immigrants. Asked by a journalist to boil the issue down to its basics, Westfield's U.S. boss said, "Well, you have all of these competing issues in circles—insurance, politics, community issues and economics," and scribbled a "mess of circles, endless round and round. 'That's it,' he says, smiling ruefully." Lowy soon walked away, but Silverstein did not.[68]

Elsewhere in the city, economic recession and fear of being targeted have frozen development. The Manhattan skyline remained as static as it was in the 1940s and 1950s. One of the few buildings going up was the replacement for 7 World Trade Center, Silverstein's rushed high-rise at the edge of the site. Financing for the $700 million building came from $800 million insurance proceeds. The architects were Skidmore, Owings & Merrill. The original 7 World Trade Center had burned uncontrollably on September 11, 2001. The new one was promoted as a "laboratory in high-rise safety."[69]

Meanwhile, hopes for transfiguration at Ground Zero continued to dim. The big news from the Port Authority in late March 2003 was that the ground level of the memorial "bathtub" was to be raised forty feet up from the actual level of Ground Zero itself. Why? Nothing to do with Libeskind's design: this called for the whole slurry wall and all the space adjacent to it to remain "sacred." Rather, the PA pragmatists need somewhere off-street to park the estimated 120 busloads of tourists who are expected to visit the site each day. Destination architecture to be sure: first the arrival point, then the point of the arrival. Architecture—even the most fraught, the most inventive—must accommodate both. The ghost of J. Paul Getty's museums returned to haunt us: at the WTC site, history is pushed upstairs (actually, it is to be shunted into a museum) in order to make space for parking. Even though this proposal was soon withdrawn after protest from the architect and the families of victims, Corian's despairing insight, cited as an epigram at the beginning of this book, echoes towards its end: even at Ground Zero, banality seems destined to merge with apocalypse, and to do so indecently.

Libeskind's relationships with his many powerful clients proved as labyrinthine as those that marked the decade-long struggle to build the Jewish Museum.[70] Contracted to the Port Authority and the LMDC for the master plan and the broad design guidelines, and to the LMDC for the memorial setting and the cultural buildings, he has oversight of the envelope of the transport terminal building, to be designed by another of the spectacle architects of late modernity, Santiago Calatrava.[71] Throughout the process he demonstrated a willingness to negotiate even the most precious aspects of his proposals that surprised many, not least *New Yorker* cartoonist Steve Brodner, who amusingly portrayed the architect, dancing in the spotlight, as a wide-eyed, media-hugging gun-for-hire, willing

55. Steve Brodner, "Rebuild Iraq? Daniel Libeskind Says, 'No Problem!'" 2003. Source: New Yorker.

to turn any upbeat symbol to any purpose—including peppering war-torn Iraq with postmodern monuments to Rumsfeld, Cheney, et al. (illus. 55).[72] The cartoonist's skepticism was matched by a burst of vitriol from rival architect Rem Koolhaas:

> From now on the most important city in the world is dominated by the tower from which first dangled an ape. What is the connection between zero tolerance and the cult of Ground Zero? In any case, the disaster resurrects Giuliani's depleted persona. New Yorkers surrender to empathy. The tragedy of 9/11 inspires a mood of collective tenderness that is almost exhilarating, almost a relief: Hype's spell has broken and the city can recover its own reality principle, emerge with new thinking from the unthinkable. But Politics interfere. In spite of Bloomberg's pragmatic sobriety, the transnational metropolis is enlisted in a

national crusade. New York becomes a city (re)captured by Washington. Through the alchemy of 9/11, the authoritarian imperceptibly morphs into the totalitarian. A competition for rebuilding Ground Zero is held, not to restore the city's vitality or shift its center of gravity, but to create a monument at a scale that monuments have never existed (except under Stalin). On March 17, at 9.30 am the winning architect rings the bell of the New York Stock Exchange. At midnight on March 20, the war starts. At 8 am, at a breakfast meeting in lower Manhattan, the "Master Design Architect," an immigrant, movingly recounts his first encounter with liberty. Instead of the two towers—the sublime—the city will live with five towers, wounded by a single scything movement of the architect, surrounding two black holes. New York will be marked by a massive representation of hurt that projects only the overbearing self-pity of the powerful. Instead of the confident beginning of the next chapter, it captures the stumped fundamentalism of the superpower. Call it closure.[73]

Entangled in this swamp of vision and bad faith are the compromises Libeskind has been obliged to make in order to accommodate the economic demands of developer Silverstein and the unrepentantly late modernist engineering and aesthetic of David Childs, Silverstein's architect. During 2003, these devolved on the design of the 1,776-foot Freedom Tower, the furled-flag shape of which—in its deliberate evocation of the Statue of Liberty's raised, torch-bearing arm—became, instantly, the iconic identifier of the entire project (illus. 56). Childs set out to trump Libeskind with a clean-lined, high modernist, singular solution: a torqued, tapering shaft that culminates in an open framework of cables, trusses, and energy-generating windmills, plus an antenna that would stretch up through 2,000 feet, beating out Taipei 101 as the world's tallest. For architects, this evoked memories of Frank Lloyd Wright's fantasy, the Illinois, a mile-high rise designed in 1956 but never built. Libeskind countered with a refurling of the upper reaches of the shape. Announced mid-December 2003, the agreed design looked like a Childs tower with a hint of Libeskind on top. By mid-2005, even this hint had gone. Child's design now looks for all the world like a spectral skeleton of one of the new Asian tiger towers. And, like them, it is full of security features: extra-strong fireproofing, chemical and biological filters in the air supply, blastproof glass, and separate stairs for firemen.[74] None of this satiates the New York hubris for the biggest and the best. Indeed, the new tower concept, like the project in its entirety, has, already, been deformed—albeit elegantly—toward impressive mediocrity.

The twisted spire at Freedom Tower's summit will emit a light beam, becoming, in Libeskind's words, "a beacon of light and hope in a world that is often dark."[75] Will such plain and simple hopefulness deflect those who might wish to make of it a target? Beneath the scrutiny of unprecedented world attention, can rhetoric such as this, when grounded in the relentless forces of compromise, be an adequate basis for the architecture for our age? Will it not drive architects to seek other, more genuinely contemporary, solutions? We can only hope.

56. David Childs for Skidmore, Owings & Merrill, and Studio Daniel Libeskind, "Freedom Tower" in the background; WTC Memorial Design, "Reflecting Absence," by Michael Arad and Peter Walker in the foreground. Both designs 2004. Photo courtesy Lower Manhattan Development Corporation.

Conclusion: *Aftermath and After*

Mourning for Manhattan

I have attempted in this book to set out the dimensions of aftermath, both negative and positive, as they relate to contemporary architecture. The perspective I have taken is broader in its scope than the stylism that is frequently employed in writing the history of architecture. Towards the end of the century—under the diverting name "Postmodernism," and in the guise of a celebration—mourning began for the Modern Movement that had, for nearly a century, built and planned so hopefully, so brilliantly, and so ordinarily well that it set the standards for good modern architecture in many countries throughout the world. (That most actual building still kept reaching backwards, or insisted on staying resolutely in place, is another, separate matter.) Late Modern architecture was one response to this prematurity. Stylistic banners were waved—Deconstructive, Past Modern, Supermodernism and engineering featurist—but none came even close to being period styles. Deeper thinkers sensed that it was modernity as a whole that had placed itself at stake and that the overarching embrace of period style was unlikely to reappear, not for some time, if ever again. They realized that the profound contradictions that had forced modernism into the light were exacerbated in contemporary conditions, yet it nevertheless remained a problematic, unshakable, still productive inheritance. Now, they search for subtle ways of rethreading contemporary architectural practice with figurations of modernism's expressive potential and with inflexions of modernity's conflicted inheritance. They also seek new programs that respond to the new demands of contemporaneity. We have explored this range of responses in the preceding chapters.

In Manhattan itself, there was mourning for the previously despised or forgotten but then so vividly attacked, so surprisingly self-obliterating World Trade Center. Whatever the initial defiance of some, most New Yorkers knew after 9.11.01 that to build anything substantial beyond the current skyline would be to erect phantasma of past glories and to invite further attacks. New York might raise a spire or two, like those that continued to spout up in striving cities all over the world. The "right" to build tall buildings—a battle vigorously fought between the front-runners, Chicago and New York, for a century, a right won in that battle—had already passed to the burgeoning economies of Asia.

These factors, when allied with others (such as where the "creative class" decides to locate itself) do add up to a sea change in how the world sees New York, and how it sees itself. They are speeding the gradual diminution of the city, its continuing decline from its high status as the modern world's greatest urban experiment. Already, and inevitably, its crown as "capital of the C20th" had been tarnished by time. Its role as the citadel of modernity, painstakingly achieved and strenuously defended, was being eroded by the world's shifting to the conditions of contemporaneity—the 9.11.01 attacks were highly visible signs of the breaching of these walls. A fear arose. Manhattan might no longer be able to draw inspiration from its deepest source of energy: its proclivity to exceed its limits, its thirst for risk. If so, this would mean an end to the idea of its rejoining the network of "global cities," those mini-Manhattans that had sprung up around the world in the last decades of the twentieth century. The miniaturization of Manhattan might, after 9.11.01, have returned home, slowly shrinking the city itself. But perhaps "global cities" had themselves become, already, a transient idea, destined, in contemporaneity, to yield to the more variegated urbanities, the more mobile kinds of concentration that deglobalization is currently engendering.

Does this profound dismembering of both building and urban form prefigure the death of architecture itself? Is this what we are, also, mourning? Are we living in the aftermath of architecture? Throughout this study we have noted the spectral underside of the spectacular, a repressed that keeps returning, often in the form of a quasi memorial, or as an urge to monumentalize, in even the most overtly celebratory projects. Now that we have moved past the postmodern moment of conspicuous indulgence, we might expect sobriety to reign, and for it to be laced with mourning for the days before uncertainty. Yet this is, as many architects have recognized, also a moment of opportunity. There is a chance, now, to conceive others kind of architecture—to begin, in the words of Rafael Viñoly (our third epigram), to "fill the void with beauty," and to go further: to reintroduce an interrogatory architecture.

What Is to Come?

In the wake of 9.11.01, and in response to the broader economic downturn, architects turned to consciously unspectacular buildings or mediating their high rises with internalizing forms—such as the Freedom Tower proposed for the WTC site—that seem to wish to hide in the light. Security became the lead item in many of the professional journals.[1] Yet design remains a hot topic in architecture magazines. Museums continue to be their focus, not the bunkers of prisons, courthouses, or storage facilities. Tadao Ando's Pulitzer Foundation for the Arts in St. Louis attracted much attention on its completion in 2002. It was designed with the goal of creating the maximal contemplative setting for the viewing of the work of just two contemporary artists—Elsworth Kelly, Richard Serra—by the least intrusive of means. It thus showcased the work of three artists: these two, plus Ando himself. Curiously, for what seems to be the purest of art museums, it bills itself as "an unmuseum." What a contrast between this architecture of exacting understatement and the form-fireworks of the Guggenheim Bilbao, where these same artists (along with many of their contemporaries) are the main attractions! Yet both buildings are, in their different ways, temples to Contemporary Art.[2]

In these strange times, private museums remain the template for even the most acultural of new buildings. Charles Gwathmey's design for the U.S. Mission to the United Nations (a reluctant embassy, if there ever was one) echoes the Huntington Hartford Museum built on Columbus Circle in 1964, a Yamasaki-like "Moorish" design by Edward Durrell Stone. Like its contemporary, the World Trade Center, this museum was, even then, an oddly tangential way to dress up a jewel box for art. In Gwathmey's projected UN mission, concrete bollards surround a police kiosk on the street, and project upwards a blast-proof steel sheath gridded with small windows that rises twenty-two stories to the helicopter escape pad on the roof. *Architecture* magazine praises its external image as "a brutally honest emblem of architecture as defense."[3] Hardly the caption language one would have been likely to read before 9.11.01.

Echoes from the era of spectacle architecture continue to resound in parts of the city. Designed before the century's end by Arquitechtonica, the first high-rise to be completed in the aftermath period was the Westin Hotel at Times Square (and penetrating the block through to Eighth Avenue). It is a Miami Vice–meets–movie billboard mix up, homage to the garishness that once used to define this site, now raised to heights—forty-five stories—previously unknown in the area. Its split structure consists entirely of advertisements turning into built forms in the lower sections, and offices and rooms in plain-speak above. The banality of the color-coding (Pre-Columbian ochres for the horizontal section, blue for the skybound stack of rooms) is ersatz Postmodernism. Venturi's decorated shed has returned with a vengeance: on the lower floors the shed is all decoration whereas on the upper floors it is all shed. Talk about the precession of the simulacrum! Times Square itself is a case study of its seemingly relentless unfolding.[4] In the Westin Hotel, simulation architecture has achieved total victory, but, it seems, too late to be of consequence.

Has 9.11.01 put a permanent hole in this fabric, or just a temporary one? If we review the projects emerging slowly from the developers' drawing boards, the effect seems closer to a distortion that exposes, yet again, the unlovely fundamentals of what drives architecture in Manhattan. By mid-2004 the top end of the market returned with bells on. All the starchitects reappeared with stunning designs for residential high-rises: Meier, Gehry, Pelli, Christian Portzamparc, and Enrique Norten. Most blatant of all is Calatrava's design for 80 South Street: an 835-foot-tall core structure, from which cantilever only twelve four-story cubes, each a custom-fitted apartment costing $30 million. Shapes such as these will recast the famous skyline, animating it again, albeit erratically, to an extent as yet unimaginable.[5]

In those economies in which modernity remains new, the drive towards erecting the biggest, most technologically advanced structure was given pause, briefly, by the spectacle of those desperate inhabitants jumping and those wounded towers imploding. The Petronas Towers were erected between 1992 and 1998 as the centerpiece of the redevelopment of a racing track site in Kuala Lampur. New York–based architect Cesar Pelli was enjoined, by booster Prime Minister Mahathir Mohammad, to design a structure that would embody "the spirit of Malaysia." When he asked what that might be, he was given an upbeat account of the country's economic aspirations, its efforts to unite its main population groups (Malay and Chinese), and he was directed to travel the villages. The result was a pair of skyscrapers, linked by a bridge that hints at those found in Chinese paintings, and a profiling of the top floors that suggests mosques seen from some distance. The eighty-eight-story structures, with the addition of a seventy-meter spire, rose ten meters higher than the Sears Tower, Chicago. As symbols of Malaysia's entry in the "Asian tiger" economic race, they quickly fulfilled their iconomic purpose. Economic success also seemed assured, but froze in the aftermath of 9.11.01. Nor did anyone involved in the design of the buildings ever imagine that both structures might become simultaneously unsafe. Evacuation drills had presumed relatively easy escape routes within each building from local fires and limited structural damage, with the sky bridge coming into use in the worst cases. It was presumed that ninety minutes would be sufficient to clear the buildings. Following a bomb scare on September 12, 2001, new procedures were quickly introduced, reducing evacuation time to thirty minutes. Confidence slowly returned. By July 2004, the towers were 87 percent occupied and the 300-store shopping center fully let, contributing 56 percent of the profits of its owners, KLCC Property Holdings, which then set out on a $284 million fund raising to finance further development of the site.[6]

Elsewhere in Asia a similar saga of briefly dented overconfidence unfolded. Taipei 101 faced down a major earthquake during its construction, as well as the new threat of being a potential target. Its design, by C. Y. Lee and Partners, incorporated a large, 660-ton steel ball suspended in its upper floors, a bold device that serves to absorb wind forces and sudden shocks as well as being, when finally painted in gold, a spectacular atrium feature. Rising like an unleashed telescope up into the skies above the city to a height of 1,667 feet (508 meters), Taipei 101 claimed the title of the world's tallest skyscraper. Advertisements promoted it as "a fitting landmark for a country with the foremost growth competitiveness in Asia."[7] China's emerging prominence as a world economic power is nowhere more strikingly evident than in the economic zones of Shenzen and Pudon. Planning for the World Financial Center building in Pudon, Shanghai, ran into impasse when the massive central hole in its upper reaches, designed by Carl Pedersen of New York firm Kohn, Pedersen and Fox, to absorb and deflect the huge wind forces at a height greater than Taipei 101's spire, was read in China as a sign for the rising sun, symbol of Japan's imperial house and expansionist ambitions—a particularly awkward factor given that the commissioner of the building was Japanese businessman Minoru Mori. The architect solved the problem by introducing a horizontal bridge to divide what he saw as an ancient Chinese "moongate" shape into more general symbol of spherical harmony. The overall design turns symbol into form with more subtlety: it twists gradually from a square base through a prism toward the slim circular disc at its top. Concerns about post-9.11.01 security were met by employing WTC engineer Leslie Robertson to devise a structural design that combined vertical megacolumns, horizontal bracing, and cage framing—a combination of support structures that has become typical for tall buildings in the region. The design of the International Finance Center in Hong Kong (known as HK 2) includes widened stairwells, separate elevators for firefighters, and a number of refuge floors. Safety standards in U.S. buildings, even that of the current pacesetter, WTC 7, do not match those in Asia.[8]

The need to build bigger than the others will not, it seems, subside. First Dubai is on the drawing board: at 800 meters it hopes to outstretch all competitors for the imaginable future. Nor has the concept of a World Trade Center evaporated from commercial consciousness: WTC builder Guy Tozzoli directs the World Trade Center Association, an organization that licenses the name and promotes such centers worldwide, most recently in Afghanistan and Saudi Arabia.[9]

Meanwhile, contemporary architects of serious intent have come to acknowledge that, while their profession has, for reasons both positive and negative, achieved unprecedented "hot story" status in the media, it is also, and for much the same reasons, faced with unprecedented challenges and opportunities. In the introduction, I noted Anthony Vidler's formulation of these concerns:

> It is as ... a star that architecture has been called upon to address, if not redress, all the intensely imbricated problems left by the attacks of September 11. It is as a star that architecture has once again entered public consciousness—architecture as advertisement, architecture as lobbyist, architecture as witness, memorial, guide to the future and sponsor of the public will; in all these roles and more architecture is being seen as a palliative, if not a solution.[10]

Does architecture today have the capacity to satisfy the widespread public expectation that goes along with such notoriety? We saw this potential in the Jewish Museum, Berlin, and in a number of similar projects. Many of the most recent high-rises acknowledge as far as possible a set of emergent principles: touch the ground lightly, favor flowing shapes that bend and twist toward the sky, offer changeable facades, design energy generation into the structure, and tend towards invisibility as the building ascends.[11] Even the much-compromised Freedom Tower parades these features.

More suggestive is the plethora of experimental buildings that prioritize ecological principles. A striking metaphorical instance was *blur*, Diller and Scofidio's exposition structure erected offshore into Lac Leman in 2002, its "skin" consisting entirely of vaporized mist. We saw hints of worlding architecture in some aspects of the Ground Zero projects, and concrete instances of specific architecture in projects such as the Knockabout Walkabout house. Altogether, an architecture of interrogation is emerging as a ferment of debate engulfs the profession. Architects are asking themselves questions about how they might meet the new social responsibilities emerging from these changed conditions. A typical example is the 2003 Berlage Institute report "109 provisional attempts to address six

simple and hard questions about what architects do today and where their profession might go tomorrow."[12] All the responses are serious ones: the collection
shows an international profession willing to question itself searchingly. A related
kind of thinking emerges in speculative work such as that of Thomas Zummer. In
response to the Bush administration's adoption of the doctrine of preemptive
strikes as a strategy in its "War on Terror," he envisaged a *preemptive architecture*,
one that invites an unspecified agency to

(1) select any site within a given city, a neighborhood, office complex, park, mer-
cantile or transportation facility. (2) suspend all laws, zoning codes, and any
other such legal determination inscribed on the landform/built environment. All
such codifications shall be null and void for an indeterminate period of time.
Legal and enforcement systems shall likewise be suspended, and any such architectural complexes supplementary to these systems, e.g. courts of law, prisons,
law and police offices, shall be vacated. (3) determine a finite perimeter. (4) devise a system of mathematical transformations, based on population density,
crowd flow, topographical or historical features, that allows for an orderly progression of any segment of any terminal border of the uncoded site into any adjacent or contingent site. Control vectors shall delimit the expansion and size of
the uncoded site, but shall not impede its progression, so that the uncoded 'territory' is mobilized and virtual. Appropriate tracking systems will trace and
record its extent. This is an abstract, hypothetical system based upon models of
contagion, parasitism and capital. It is conceived as coextensive with the contemporary inhabited/built environment.[13]

Zummer makes his point with Borgesian irony, yet the impulse to an-architecture
is rippling through the profession. The question of architecture's social contract
has returned to center stage. This raises sharp issues as to ethical practice, ones
familiar in the world of contemporary art. In his appreciation of Gerhard Richter,
on the eve of his 2002 MoMA retrospective, art critic Michael Kimmelman transformed him before our eyes into an always-already high modernist, an aesthetic
beautician.[14] This had, one hopes, less to do with Richter's project, and more to do
with Kimmelman fulfilling, expertly, his Faustian compact as a critic mediating
difficult art to a public that does not wish to do the work to know this art: the
popular critic's job, he knows, is to present even the most radical art as, ultimately,
harmless. Rem Koolhaas did this to himself, in his book about his design for the
Prada store in Manhattan (downtown on Broadway at Prince, it replaced the
failed Guggenheim SoHo): "If museums now tend towards the store, why not
stores that serve, at least in part, as museums?"[15] Hal Foster's comment is an
ironic "Yeah, right," and then he cites Koolhaas's response to his critics:

I have never thought of our activity as "affecting change." I'm involved with how
"everything" changes in ways that are radically at odds with the core values of
architecture. In spite of its apparent success, I see "architecture" as an endangered brand, and I'm trying to reposition it. To me, it is ironic that the (I would

almost use the word "innocent") core of our activity—to reinvent a plausible relationship between the formal and the social—is so invisible behind the assumption of my cynicism, my alleged lack of criticality, our apparently never-ending surrender.[16]

Can you hear, in these words, in their sliding between language worlds, in their overlaying of value sets, the talisman waxing and waning, mostly waning? The talisman in this case is, of course, the second "core" identified by Koolhaas, the obligation to "reinvent a plausible relationship between the formal and the social" and to do so from a position of radical otherness to the first "core," the all-too-plausible relationship between art and social power that maintains its iniquitous grip on the structure as a whole.

Architecture in the service of power might seem to hold all the cards, but it has failed to look up and out, to grasp the changed nature of the game. It has only a partial purchase on the post-9.11.01 world. Surely the point is that there is no point any longer in striving to learn from Las Vegas as if the consumer-driven market had, in the end, all the answers. Las Vegas itself is not the fastest-growing city in the U.S. because of its success in solving all the issues of amenity for communal living. It is centered on an industry of exploitation, greed, money laundering, and fantasy. Its expansion is a violent consumption of a fragile desert environment. Due to its ubiquity, and the wearing of time, the decorated shed has become a duck there, too. From Las Vegas we should learn what not to do. The single building that attracted most attention in 2003 was the newly opened Walt Disney Concert Hall, a compacted Bilbao devised by Frank Gehry that is already touted as having finally given Los Angeles an unmistakable icon. For all its successes as a work of architecture, Disney Hall may be an elegant, ethereal dinosaur, a simulacrum of a time when the claim could plausibly be made by an act, a style, an idea, or a building that it represented its time. Such claims will continue to be made, and spectacles will be always be staged. Modernism will be revived, again and again, in novel forms, each more vapid than the last.[17] These revivals and novel declarations will be high voices among a crowd of attention-seeking claimants. But the times of staking claim to be able to define the times are past. We build in the aftermath of such excesses and the specter of their implosion.

Visible Cities

At the conclusion to his novel *Invisible Cities* (1972), Italo Calvino brings us back to ethical ground zero. The much-traveled Paolo responds to the despair of the Great Kahn, who believes that "the infernal city" is our only destination, with this:

> The inferno of the living is not something that will be; if there is one, it is what is already here, the inferno we live every day, that we form by being together. There are two ways to escape suffering it. The first is easy for many: accept the inferno and become such a part of it that you can no longer see it. The second is

risky and demands constant vigilance and apprehension: seek and learn to recognize who and what, in the midst of the inferno, are not inferno, and then make
them endure, give them space.[18]

Yamasaki's daydream, that his WTC buildings would stand as a "monument to
world peace," seems now a predestination of exactly the reverse: in their absence,
they have become the mausoleum of the dream of world peace, an icon of its pastness, its apparent impossibility. Yet, just as the imaginary logic of destination is
predestined to entail its own ending, so too does predestination entail the issu-
ing of new beginnings, other aspirations, still further destinations. The great message of the pilgrimage-based religions can be seen in the etymology of the word
"pilgrim" itself. It builds into the Latin word "peregrinus," meaning foreigner, an
elision to "pelegrinus," a shift of nomination: from someone who passes through
our lands, our fields, our places, to someone who comes to them, respectfully, and
then leaves in the same spirit. I see this as a subtle and softening shift, one that
prefigures the kinds of relationships that now seem predestined for all of us: relationships based in understanding the unknowable, rejecting reductiveness of all
kinds, and in forgiving even the unforgivable. These are the principles for the
architecture of contemporaneity as well.

The rebuilt site at Ground Zero—all architecture to come—should be shaped
by heterogeneity, and designed in such a way that it never becomes a single,
supreme symbol of any one ideology, way of life, or faith (and thus a target). It
should never become an iconotype. From inside the ruination of Sarajevo
Lebbeus Woods reminded us that:

> For many today the heterarchical offers the best chance to realize the potential of
> the human. To a religious fundamentalist, the very opposite is true. One differ-
> ence exists, however—the two points of view are neither equivalent nor inter-
> changeable. The heterarchical of necessity embraces the hierarchical, but the
> hierarchical cannot, of necessity, embrace the heterarchical, and will suppress it
> by any means, including international violence and war.[19]

To counter fundamentalism wherever it occurs, the contemporaneity to come
requires an architecture that is no longer subject to spectacle, to none of its many
imperatives, to the specters of its forms. Nor should it retreat into compromise: the
languages of architecture and design after the spectacle are emergent. We are wit-
nessing their difficult birth. At the WTC on 9.11.01, 2,383 civilians, 343 firefighters,
23 police officers, and 10 hijackers died. Many people throughout the world still
feel confident enough to apportion these dead among the labels "hero" or "savior,"
"victim," "martyr," or "coward," confining them neatly into just one each of these
categories—or they do so unthinkingly. In the memorializing process at Ground
Zero, great care has been taken to exclude the attackers—including DNA testing of
body parts. Yet there are millions of others in the world who distribute the same list
of words differently to describe exactly the same human beings. This should give
us pause. If something so blatantly out there—an event and a place about which

57. Djenné, ruins of the ancient mosque. Postcard issued by the Collection Générale Fortier, Dakar, 1895. [public domain]

the illusion exists that almost everything is not only known but is repeated end-lessly in multiple media—can be seen in such utterly opposite ways, then perhaps it just is complex, even heterogeneous, and should remain so. The conditions of contemporaneity cannot be wished away. If it is inevitable that the former WTC site contain a temple of the money-managers, and a bazaar, then there should also be in among its mix a great—in the religious sense—but modest—in its stance to the world—mosque.

If I think of a mosque in this context, I think of the Great Mosque, or Friday Mosque, at Djenné, in Mali (illus. 57). It has emerged from a long and complex history to become an architectural iconotype for West Africa. It has been destroyed by non-Muslims, and by a Muslim emperor who wished to replace it with a more modest structure reflective of his regime, who bypassed the prohibition against destroying holy places by ordering the blocking of its drains, thus allowing the rain to erode it. French colonists have claimed its authorship, it has been reproduced frequently in the French African sections of world expositions, and a to-scale copy of it was built on the Cote d'Azur. More importantly for the approach I am proposing, the actual Great Mosque at Djenné is a structure that requires that parts of it, especially its stucco covering, be continuously rebuilt, by those who use it, year after year. This is commonly done on feast days each year (illus. 58). It is, then, a building that requires communal effort to keep its shape in the climate, a determined, selfless application of collective will to keep it stand-ing. In this sense, it symbolizes its community, embodies that community; it is the material form of shared effort.[20] When asked what he would build on Ground Zero, Frank Gehry did not give a direct answer. But he did say that he had set his

students the task of designing a structure to house a "soaring public space . . . imagine Central Park with a roof over it," a spiritual (although not religious) space, "a symbol of openness and tolerance" (perhaps not unlike, in feeling, Christo and Jean-Claude's *The Gates* project, realized in the Park during February 2005). For inspiration, Gehry took his students to see the Hagia Sofia.[21] And in October 2004 he, too, joined the galaxy of starchitects accumulating at Ground Zero, as designer of the performing arts center.[22]

When it comes to building, there is a world of difference between the people of Djenné and Frank Gehry. Building up and out of difference is what distinguished the conceptual underpinning of the Jewish Museum, Berlin. Libeskind's WTC design has some of the same elements, and the potential for many more. The step he is being asked—by the world—to take is one that he took in Berlin but that will require, in the chimera of aftermath, the stunned anger of the survivors, and the implacability of the economists and the security freaks, extraordinary tact, judgment, and inventiveness: to design into the project forgiveness of the attackers, and to do so within a framework that will show

58. Carollee Pelos, market day at Djenné, Mali, 1983. 1983, photograph. Source: Carollee Pelos Estate. From Jean-Louis Bourgeois, *Spectacular Vernacular* (New York: Aperture, 1989), 75.

to the world the advantages of reaching for reconciliation in spite of the rush of events towards the irreconcilable. In the conditions of contemporaneity, it is precisely from this world of difference that the architecture of contemporaneity is to come.

Two Sightings: Visual Culture and Iconomy

> They broke our city. I'm among the newest of New Yorkers, but even people who have never set foot in Manhattan have felt their wounds deeply, because New York in our time is the beating heart of the visible world, tough-talking, spirit-dazzling, Walt Whitman's "city of orgies, walks and joys," his "proud and passionate city—mettlesome, mad, extravagant city!" To this bright capital of the visible, the forces of invisibility have dealt a dreadful blow. No need to say how dreadful; we all saw it, we are all changed by it, and must now ensure that the wound is not mortal, that the world of what is seen triumphs over what is cloaked, what is perceptible only through the effects of its awful deeds.[23]

Novelist Salman Rushdie speaks on these matters with a double authenticity. His novels conjure the desperate operatics of cultural difference and transference, and he has braved fatwas calling for his head. In his novels and in his life, he has shown a subtlety that is less evident in the metaphors for which he reached after 9.11.01. Light against darkness, in this context, trips a chain: Enlightenment against Superstition, democracy versus despotism, the West over the East. Art historian Otto Karl Werckmeister was equally moved, but more precise. Writing in Berlin, also in October 2002, after a lifetime devoted to the study of medieval imagery of apocrypha, he was alert to recurrence over a longer span and across more of the world:

> The color pictures of September 11 seem to face us as testimony of an incontrovertible reality that legitimates the invisible military campaign [the "War on Terror" in Afghanistan] in the public sphere. Distributed by agencies, they are not attributed to an individual photographer, are linked to no subjective perspective. All the more transcendent is their effect. In the real time of the television reports, the aerial attacks on the World Trade Center transpired as though in a panorama. After that, the videotapes of the reports were repeated endlessly. The visual symbolism of reality was perhaps foreseen by the attackers. In any case, it corresponds to an Islamic form of apocalyptic thinking to which the ideals of the Holy War and Martyrdom are linked. This symbolism finds its ready-made resonance in the Christian apocalyptic notions of the victims under attack. They offer both sides in the conflict totally believable symbolic scenery, both for the attack on the globalized capitalist system and for its defense. It is unnecessary for one to consider what is at stake in the conflict. The apocalyptic pictures of catastrophe outshine the darkness in which the planning and the execution of terror attacks have remained up to this day, just as they outshine the political opacity of the counterattack.[24]

In this account, visual culture is recognized as thoroughly embedded in all the relevant economic, political, social, and psychic formations, in all these forces as they contend, but also as specifically visual in its workings. And as significantly so—that is, with effects in all these other spheres as a consequence of the specifics of its visuality. What Rushdie presents as a universal battle between the forces of good and evil, however mitigated with elements of the other each might be, Werckmeister shows to be a multiplicitous global struggle, with at once an ancient lineage and a very contemporary presence. Iconophilia and iconoclasm, a warring over the long haul, and across vast tracts of indifference to the visual, has come home to the iconozone—playground of capitalism triumphant—with a bang. Two, in fact. One after each other. And then, again and again, seemingly forever.

In this book I have explored the role of a visual art, contemporary architecture, in three distinct settings—negotiated cultural exchange, mutual destruction, and aftermath, recovery, and reinvention. Intertwined with this has been an examination of how different tendencies in contemporary architecture stood in both contrast and complicity with the event architecture of a particular act of spectacular terrorism. From a methodological point of view, explorations such as this one throw the productive tension between the conventional disciplines devoted to the study of the visual arts not just out of gear but into fast-forward, imminent crash mode. Novelist J. G. Ballard had it right: contemporary experience just is like this.

Aby Warburg saw much of this over a century ago. Visual culture studies have come a long way since then.[25] In the case of the 9.11.01 attacks we face an emergent phenomenon—not an unprecedented one by any means, but a striking reconfiguration of long-running forces of destination and predestination, of ordering, destruction, and, we can only hope, reconciliation. This kind of "object" will call more and more for our understanding, and to achieve that, I submit, we will need to show more and more disciplinary flexibility. We cannot expect the discourses of art and architectural history or criticism, even at their most reconstituted, their most engaged, to entirely (and from within their own traditions) encompass the 9.11.01 "image-event" and all the flows of which it is an instance. Nor would we expect cultural, film, and media studies to do so, not when they remain in isolation from reconstituted art and architectural history and from engaged criticism (although we would expect them to cover more of the implications). But we have a right to expect that a judicious fusion of reconstituted art history, engaged criticism, and critical cultural, film, and media studies, along of course with all other appropriate interpretive schemas (from political science to raw gut reactions), would do so. It is this judicious fusion, this careful blend of precise judgments, which I am advocating as not only a more effective methodology but also a necessary one. It would be a study of visual culture worthy of the name. To invoke the maxim of La Rochefoucauld with which I began: such a scholarly enterprise would be one that looks at both the sun and death, straight in their faces.

These are old issues—indeed, ancient ones. The point is that they are incessantly, unevenly updated. In our current situation, not that of postmodernity but of contemporaneity, the persisting elements—time, power, and picturing—are reshaped by the basic qualities of contemporaneity—the untimely, inequity, and multiplicity. It is these processes that we see at work all around us these days. They are reconstituting our objects of inquiry around issues of temporality, struggle, and figuring as fast as—it seems, at times, faster than—we can revise our methods of understanding them.

Waiting . . .

9.11.01 was, among much else, a meeting of spectacular terrorism with spectacle architecture, a fatal but also generative clash between two of the many formations and deformations that, taken together, constitute the iconomy in the era of contemporaneity. Usually, these two keep their distance across the iconoscape. For a moment, however, they were the flashpoint at which the two-sided mirror of cultural difference exploded into everybody's real.

As the fissure seals over, while larger forces go into direct conflict, as displacement occurs and forgetting takes place, the 9.11.01 eruption will echo throughout the iconozone, and far beyond it. Spectacular terrorism went into hiding, for a time, only to reappear—albeit in smaller, more individuated forms—in the Palestine/Israel struggle and in occupied Iraq, the new target opportunity par excellence. In response, state terrorism is out there, waving its bludgeon about its head. For all of us, waiting for the next attack is now a permanent part of everyday life. New York has been the central city in this story so far, but 9.11.01 gave an obvious warning that the iconotypes of Washington were the main target. Washington is, after all, the fastest-growing concentration of the kinds of power most central to the mechanics of the U.S. Emperium. The war launched in Iraq in March 2003 was actually a battle in a larger ongoing and probably ceaseless war, the economic bases and iconomic form of which are out there for all to see. Waiting for the emperium to strike again is, now, an expectation shared by peoples all over world. So is waiting for the next attack by a special-interest group, which can—as the March 2004 explosions in Madrid and those of July 2005 in London show—occur anywhere that the emperium is seen to reach. It can occur within the heart of the emperium itself, where the language of iconomy reigns, and where a consciousness that it is a war zone has finally penetrated. On releasing its long-awaited, oft-deferred report in July 2004, the chairman of the Commission of Inquiry commented on the impact of the attacks: "They inflicted unbearable trauma on our people, and at the same time turned the international order upside down."[26] Soon after, Homeland Security Secretary Tom Ridge issued an official warning to prepare for attacks on "iconic" financial institutions in New York City, Washington, and Newark, N.J.[27] That these advisories seemed timely, in an election campaign, as a counter to a successful Democratic Party convention, and that it soon emerged that they were based mostly on pre-9.11.01 information, blunted their impact somewhat. Yet the larger picture remains constant. Persisting between strikes is a state of being in the present that 9.11.01 has made sure we all share. Just in case anyone might forget that fact, Osama bin Laden himself intervened in the 2004 U.S. Presidential campaign, via a video broadcast on Al-Jazeera on October 28, with a direct appeal to the American people to turn against their warmongering leadership and an implied threat to repeat large-scale attacks unless those on Muslims in the Middle East desisted.[28] We no longer need bin Laden to remind us that we live perpetually between events, linked by the iconomy, trapped in the trailings of aftermath. With so many well-targeted, highly significant, yet messy and unfinished events accumulating, it may be that we will live in contemporaneity forever, and that there might never again be an after to aftermath.

Contemporary architecture is striving to regroup itself, and to do so under the most intense media scrutiny, as a spectacle of recovery and reinvention. To what degree it will succeed at this is less important than how it does so. Attractor architecture will retreat before the quieter, more reflective, and longer-term requirements of community. Open communality will have to find ways of negotiating the tendency to all-pervasive control in governmentalities built increasingly around surveillance, security, and militarization. Interrogatory architecture will have to acknowledge, far more than it has to date, the demands of the conditions of contemporaneity. The rest of the world beyond the brief can no longer be ignored, or merely alluded to via design details. The multiplicity, the untimeliness, and the inequities of the world are not contextual factors. For a critical architecture, they never have been. They are the labyrinthine fundament of contemporaneity, at once its ground plan and its interstitial passaging. They have always been there and will be there at the end, when actual structures have disappeared into the background of everyday life, succumbed to violence, collapsed into ruin or simply, ultimately, returned to the earth.

NOTES

INTRODUCTION

1. Staehle's *Untitled*, 2001, is illustrated and described in Alexi Worth, "Centerfold: Wolfgang Staehle's *Untitled*, 2001," *Artforum*, November 2001, 129. A sequence of stills from James Naudet's film for Gamma is reproduced in Giorgio Baravalle/A de. MO, *newyorkseptembereleventwothousandandone* (New York: de. MO, 2001, np.). For Pavel Hlava's story, see James Glanz, "A Rare View of Sept.11, Overlooked," *New York Times*, September 7, 2003, pages 1, 27. I thank Patricia Leighton for alerting me to the imagery of the words on the sides of the airplanes on 9.11.01.

2. This image was often reproduced, beginning with the front page of the *New York Times* itself, on September 12. For a sample of newspaper coverage, mainly in the U.S., see the Poynter Institute, *September 11, 2001: A Collection of Newspaper Front Pages* (Kansas City: Andrew McMeel Publishing, 2001). See also the New York Times, *A Nation Challenged: A Visual History of 9/11 and Its Aftermath* (New York: Callaway, 2002). For the Fairbanks video see Magnum Photos, *New York September 11 by Magnum Photographers* (New York: powerHouse Books, 2001), 4–5.

3. Interview with bin Laden, conducted November 8, 2001, in *Guardian Weekly*, November 15–21, 2001, 3.

4. I allude here to Sheldon Rampton, *Weapons of Mass Deception: The Uses of Propaganda in Bush's War on Iraq* (New York: Jeremy P. Tarcher/Penguin, 2003). The study details the Renton Group's involvement in Republican politics over a long period, and in the War in Iraq in particular.

5. The story was thoroughly pursued by Seymour M. Hersh, "Annals of National Security: Torture at Abu Ghraib," *New Yorker*, May 10, 2004, 42–47. The place of these photographs in the image war over Iraq is analyzed in Frank Rich, "Saving Private Englund," *New York Times*, May 16, 2004, AR 1, 8. See Steven Strasser, *The Abu Ghraib Investigations: The Official Report of the Independent Panel and Pentagon on the Shocking Prisoner Abuse in Iraq* (New York: Public Affairs, 2004), and Mark Danner, *Torture and Truth: America, Abu Ghraib, and the War on Terror* (New York: New York Review Books, 2005).

6. See, for example, Anthony Giddens, *Runaway World: How Globalisation Is Reshaping Our Lives* (London: Profile Books, 2000). Aspects of the pivotal role of visual culture in these developments are canvassed in Naomi Klein, *No Logo* (London: Flamingo, 2001). An important trigger to the idea of iconomy was Arjun Appadurai's concept of the changed "landscapes of experience" under the impacts of globalization and his account of the definitive importance of both their internal dynamics and the trafficking between them. He distinguishes "ethnoscapes," "ideoscapes," "technoscapes," "financescapes," and "mediascapes." See his Appadurai, "Disjuncture and Difference in the Global Cultural Economy," *Public Culture* 2 (spring 1990): 1–24, and his *Modernity at Large: Cultural Dimensions of Globalization* (Minneapolis: University of Minnesota Press, 1997). An approach complementary to mine is Retort, *Afflicted Powers: Capital and Spectacle in a New Age of War* (London: Verso, 2005).

7. *Oxford English Dictionary Online*, 2002, derived from many earlier print versions, such as that of the *Complete Oxford English Dictionary*, 2nd ed., 1989.

8. This begins to be an answer to the conundrum posited in Fredric Jameson, *A Singular Modernity: Essay on the Ontology of the Present* (London: Verso, 2002).

9. Terry Smith, "The Political Iconomy of Iconotypes and the Architecture of Destination," *Architecture Theory Review*, vol. 7, no. 2 (2002): 1–44.

10. Ada Louise Huxtable, "An Exercise in Culture Shock," in *Goodbye History, Hello Hamburger: An Anthology of Architectural Delights and Disasters* (Washington: Preservation Press, 1986), 81.

11. Anthony Vidler, "Redefining the Public Realm," in "109 provisional attempts to address six simple and hard questions about what architects do today and where their profession might go tomorrow," *hunch, the Berlage institute report,* no. 6/7 (summer 2003): 469. On the buzz that contemporary architecture attracts, see Hal Foster, *Design and Crime (and Other Diatribes)* (London and New York: Verso, 2002).

12. Peter Eisenman and Cynthia Davidson, "The End of the Spectacle," in "109 provisional attempts to address six simple and hard questions about what architects do today and where their profession might go tomorrow," *hunch, the Berlage institute report,* no. 6/7 (summer 2003), 168.

13. Kenneth Frampton, "On the Predicament of Architecture at the Turn of the Century," *Labour, Work, and Architecture* (London: Phaidon, 2002), 18.

14. Collingwood's warning is this: "Contemporary history embarrasses a writer not only because he knows too much, but also because what he knows is too undigested, too unconnected, too atomic. It is only after close and prolonged reflection that we begin to see what was essential and what was important, so see why things happened as they did, and to write history instead of newspapers." R. G. Collingwood, *Speculum Mentis, or The Map of Knowledge* (Oxford: Clarendon Press, 1924), 236. Another Englishman made the same point, much earlier, and more pointedly: "who-so-ever in writing a moderne Historie, shall follow the truth too near the heeles, it may happily strike out his teethe." Sir Walter Raleigh, *The History of the World* (Temple University Press, 1971), 80.

CHAPTER 1

1. Blake Eskin, "The Incredible Growing Art Museum," *Artnews,* vol. 100, no. 9 (October 2001): 142–45.

2. Glenn D. Lowry, cited by Nicolai Ouroussoff, "Art for Architecture's Sake," *Los Angeles Times,* March 31, 2002, F4.

3. See Adrian Ellis, "Museum Boom Will Be Followed by Bust," *Art Newspaper,* no. 116 (July–August 2001): 14. For sober assessments of the same phenomenon at the earliest stage of its development, see Martin Feldstein, ed., *The Economics of Art Museums* (Chicago: University of Chicago Press, 1991), and Olin Robison, Robert Freeman, and Charles A. Riley eds., *The Arts in the World Economy* (Hanover: Salzburg Seminars and University Presses of New England, 1994).

4. On Kahn see Terry Smith, *Making the Modern: Industry, Art, and Design in America* (Chicago: University of Chicago Press, 1993), ch. 2, and Brian Carter, ed., *Albert Kahn: Inspiration for the Modern* (Ann Arbor: University of Michigan Museum of Art, 2001).

5. A sloping ramp appears in Wright's preliminary sketches for the Guggenheim Museum, New York, as early as September 1943, and comes to dominate its design agenda from then onwards. Wright spoke and wrote often of his intention to change the traditional museum plan, with its sequence of rooms arranged as if in a palace, and of his objections to the "white cube" favored by modernist curators and artists. Instead, he sought an open plan within which a viewer could choose his or her own pathway through essentially domestic spaces. A letter of 1958 is perhaps the clearest statement: "Walls slant gently outward to form a giant spiral for a well-defined purpose: a new unity between beholder, painting and architecture. As planned, in the easy downward drift of the viewer on the giant spiral, pictures are not to be seen bolt upright as though painted on the wall behind them. Gently inclined, faced slightly upward to the viewer and to the light in accord with the upward sweep of the spiral, the paintings themselves are emphasized in themselves and not hung 'square' but gracefully yield to movement as set up by these slightly-curving massive walls." Manuscript, June 1958, FLW Archives, cited in Bruce Brooks Pfeiffer, "A Temple of Spirit," in Solomon R. Guggenheim Foundation, *The Solomon R. Guggenheim Museum* (New York: Solomon R. Guggenheim Foundation, 1995), 7. See also Frank Lloyd Wright, *The Guggenheim Correspondence,* selected and with commentary by Bruce Brooks Pfeiffer (Fresno: California State University Press; Carbondale: Southern Illinois University Press; London: Architectural Press, 1987). Interesting here is Wright's deep insight into the spatial conceptions of the artists most assiduously collected in the days of the Guggenheim's earlier incarnation, the Museum of Non-Objective Painting, in particular its concentration on Constructivist painting. This art was calibrated in such ways as to banish its framing edges from the viewer's perception in

order to engage his or her consciousness in the interplay of interior surfaces, forms, colors, suggestions. Wright's sketches show that he thought of quite close hangings, in which these spatial concentrations could interact with others nearby. When the museum opened, however, director James Johnson Sweeney insisted on flat white walls (Wright commented that this was equivalent to taking the high C as the background for all orchestral tonality), and the isolated hanging of paintings projected out from the walls on spikes, a jarring that has haunted the museum ever since. On this matter, and the subsequent fate of this much-modified building, see Neil Levine, *The Architecture of Frank Lloyd Wright* (Princeton: Princeton University Press, 1996), ch. 10, and Victoria Newhouse, *Towards a New Museum* (New York: Monacelli Press, 1998), 162–68. Wright's comment is in *The Guggenheim Correspondence*, 248.

6. Cited in Margaret J. King, "Theme Park Thesis," *Museum News* (September/October 1990): 60–62.

7. Interview with Philip Jodidio, *Connaissance des Arts, Guggenheim Bilbao* (special issue, 2000): 19.

8. Kurt W. Forster, "Frank O. Gehry Guggenheim Museum," in Vittorio Magnago Lampugnani and Angeli Sachs, *Museums for a New Millennium: Concepts Projects Buildings* (Munich, London, and New York: Prestel, 1999), 129.

9. Guy Debord, *Society of the Spectacle* (Detroit: Black and Red, 1977; New York, Zone Books, 1994).

10. For an example of bedazzlement by technology, see Kurt Forster, "The Museum as Civic Catalyst," in *Frank O. Gehry: Museo Guggenheim Bilbao* (Stuttgart: Edition Axel Menges, 1998), 11.

11. Sabine Theil-Siling, ed., *Icons of Architecture, The Twentieth Century* (Munich, London, and New York: Prestel, 1998), 182–83.

12. Newhouse, *Towards a New Museum*, 259.

13. Cited in Cossje van Bruggen, *Frank O. Gehry Guggenheim Bilbao* (New York: Solomon R. Guggenheim Foundation, 1997), 115.

14. Van Bruggen, *Frank O. Gehry Guggenheim Bilbao* is the most complete presentation of the building itself and its design process.

15. Cited in *Connaissance des Arts, Guggenheim Bilbao* (special issue, 2000): 22. Chartres was actually built 1194–1260 CE.

16. A dramatic view up into the atrium is the front cover image on Newhouse's *Towards a New Museum*. This neatly encapsulates her argument. An external view of the titanium sails at sunset shares the cover of the fourth edition of David Wilkins, Bernard Schultz, and Kathryn M. Linduff, *Art Past, Art Present* (Englewood Cliffs, N.J.: Prentice Hall, 2001). And alongside Richard Meier's Getty Museum of Art, it is the culminating work considered in the 2000 edition of Sam Hunter, John Jacobus, and Daniel Wheeler, *Modern Art: Painting, Sculpture, and Architecture* (New York: Abrams, 2000), 440.

17. The phrasing in Osama bin Laden's, used in describing the nature of the Al Qaeda targets in the United States on September 11, 2001, during an interview with him conducted on November 8, 2001, and published in the *Guardian Weekly*, November 15–21, 2001, 3.

18. *Connaissance des Arts, Guggenheim Bilbao* (special issue, 2000): 40.

19. Stanislaus von Moos, "A Museum Explosion: Fragments of an Overview," in Lampugnani and Sachs, *Museums for a New Millennium: Concepts Projects Buildings*, 17.

20. For details as to the local circumstances, see "Negotiating the Center in Bilbao," in Selma Holo, *Beyond the Prado: Museums and Identity in Democratic Spain* (Washington: Smithsonian Institution Press, 1999), ch. 6, and Joseba Zulaika, *Crónica de una seducción: El museo Guggenheim Bilbao* (Madrid: Editorial Nevea, 1997).

21. Philip Jodidio, "Architecture," *Guggenheim Bilbao* (special issue of *Connaissance des Arts*, 2000): 27.

22. Allan Sekula, "Between the Net and the Deep Blue Sea (Rethinking the Traffic in Photographs)," *October* 102 (fall 2002): 18.

23. Ibid., 20.

24. Ibid., 20. Guggenheim Bilbao director Juan Ignacio Vidarte responded to Sekula's criticisms in *October* 104 (spring 2003): 157–59.

25. David van Zanten, private communication, April 2003. From this perspective, the museum might seem—to reverse Deleuze and Guattari and to invoke a trope from sci-fi animation—a creature that was only organs.

26. Sekula, "Between the Net and the Deep Blue Sea," 21.

27. In *Frank Gehry Architect, 2002 Guggenheim Museum*, a calendar published on the occasion of the exhibition "Frank Gehry Architect," Guggenheim Museum, May–August 2001, models of the proposed design are pictured in situ on the page for the month of March. The relevant text reads: "The rigid forms characteristic of a skyscraper—the quintessence of New York architecture—are fractured and recombined with a curvilinear body suggestive of the water's fluid movement and the energy of the city." The project was aborted in January 2003. We will return to it in chapter 3.

28. Former director of the Los Angeles Museum of Contemporary Art Richard Koshalek is not alone in boosting Gehry as the only architect of the turn of the twenty-first century, and his design for the $274 million Disney Hall as better than that of Bilbao. See his essay in *Symphony: Frank Gehry's Walt Disney Concert Hall*, introduction by Frank Gehry, preface by Deborah Borda, photographs by Grant Mudford, essays by Richard Koshalek et al. (New York: Whitney Museum of American Art/Abrams, 2003). The central concern of Gehry's design for the hall was to create an instrument for listening. Thus, much effort went into hiring the best possible acoustician. The centerpiece is the acoustic box. (On its qualities as a music hall, see Alex Ross, "Kingdom Come: The Magic Sound of Disney Hall," *New Yorker*, November 17, 2003, 164–67.) Once we get outside the main hall, however, it is notable that volumes and spaces are created by adaptation from the signature style of several contemporary artists. The inner foyers and walkways elaborate the heavy metal assemblages of Mark di Suvero. The overall, external "composition" is "resolved"—to use Gehry's own terms—by covering these spaces with—to use my own parallels—the tensioned steel of Richard Serra according to a rhythmic logic in the manner of the swirling scallops of David Reed. Is it too much of a stretch to see, in these billowing shapes, an echo of an iconic image of Hollywood eroticism: Garry Winogrand's famous 1957 photograph of Marilyn Monroe, on the set of *The Seven-Year Itch*, delighted as she scarcely manages to stop the subway draft blowing up her skirt? Such fusions are common in contemporary design but are barely conceivable within the most committed contemporary sculpture and painting (including that of Serra). They come alive in Gehry's extraordinary synthetic drive. A distinctively Gehry work of art, one that exceeds the atrium at Bilbao as a dazzling, breathtaking invitation to transcendence, is the "ceiling" of the Patrons Room. Unfortunately, it is accessible only to a few. As an image, Disney Hall reprises the look of the Sydney Opera House and is being so assiduously boosted by local publicists that it is only a matter of time before it attains a similar degree and depth of iconicity. Among review essays, see Martin Filler, "Victory at Bunker Hill," *New York Review of Books*, October 23, 2003, 55–60, and Alexander Linklater, "Frank Gehry: The Master Builder," *Prospect* 89 (August 2003), www.prospect-magazine.co.uk.

29. Forster, "Frank O. Gehry Guggenheim Museum," in *Museums for a New Millennium*, 129.

30. As set out by Martin Jay, *Downcast Eyes: The Denigration of Vision in Twentieth-Century French Thought* (Berkeley: University of California Press, 1993), and explored by Jonathan Crary in *Techniques of the Observer: On Vision and Modernity in the Nineteenth Century* (Cambridge: MIT Press, 1990).

31. Gilles Deleuze and Felix Guattari, *Anti-Oedipus* (Minneapolis: University of Minnesota Press, 1983), 9–16.

32. Designed in the 1230s, the cathedral at Beauvais is perhaps the most famous cautionary tale in the history of European architecture. Its builders strove to raise its choir vaults to such unprecedented heights that it collapsed. Instead of turning to the transept and nave, they recommenced the choir, completing that work at the end of the fourteenth century. In the mid sixteenth century work began on a huge tower and spire, which also quickly collapsed. Repairing it used up resources that might have gone to building the nave (and which, technically, should have preceded the tower and spire). Only a portion of the nave was ever built, yet that rose to 157 feet, in a height-to-width proportion of 3.36:1. Outreaching Amiens, the choir remained the tallest of all Gothic buildings, and brought the High Gothic phase to an end. See Jean Bony, *French Gothic Architecture of the 12th and 13th Centuries* (Berkeley: University of California Press, 1983), 289–95. This dramatically truncated structure seemed destined, from its inception, to become a self-perpetuating ruin.

33. See Robert Shiller, *The New Financial Order: Risk in the 21st Century* (Princeton: Princeton University Press, 2003). More broadly, see Ulrich Beck, *Risk Society: Towards a New Modernity* (London: Sage, 1992).

CHAPTER 2

1. Peter Hall, *Great Planning Disasters*, 2nd ed. (Berkeley: University of California Press, 1982), 138.

2. Ibid. Hall's other chapters include studies of London's third airport, its motorways, the Concorde, the BART system in San Francisco, and what he terms the "near-disasters" of California's new campuses and the British National Library.

3. Research published on the SOH website, www.soh.nsw.gov.au, "Our Past", was helpful for this section.

4. See Laila Haglund, "Sydney Harbour: Aboriginal Context," in *Sydney Opera House in Its Harbour Setting: Nomination ... for Inscription on the World Heritage List ...*, jointly prepared by the Commonwealth Department of the Environment, Sports and Territories and the New South Wales Department of Urban Affairs and Planning, unpublished, 1996. See also Isabel McBryde, *Guests of the Governor: Aboriginal Residents of the First Government House* (Sydney: Friends of the First Government House Site, 1989).

5. The requirements were spelt out as follows:
There shall be two halls—one large and one small hall. The large hall should seat between 3,000–3,500 persons. The small hall should seat approximately 1,200 persons.
    1. The large hall to be designed for use for the following purposes:
        (a) Symphony Concerts (including organ music and soloists).
        (b) Large-scale Opera.
        (c) Ballet and Dance.
        (d) Choral.
        (e) Pageants and Mass Meetings.
    2. The small hall to be designed for use for the following purposes:
        (a) Dramatic Presentations.
        (b) Intimate Opera.
        (c) Chamber Music.
        (d) Concerts and Recitals.
        (e) Lectures.
From *An International Competition for a National Opera House at Bennelong Point, Sydney, NSW, Australia* (Sydney: Government Printer, [1955]).

6. New South Wales Government, *Opera House Competition: Memorandum to Competitors* (Sydney, 1956), 1. On the Sydney Harbour Bridge see, for example, Peter Spearritt, *The Sydney Harbour Bridge* (Sydney: George Allen & Unwin, 1982). Bridges have, of course, been used to unite, or mark the divisions, between different peoples for centuries. An example relevant to this discussion is the Stari Most over the Neretva River at Mostar, built in 1566 to connect the outer reaches of the Ottoman Empire to Ragusa, a wealthy city-state we know as Dubrovnik. Its masons cut the marble stone in both the Ottoman and European manner—the one straight on, the other sideways—yet created a structure ever since admired, by visitors from all cultures, for its beauty. After the fall of the Ottoman Empire in 1870, the Stari Most connected the contending ethnicities of the region until November 9, 1993, when, in the midst of the Croat-Muslim madness of the time, two days of sustained artillery fire managed to bring it down. Now, it is being rebuilt under the direction of a French engineer. Whether it will become the agency of reconciliation that it once seemed to be remains to be seen. See Michael Ignatieff, "When a Bridge Is Not a Bridge," *New York Times Magazine*, October 27, 2002, 56–59.

7. New South Wales Government, *Opera House Competition: Memorandum to Competitors* (Sydney, 1956), 2. The idea that Saarinen may have been inspired by Utzon is advanced in Peter Meyers, "The First Monument of the Third City: Harry Ingham Ashworth's International Architectural Competition for the Sydney Opera House," lecture to Utzon Symposium, Aalborg University, August 2003. In 1957 Saarinen prepared two crayon perspective sketches of Utzon's design for the state premier to assist in his comprehension of the design. That he was thinking of his New York commission is evident in the southern perspective, reproduced by John Murphy, *The Studio of Jørn Utzon: Creating the Sydney Opera House* (Sydney: Historic Houses of Trust, 2004), 3.

8. *Sydney Morning Herald*, cited by John Yoemans, *The Other Taj Mahal* (Camberwell: Longmans, 1973), 35–36. For further information on the design and reception of the opera house, see the following: the Dennis Wolanski Archive of the Sydney Opera House, held by the Sydney

Opera House Trust; State Records, New South Wales; Michael Baume, *The Sydney Opera House Affair* (Sydney: Nelson, 1967); Yeomans, *The Other Taj Mahal*; Pat Westcott, *The Sydney Opera House* (Sydney: Ure Smith, 1965); Francis D. K. Ching, *Architecture: Form, Space, and Order* (New York: Van Nostrand Reinhold, 1979); Roger H. Clark and Michael Pause, *Precedents in Architecture* (New York: Van Nostrand Reinhold, 1985); Phillip Drew, "Utzon, Jørn," *International Dictionary of Architects and Architecture*, vol. 1, *Architects* (Detroit: St. James Press, 1993); Phillip Drew, Jørn Utzon, and Anthony Browell, *Sydney Opera House* (London: Phaidon Press, 1995); Françoise Fromonot, *Jørn Utzon: The Sydney Opera House* (Milan: Electa/Ginko, 1998); Richard Weston, *Utzon: Inspiration, Vision, Architecture* (Hellerup: Edition Bløndal, 2002). See also note 12 below.

9. Utzon, "The Sydney Opera House," *Zodiac* 14 (1965): 49.

10. Ibid.

11. Ibid.

12. Lucy Grace Ellem, "Utzon's Sydney Opera House," *Australian Art and Architecture*, ed. Anthony Bradley and Terry Smith (Melbourne: Oxford University Press, 1980), 192–209. If Ellem's critique is accepted, the tiles may be regarded as an attempt to capture the bedazzlement of purely aesthetic response, after the reality of it has been conceded to design compromise.

13. Utzon's comment was made in a television interview, *This Day Tonight*, ABC Television, 1972. An interesting polemic, written close to the events, and full of documents, is Elias Duek-Cohen, *Utzon and the Sydney Opera House: Statement in the Public Interest* (Sydney: Morgan Publications, 1967; new edition with addenda 1998). Hall, *Great Planning Disasters*, ch. 6, covers the details of the dispute, as do Baume, *The Sydney Opera House Affair*, and Yeomans, *The Other Taj Mahal*.

14. This interpretation is most powerfully argued in Sylvia Lawson, *The Outside Story: A Novel* (South Yarra: Hardie Grant Books, 2003).

15. It could be argued that the lottery was an elaborate mechanism to induce the Australian working and lower middle classes—overwhelmingly the main ticket buyers—to pay for a venue that staged high culture for the Australian upper classes. There is much to this, but its edge is blunted somewhat by three things. The SOH has evolved into an event center for Sydney, staging a wide range of entertainment (with opera being among the least of its regular offerings). Second, surveys of public opinion have for decades shown a willingness—on instinctive grounds of the social good—by Australians of broad tastes to support aspirations to high culture on the part of their fellow citizens, even to fund, through their taxes, elite cultural activity from which they feel excluded. Indeed, with the lottery ticket Australians whose taste in entertainment did not include opera could win, symbolically, twice: they could register an imaginary membership in a class to which they did not belong, while at the same time buy out of having to attend an art performance not intended for them and avoid having to spend their leisure time in the company of people with whom they would not wish to associate. More broadly, there is the win for everybody: the sight of the building itself, an experience open to all who go to Sydney Harbour or who catch an image of it on television, in a magazine, or on a postcard.

16. Hall, *Great Planning Disasters*, xvii.

17. Paraphrased from C. P. Mountford, *Ayers Rock: Its People, Their Beliefs, and Their Art* (Sydney: Angus & Roberston, 1965) by A. W. Reed and published in A. W. Reed, *Aboriginal Myths, Legends, and Fables* (Sydney: Reed New Holland, 2003), 154–56. Spelling of the names of Aboriginal tribes and ancestor figures varies according to three systems of transliteration. More recent accounts of the history of the Rock include Mititulu Community and Parks Australia, "Uluru-Kata Tjuta National Park," in *The Oxford Companion to Aboriginal Art and Culture*, ed. Sylvia Klienert and Margo Neale (Melbourne: Oxford University Press, 2000), 52–56; anonymous, *Some Anangu Perceptions of Uluru, Uluru (Ayers Rock-Mount Olga) National Park* (Canberra: Australian National Parks and Wildlife Service, 1987); and Robert Layton, *Uluru, An Aboriginal History of Ayers Rock* (Canberra: Aboriginal Studies Press, 1989). Further information may be found in Kerry Williams, *Ayers Rock and the Olgas* (Alice Springs, NT: Barker Souvenirs, 1993); *Sharing the Park: Anangu Initiatives in Ayers Rock Tourism* (Canberra: Institute for Aboriginal Development, Australian National Parks and Wildlife Service, 1991); Uluru-Kata Tjuta Board of Management, *Uluru (Ayers Rock-Mount Olga) National Park, Plan of Management* (Canberra: Commonwealth of Australia, 1991); *Uluru & Kata Tjuta: A Geological History* (Canberra: Commonwealth of Australia, 1992); Australian National Parks and Wildlife Service in association with the Mutitjulu Community Inc., *The Mala Walk and*

the Mutitjulu Walk: An Insight into Uluru (Canberra: Australian National Parks and Wildlife Service, 1990).

18. For example, the issues of October 1941, January 1949, and October 1950.

19. Tim Rowse, "The Centre: A Limited Colonization," in *Australia from 1939*, ed. Ann Curthoys, A.W. Martin, and Tim Rowse (Sydney: Fairfax, Syme and Weldon, 1987), 161–65. See also "Cultural Tourism at Uluru: Ananguku Tjukurpa," in *Oxford Companion to Aboriginal Art and Culture*, 398–99.

20. *The Australian*, December 27, 2000.

21. "The Centenary of Australia's Federation: What Should We Celebrate?" *Sydney Morning Herald*, January 27, 2001.

22. AATKings, a company that led in the promotion of visits to Uluru, Kings Canyon, and Kata Tjuta, bills itself as "Australia's No. 1 Tour Operator." It offers international visitors a twelve- or sixteen-day "Icons of Australia" package. The tour begins with "breathtaking views of the Sydney Opera House" and a bus tour to the Blue Mountains outside Sydney. Stage two is the MacDonnell Ranges and "Aboriginal Culture" (visits to a camp, boomerang and spear throwing demonstrations, etc.) near Alice Springs. The centerpiece: "Enjoy a glass of wine this evening while watching sunset over Ayers Rock (Uluru) from the special viewing area known as 'sunset strip.' Don't forget your camera!" and, next day, "Rise early to view Ayers Rock at sunrise." The tour then moves to Northern Queensland, to the rain forests and island of the Great Barrier Reef area. See AATKings, *Australia & New Zealand Fiji & Hawaii Stopovers* (South Melbourne: AAT Kings, 2002), 16–17.

23. Michael Tawa makes important comments on these matters in his "Place, Country, Chorography: Towards a Kinesthetic and Narrative Practice of Place," *Architectural Theory Review*, vol. 7, no. 2 (2002): 45–58.

24. "Muruku Arts and Crafts," in *Oxford Companion to Aboriginal Art and Culture*, 640–41. See also Stephen Dobney, ed., *Cox Architects: Selected and Current Works* (Sydney: Craftsman House, 1997), 80–82, and Greg Burgess Architects, *Uluru National Park: Project Brief and Concept Design* (Melbourne: Burgess Architects, 1990).

25. For one perspective on these issues, see Terry Smith, *Transformations in Australian Art*, vol. 2, *The Twentieth Century: Aboriginality and Modernism* (Sydney: Craftsman House, 2002), ch. 7.

26. See story *Sydney Morning Herald*, July 25, 2001, 14, and Peter Meyers, "Knockabout Walkabout," *Architecture Australia* (March/April 2000), 72–5.

27. A phrase coined by historian Geoffrey Blainey to caricature this position, and adopted by Liberal Party prime minister John Howard as part of his government's refusal of reparation and reconciliation. See Geoffrey Blainey, "Drawing Up the Balance Sheet of Our History," *Quadrant* (July–August 1993): 10–15, and John Howard, Sir Thomas Playford Memorial Lecture, July 5, 1996. For balanced commentary on both see Graeme Davison, *The Use and Abuse of Australian History* (Sydney: Allen & Unwin, 2000), introduction.

28. When popular artist-designer Ken Done produced a sequence of paintings that visually metamorphosed the red sun over Uluru (itself echoing the colors and design of the Aboriginal flag) into the sharper-edged shapes of the opera house, and vice versa, he was sharply criticized by Djon Mundine, an Aboriginal arts advisor and curator. Mundine complained that the image of Uluru was not Done's to appropriate, and that he had no right to transform it, especially not into something so culturally other. Done replied that he was trying to do his best for reconciliation between the races, the most contentious issue in Australian polity at the time and since. See Djon Mundine, *The Bulletin*, July 29, 1997, 22–23, and Done's reply, cited in Leonore Nicklin, "Dream Meets Reality," *The Bulletin*, August 19, 1997, 7. (Done has established, over twenty years, a very successful souvenir, homeware, and clothing business based on marketing his brightly colored and attractive imagery of Sydney harborside life and other instantly recognizable Australian symbols.)

29. Cited by Les Murray in his contribution to "Whitefella Jump Up Correspondence," in David Malouf, "Made in England, Australia's British Heritage," *Quarterly Essay* 12 (2003), 68.

CHAPTER 3

1. Cited in Deborah Solomon, "Is the Go-Go Guggenheim Going?" *New York Times*, June 30, 2002, 41.

2. John Walsh and Deborah Gribbon, *The J. Paul Getty Museum: A Museum for the New Century* (Los Angeles: J. Paul Getty Museum, 1997), 7.

3. David Carrier, "The Art Museum as a Work of Art: The J. Paul Getty Museum," *Source* XXII/2 (winter 2003): 43. The conservatism of the trustees is picked up here: an assumption that most of the world's really wonderful art was made in Europe in ancient times and in the three centuries after the Renaissance—and nowhere else, nor at any other time.

4. Walsh and Gribbon, *The J. Paul Getty Museum*, 87–88.

5. J. Paul Getty, *As I See It* (Englewood Cliffs, N.J.: Prentice-Hall, 1976), 281–82. The story of the Getty finances is a complex one; it may be pursued in Robert Lenzer, *The Great Getty* (New York: Crown Publishers, 1985), appendix 1 ("Getty's Annual Income and Federal Tax Paid, 1923–75") and appendix 2 ("Chronicle of Getty Fortune"). There is a persistent belief that Getty himself, and subsequently the Getty Museum and Center, were and are driven by the necessity to spend each financial year a vast chunk of the fund lest—horror of horrors!—the entire fortune evaporate in taxes. Long-term chairman Harold Williams has repeatedly refuted this by pointing out that the only requirement on the Getty Trust, which runs all the Getty Center activities, is to spend 4.5 percent of interest coming from the funds in three out of every four years. Spending is confined to the goals that the trust sets itself. See the preface by Williams in Walsh and Gribbon, *The J. Paul Getty Museum and Its Collections*, and the interview with him in "The New Getty," *Los Angeles Times*, December 7, 1997.

6. Getty, *As I See It*, 283. Walsh and Gribbon, *The J. Paul Getty Museum*, 43–62, discuss this project in detail.

7. *Guidebook*, J. Paul Getty Museum, Malibu, 1974, cited in *As I See It*, 284.

8. A connection made by Kurt W. Forster, "A Citadel for Los Angeles and an Alhambra for the Arts," *a+u, Architecture and Urbanism* 11 (1992): 6–15. As director of what was then the Getty Center for the History of Art and the Humanities, Forster was in effect the client for what is now the Getty Research Institute, by far the most successful building on the site.

9. Stanislas von Moos, "A Museum Explosion: Fragments of an Overview," in Lampugnani and Sachs, *Museums for a New Millennium*, 18.

10. Definition drawn from Brian Graham, G. J. Ashworth, and J. E. Tunbridge, *A Geography of Heritage* (London: Arnold, 2000), 2.

11. In this broad sense, the Getty echoes faintly the educative spirit that animated the Hall of Architecture in the Carnegie Museum of Art, Pittsburgh, where plaster replicas of famous ancient Greek and Roman sculptures are surrounded by, among much else, life-size casts of a Pisano altar, a section of the Erectheon, and the entire entrance façade of St.-Gilles-du-Gard. The Getty is a late, pale reflection of the urge, so common in the United States during the later nineteenth century and the early twentieth, to clad educational and cultural edifices in classical garb. Thomas Cole's painting of 1840, *The Architect's Dream*, imagines this as a fantasy. No more extreme instance exists than the 1900 proposal for a National Museum of Art and History, submitted to Congress by architect F. Webster Smith. It took the form of a great city that would fill the Washington Mall with serried ranks of actual size, exact reconstructions of the most important monuments from a number of ancient civilizations, beginning with the Sumerian and the Egyptian, and culminating at the Capitol with a perfect Parthenon.

12. On the architecture of the Getty Center see Richard Meier, Ada Louise Huxtable, Stephen D. Rountree, and Harold M. Williams, *Making Architecture: The Getty Center* (Los Angeles: J. Paul Getty Trust, 1997); Richard Meier, *Building the Getty* (New York: Knopf, 1997), 112–13; *Richard Meier The Getty Center*, a special issue of *a+u, Architecture and Urbanism* (November 1992); and the film by Albert Maysles, Susan Froemke, and Bob Eisenhardt, *Concert of Wills: Making the Getty Center* (U.S.A., 100 minutes, 1997).

13. Meier may have been familiar with a once famous but long since forgotten text by art historian Alois Riegl, "the modern cult of monuments." Written in 1903, it was first published as "Der moderne Denkmalkultus, sein Wesen, seine Entstehung," in Alois Riegl, *Gesammelte Aufsätz* (Augsburg-Vienna, Dr Benno Filser, 1928). An English translation by Kurt W. Forster and Diane Ghirardo appeared in *Oppositions* 22 (Fall 1985), 21–51. The historicist blend at the Getty Center melds the three major categories under which us moderns, Riegl believed, value monuments: their age-value, history-value and newness-value, and does so under the framework of what Riegl also saw to be the over-arching preference in modernity: art value. Although he did not name it so,

Riegl was the first theorist of the past-modern. For an elaboration of Riegl's views in the context of the debates of his moment, see chapters II and III of Margaret Iverson, *Alois Riegl: Art History and Theory* (Cambridge: MIT Press, 1993). See also Ignasi de Solà-Morales, "Towards a Modern Museum: From Riegl to Gideon," *Oppositions* 22 (Fall 1982), 69–77, and Alan Colquhoun, "Thoughts on Riegl," *Oppositions* 22 (Fall 1982), 79–83.

14. Carrier, "The Art Museum as a Work of Art," 41.

15. Ibid., 42.

16. Richard Meier, cited in "Building for the Future," *Getty Bulletin*, vol. 1, no. 1 (fall 1986): 4.

17. Reyner Banham, *Los Angeles: The Architecture of the Four Ecologies* (New York: Harper & Row, 1971).

18. The best start is still Mike Davis, *City of Quartz* (London: Vintage, 1990).

19. Le Corbusier, *Towards a New Architecture*, trans. Frederick Etchells (New York: Payson & Clark, 1927); originally *Vers une architecture* (Paris: 1923).

20. Robert Venturi, *Complexity and Contradiction in Modern Architecture* (New York: Museum of Modern Art, 1966).

21. On the Athenaeum, see Martin Filler, "Modernism Lives: Richard Meier," *Art in America* (May 1980): 123–31.

22. Jacques Derrida, *Specters of Marx, The State of the Debt, the Work of Mourning, and the New International* (New York: Routledge, 1994).

23. *Art Newspaper*, June 2002, 26.

24. I evoke here the arguments about the labyrinthine narcissism that underlies the contemporary approach to historical monuments, and to heritage in general, advanced by Françoise Choay, *The Invention of the Historic Monument* (New York: Cambridge University Press, 2001).

25. See, for example, Christina Bechtler, ed., *Frank O. Gehry/Kurt W. Forster, Art and Architecture–A Dialogue* (Ostfildern-Ruit: Cantz, 1999). For a comprehensive record of Gehry's work up to Bilbao, see Francesco dal Co and Kurt W. Foster, *Frank O. Gehry: The Complete Works* (New York: Monacelli Press, 1998).

26. Cited in Anthony Alofsin, "Putting a Shine on Things," *Times Literary Supplement*, November 2, 2001, 16.

27. Ouroussoff, "Art for Architecture's Sake," *Los Angeles Times*, March 31, 2002, F4.

28. Alofsin, "Putting a Shine on Things," 16.

29. Hal Foster, *Design and Crime (And Other Diatribes)* (London: Verso, 2002), 32.

30. Quotations in this paragraph from ibid., 32, 35, 39 and 40.

31. See Alan Hess, *The Architecture of John Lautner* (New York: Rizzoli, 1999), and Barbara-Ann Campbell-Lange, *John Lautner* (Cologne and New York: Taschen, 1999).

32. See Russell Bowman and Franz Schulze, *Building a Masterpiece: Milwaukee Art Museum* (New York: Hudson Hills Press, 2001).

33. Rob Klins, Spencer Olin, and Mark Poster, eds., *Postsuburban California: The Transformation of Orange County since World War II* (Berkeley: University of California Press, 1991).

34. Sharon Zurkin, *Landscapes of Power, From Detroit to Disney World* (Berkeley: University of California Press, 1991), 217 ff. She also cites Henry James on the "great glittering, costly caravansary" of "the universal Waldorf Astoria" as an acute prefiguration of Fredric Jameson on the Hotel Bonaventure (53–54).

35. *Frank Gehry Architect, 2002 Guggenheim Museum*, a calendar published on the occasion of the exhibition "Frank Gehry Architect," Guggenheim Museum, May–August 2001; text cited is the caption for the month of March.

36. Michael Hardt and Antonio Negri, *Empire* (Cambridge: Harvard University Press, 2000), pt. 1.3, 205 ff, and passim.

CHAPTER 4

1. On the building itself and the new artworks in it, see Sebastian Redecke and Andreas Kernbach, *Das Reichstagsgebäude: Architektur und Kunst* (Berlin: Deutsche Bundestag, 2001). On Haacke's work *Die Bevolkerung*, see Hans Haacke, "Thoughts on the Project 1999–2000," in Walter Grasskamp, Molly Nesbit, and Jon Bird, eds., *Hans Haacke* (London: Phaidon, 2004), 138–43.

2. Adorno's doubts are set out in his 1931 inaugural lecture at the University of Frankfurt. See "The Actuality of Philosophy," *Telos* 31 (spring 1977): 120–33. They are amplified throughout his

work, notably in *Negative Dialectics* (1966) (London: Routledge & Kegan Paul, 1973) and *Aesthetic Theory* (1970) (London: Routledge & Kegan Paul, 1984).

3. "Art, Culture, and Society," *Prisms* (Cambridge: MIT Press, 1981), 17–34; in *The Adorno Reader*, ed. Brian O'Connor (Oxford: Blackwell, 2000), 210.

4. See "Commitment," in Adorno, *Notes to Literature*, vol. 2 (New York: Columbia University Press, 1992), 85–86.

5. "Trying to Understand Endgame" (1961), *New German Critique* 26 (spring–summer 1982): 119–50; in *Adorno Reader*, 343.

6. Adorno, *Negative Dialectics*, 362.

7. Ibid., 380. To Adorno, the effects of Auschwitz were almost infinite in range and in their recursive negativity. They are pursued in detail in Rolf Tiedemann, ed., *Theodor W. Adorno, Can One Live after Auschwitz?* (Stanford: Stanford University Press, 2003).

8. Gene Ray, "Mirroring Evil: Auschwitz, Art, and the 'War on Terror,' " *Third Text*, vol. 17, no. 2 (2003): 119. This essay is an excellent application of Adorno's admonitions to the 2002 exhibition at the Jewish Museum, New York, *Mirroring Evil: Nazi Imagery/Recent Art*. On the more general setting of post-Holocaust visual art, see James E. Young, *At Memory's Edge: After-Images of the Holocaust in Contemporary Art and Architecture* (New Haven: Yale University Press, 2000). There are important special studies as well, such as Lisa Salzman, *Anselm Kiefer and Art after Auschwitz* (Cambridge: Cambridge University Press, 1999).

9. Robert Jan van Pelt, "Auschwitz: From Architect's Promise to Inmate's Perdition," *Modernism/Modernity*, vol. 1, no. 1 (1994): 82.

10. Ibid., 106–7. A thorough history of the city up to and including its infamy is given in D. Dwork and R. J. van Pelt, *Auschwitz: 1270 to the Present* (New York: W.W. Norton & Co., 1996). For an account of the direct links between the concentration camp system and the Nazi architectural program—above all through the production of building materials—see Paul B. Jaskot, *The Architecture of Oppression: The SS, Forced Labor and the Nazi Monumental Building Economy* (London and New York: Routledge, 2000).

11. Berlin Museum, *Architect's Competition Brief* (Berlin: Berlin Museum, 1988), n.p.

12. Michael Spens, "Berlin Phoenix," *Architectural Review*, no. 1226 (April 1999): 40. In a lecture delivered in Berlin in 1997, Libeskind relates the story of his interview with key members of the Berlin Senate, including his astonishment and delight that their questioning was confined to matters to do with music: see "Chamberworks: Architectural Meditations on the Themes from Heraclitus," in Daniel Libeskind, *The Space of Encounter* (New York: Universe, 2000), 54.

13. Other complications included controversy around the curatorial appointments and direction and the massive budget reduction partway through—from DM 178.5 million to DM 77 million. See James Russell, "Project Diary: Daniel Libeskind's Jewish Museum in Berlin," *Architectural Record*, vol. 287, no. 1 (1999): 76–98. See also Daniel Libeskind, *Jewish Museum Berlin: Between the Lines* (Munich and New York: Prestel, 1999). Libeskind devotes two chapters of his autobiography to his experiences in connection with the museum: *Breaking Ground: Adventures in Life and Architecture* (New York: Riverhead Books, 2004), 77–104, 133–52.

14. Daniel Libeskind, "Between the Lines," manuscript in *Commemorative Book*, Daniel Libeskind Papers, 1970–1992, Getty Research Institute, Los Angeles, Special Collections, 920061: 1.5. Reproduced in Libeskind, *The Space of Encounter*, 29. All subsequent citations in this paragraph are from this page. Adorno is mentioned at Libeskind, *Breaking Ground*, 82.

15. Libeskind, "Between the Lines, Jewish Museum, Berlin, 1988–99," in Libeskind, *The Space of Encounter*, 26.

16. This connection has been suggestively noted by Anthony Vidler, afterword, in Libeskind, *The Space of Encounter*, 222–24, and Naomi Stead, "The Ruins of History: Allegories of Destruction in Daniel Libeskind's Jewish Museum," *Open Museum Journal*, vol. 2 (August 2000): 1–17.

17. The relevant key text is Benjamin's unfinished Arcades Project (*Das Passagen-Werk*), vol. 5 of the *Gesammelte Schriften*, Rolf Tiedemann and Herman Schweppenhäuser, eds. (Frankfurt: Suhrkamp Verlag, 1982); in English as *The Arcades Project* (Cambridge: Belknap Press of Harvard University Press, 1999). See also the useful introduction by Susan Buck-Morss, *The Dialectics of Seeing: Walter Benjamin and the Arcades Project* (Cambridge: MIT Press, 1989).

18. Walter Benjamin, *One-Way Street and Other Writings* (London: New Left Books), 1979.

19. "Architecture Intermundium: An Open Letter to Architectural Educators and Students of Architecture," in Libeskind, *The Space of Encounter*, 20.

20. Libeskind, *The Space of Encounter*, 49–55 and 55–57 respectively.

21. Libeskind, *The Space of Encounter*, 92–96. Another compilation of projects such as these is Daniel Libeskind, *Radix-Matrix: Architecture and Writings* (Munich and New York: Prestel, 1997).

22. Libeskind, "Between the Lines, Jewish Museum, Berlin, 1988–9," 23.

23. Both sheets in Daniel Libeskind Papers, 1970–1992, Getty Research Institute, Los Angeles, Special Collections, 920061: FF 16. Libeskind would devote an entire notebook to sketches in which a falling stack of books—Torahs, burned books—are abstracted into a variety of Malevich-style Suprematist images. See the notebook entitled *Uncertainty* in Special Collections, 920061-5.

24. Ink on tracing paper, Libeskind Papers, 1970–1992, Getty Research Institute, Special Collections, 920061: FF 15.

25. Libeskind, "Between the Lines, Jewish Museum, Berlin, 1988–9," 23.

26. Kurt W. Forster, "Frank O. Gehry Guggenheim Museum," in Vittorio Magnago Lampugnani and Angeli Sachs, *Museums for a New Millennium: Concepts Projects Buildings* (Munich, London, and New York: Prestel, 1999), 129.

27. Remarks in Libeskind, *The Space of Encounter*, 26; diagram, 23. There is a drawing in a sketchbook at GRI Special Collections 920061-6 that shows five major Berlin landmarks—the Brandenburg Gate, the Angel, the Bismarck memorial, etc.—forming all but one of the points of a Star of David with the word "Jude" inscribed inside it. The sixth point may be a standing man.

28. GRI Special Collections 920061, box 31*.3.

29. GRI, Special Collections, 920061, FF 15. This is the sketch for the diagram in the *Commemorative Book*, GRI, Special Collections, 9260061, 1.5.

30. GRI, Special Collections, 920061, box 31*.3.

31. GRI, Special Collections, 920061-9.

32. Ibid.

33. Ibid.

34. GRI, Special Collections, 920061-8.

35. Libeskind cites a survivor: " 'What do you suppose that white light you saw from the crack in the cattle car on your way to Stutthof really was?' the interviewer asked Elaine some thirty years later in her Brooklyn home. 'You see in order to survive you must believe in something, you need a source of inspiration, of courage, of something bigger than yourself, something to overcome reality. The line was my source of inspiration, my sign from Heaven. Many years later, after liberation, when my children were growing up, I realized that the white line might have been fume from a passing airplane's exhaust pipe, but does it really matter?' " From Yaffa Eliach, *Hasidic Tales of the Holocaust* (New York: Oxford University Press, 1982), quoted in Libeskind, *The Space of Encounter*, 49.

36. Anthony Vidler, "Warped Space: Architectural Anxiety in Digital Culture," in *Impossible Presence: Surface and Screen in the Photogenic Era*, ed. Terry Smith (Sydney: Power Publications; and Chicago: University of Chicago Press, 2001), 294–95. These ideas are developed further in his *Warped Space: Art, Architecture, and Anxiety in Modern Culture* (Cambridge: MIT Press, 2000).

37. Ignasi de Solà-Morales, *Differences: Topographies of Contemporary Architecture* (Cambridge: MIT Press, 1997), 56–70.

38. Vidler, "Warped Space," 296.

39. Ibid., 297.

40. Ibid., 298.

41. Ibid.

42. Ibid.

43. Andrew Benjamin, "The Architecture of Hope: Daniel Libeskind's Jewish Museum," in Benjamin, *Present Hope: Philosophy, Architecture, Judaism* (London: Routledge, 1997), 103–18.

44. Libeskind, *The Space of Encounter*, 26.

45. Benjamin, "The Architecture of Hope," 112.

46. Ibid., 115–16, 118.

47. See Ken Corby, *Discovering the Jewish Museum Berlin* (Berlin: Stiftung Jüdisches Museum Berlin, 2001).

48. Is this overdetermination? Some have thought so. In *Der Knabentanz* (Berlin: Künstlerhaus Bethanien, 2000), artist Adam Geszy provocatively compares the Jewish Museum to a Nazi-era official building by Heinrich Tessenow. On this and related issues in connection with the Washington Holocaust Museum, see Naomi Miller, "Building the Unbuildable: The U.S. Holocaust Memorial Museum," in Wessel Reinink and Jeroen Stumpel, eds., *Memory and Oblivion: Proceedings of the XXIXth International Congress of the History of Art* (Dordrecht: Kluver, 1999), 1091–1101.

49. Vidler, "Warped Space," 299.

50. See Anthony Vidler, *The Architectural Uncanny: Essays in the Modern Unhomely* (Cambridge: MIT Press, 1992).

51. Romi Khosla, *The Loneliness of a Long Distant Future: Dilemmas of Contemporary Architecture* (New Delhi: Tulika Books, 2002).

52. See Daniel Bertrand Monk, *An Aesthetic Occupation: The Immediacy of Architecture and the Palestinian Conflict* (Durham: Duke University Press, 2002), introduction and passim.

53. Lin may have seen Serra's *Shift* 1970–72, a set of six extended finlike shapes set at dynamic angles to each other in a field in King City, Ontario. Of this and similar works, Serra has said that they point to "the indeterminacy of landscape . . . The dialectic of walking and looking into the landscape establishes the sculptural experience." Cited in "Interview: Richard Serra and Lisa Bear," *Richard Serra: Interviews, Etc. 1970–80* (Yonkers, N.Y.: Hudson River Museum, 1980), 72.

54. Ironically, this situation plays out, twenty years later and in reverse, the impassioned attack on Minimal sculpture launched by the modernist critic Michael Fried in his famous essay "Art and Objecthood" (1967) in Michael Fried, *Art and Objecthood* (Chicago: University of Chicago Press, 1998). In defense of the high modernism of sculptors such as Anthony Caro, Fried labeled the work of Donald Judd, Carl Andre, Robert Morris, Tony Smith, and others "literalist" as art and "theatrical" in its address to the spectator. Fried's critique failed to recognize that the work of the very artists he was attacking was the most effective, and art-historically acute, high modernism of its moment—a fact that conceptualism was already, to some, making clear. Now, however, Fried's account reads like a prediction of the capacity of Minimalist art language—a generation later, and, importantly, when spoken by architects—to dramatically articulate widespread and profound social feeling.

55. See Louis Menand, "The Reluctant Memorialist: Maya Lin and the World Trade Center," *New Yorker*, July 8, 2002, 54–65. See also "The Mail," *New Yorker*, July 29, 2002, 12, including two letters from veterans attesting to their role in recognizing the nature and protecting the integrity of Lin's intentions from those, led by conservative presidential candidate Ross Perot, who wanted the wall "white and above the ground" with a flagpole at its apex.

56. Jack Hitt, "The American Way of Death Becomes America's Way of Life," *New York Times*, August 18, 2002, Week in Review, 6.

57. "Notebook 28 Mai 92 to 15 June 92," Lebbeus Woods Papers, Special Collections, Getty Research Institute, Los Angeles, 970081, box 1.

58. Lebbeus Woods, *War and Architecture* (New York: Princeton Architectural Pamphlets, 1993), 3.

CHAPTER 5

1. Marshall Berman, *All That Is Solid Melts into Air: The Experience of Modernity* (1982; reprint, New York: Penguin, 1998), 298.

2. Ada Louise Huxtable, *The Tall Building Artistically Reconsidered: The Search for a Skyscraper Style* (New York: Pantheon Books, 1982), 7.

3. Judith Dupré, "Introductory Interview with Philip Johnson," in *Skyscrapers: A History of the World's Most Famous and Important Skyscrapers* (New York: Black Dog and Leventhal, 2001), 7.

4. "World Trade Center Destroyed," *ArchitectureWeek*, September 12, 2001, N1.

5. Sayyid Qutb, *Milestones* (Cedar Rapids, IA: Mother Mosque Foundation, 1981).

6. The warning by bin Laden was broadcast by Al-Jazeera, October 7, 2001, cited in Mohammed El-Nawawy and Adel Iskandar, *Al-Jazeera: How the Free Arab News Network Scooped the World and Changed the Middle East* (Cambridge, Mass.: Westview, 2002), 146. His videotape intervention into the U.S. election campaign was broadcast by Al-Jazeera on October 29, 2004; full text translation provided by the U.S. government, published *Washington Post*, November 2, 2004,

A.02. One indicator of the labyrinthine strangeness of the intertexts with which we are dealing is that this was the first time bin Laden publicly acknowledged his personal role in the conception of the 9.11.01 attacks.

7. James Glanz and Eric Lipton, *City in the Sky: The Rise and Fall of the World Trade Center* (New York: Times Books, 2003), 5.

8. They are brought out by Andrew Ross, "The Odor of Publicity," in Michael Sorkin and Sharon Zukin, eds., *After the World Trade Center: Rethinking New York City* (New York and London: Routledge, 2002), 121–30. For the most thorough pre-9.11.01 accounts see Robert Fitch, *Assassination of New York* (London and New York: Verso, 1993), Eric Darton, *Divided We Stand: A Biography of New York's World Trade Center* (New York: Basic Books, 1999), and Angus Kress Gillespie, *Twin Towers: The Life of New York City's World Trade Center* (New Brunswick, N.J.: Rutgers University Press, 1999). The last two are reviewed by Michael Tomasky in the *New York Review of Books*, March 14 and 28, 2002. Among the many post-9.11.01 accounts, Glanz and Lipton, *City in the Sky*, offers the most engaging mixture of personality profiles and relevant information.

9. See I. N. Phelps Stokes, *The Iconography of Manhattan Island, 1498–1909*, unpublished, New York Historic Society. This is the major source for Cathleen Schine, "That was New York: The 'Holy Ground'", *New Yorker*, September 16, 2002, 46–51, on which I draw in the following paragraphs. She concludes her useful history with this observation: "An icon, when it is not an exquisite painting of an Eastern Orthodox saint, is generally understood to be an important and enduring symbol. How wonderful that the icons of I.N. Phelps Stokes are not only the grand and majestic images we associate with memorials but also the documents of thousands of daily events, disagreements, compromises, and mundane decisions—the shells and sand that shaped New York City."

10. *Encyclopaedia Britannica Online*, s.v. Manhattan.

11. See John Kuo Wei Tchen, "Whose Downtown?!?" in Sorkin and Zukin, *After the World Trade Center*, 41–43.

12. This is the argument of Edwin G. Burrows, "Manhattan at War," in Sorkin and Zukin, *After the World Trade Center*, 3–32.

13. Robert Moses, *Public Works: A Dangerous Trade* (New York: McGraw-Hill, 1970), cited in Robert Caro, *The Power Broker: Robert Moses and the Fall of New York* (New York: Knopf, 1974), 876.

14. See James Glanz and Eric Lipton, "The Height of Ambition," *New York Times Magazine*, September 8, 2002, 34–36; David Rockefeller, *Memoirs* (New York: Random House, 2002); and Glanz and Lipton, *City in the Sky*, ch. 1.

15. Cited in Eric Darton, "Visible City: The Center That Would Not Hold," *Metropolis*, November 1995, 50.

16. Eric Darton, cross-referencing Moses's 1950s downtown slum clearance plans with the DLMA's 1960s scale model of Lower Manhattan on view at the Skyscraper Museum at Wall Street. Darton, "Visible City," 47.

17. Berman, *All That Is Solid Melts into Air*, 290. In contrast, New York was capable of providing sites of, on balance, positive self-regeneration, as Berman shows in his essay "Too Much Is Not Enough: Metamorphoses of Times Square," in Terry Smith, ed., *Impossible Presence, Surface and Screen in the Photogenic Era* (Chicago: University of Chicago Press; Sydney: Power Publications, 2001). Berman's comments on 9.11.01 may be found in his "When Bad Buildings Happen to Good People," in Sorkin and Zukin, *After the World Trade Center*, 1–12.

18. Louis Mumford's earlier condemnation of the Port Authority of New York as the body most responsible for "the destruction of New York" was couched in these terms:

> The part that this quasi-public body has played in furthering the disintegration of New York as a going metropolis has not been sufficiently appreciated. The Port Authority was created as an adjunct to our state-bounded governmental units, to promote the welfare of our whole vast port area by treating it as a single unit. Because this activity was regarded as a public benefit, the Authority was granted public powers denied to a private corporation ... In the course of time, the Port Authority has turned increasingly into a money-making enterprise, using public-planning activities of the widest order to further ends not easily identified with the health, welfare or prosperity of the New York region ... In short, this is the subsidization of chaos, and the result is already predictable—a sprawling mass of expressways, cloverleaves, bridges, viaducts, airports, garages, operating in an urban

wasteland, with the municipality sinking ever deeper under the burden of taxes imposed to bring even the illusion of relief from the inevitable congestion and disorder." Lewis Mumford, *The Highway and the City* (New York: New American Library, 1963), 230–31.

19. Glanz and Lipton, *City in the Sky*, 40.

20. One of the ways in which the void created by the absent towers has been filled is through stories of their creators. Profiles of most of the major players have been written, and rewritten, extensively, since the attacks. See, as one example among many, James Glanz and Eric Lipton, "Towering Ambition, The Rise of the World Trade Center: A History, with Life and Death Implications," *New York Times Magazine*, September 8, 2002, 32–44, 59–63, and their book, *City in the Sky*.

21. Paul Goldberger, "Building Plans," *New Yorker*, September 24, 2001, 76.

22. See Kevin Phillips, *American Dynasty: Aristocracy. Fortune and the Politics of Deceit in the House of Bush* (New York: Viking, 2004). Michael Moore pointed to these connections in his 2004 film *Fahrenheit 9/11*.

23. Minoru Yamasaki, untitled statement, *Contemporary Architects*, 1st ed. (London: St James Press, 1980), 912. See also Minoru Yamasaki, *A Life in Architecture* (Tokyo and New York: Weatherhill, 1979), and Robert B. Harmon, *Serenity and Delight in the New Architecture as Exemplified in the Work of Minoru Yamasaki* (Monticello, Ill.: Vance Bibliographies, 1981).

24. Cited in James Glanz and Eric Lipton, "The Height of Ambition," *New York Times Magazine*, Sept. 8, 2002, 38.

25. Christopher Gray, *The Chrysler Building: Creating a New York Icon, Day by Day* (Princeton: Princeton Architectural Press, 2002), contains a photographic record of this competition.

26. Dupré uses icons to compare the height of each building she illustrates to the Sears Tower, the Empire State Building, and the Eiffel Tower, and appends a list of "The 100 Tallest Buildings in the World" (*Skyscrapers*, 120–21). Zukowsky and Thorne add an epilogue that briefly reviews the history of the race to build the tallest, then profiles the dozen or so tallest buildings under construction or projected in 2000. John Zukowsky and Martha Thorne, *Skyscrapers: The New Millennium* (Munich, London, and New York: Prestel, 2000), 122–29.

27. Cited in Aaron Betsky, "Babylon Revisited: The Latest Skyscraper Designs Offer Mixed Hopes for a Towering Aesthetic," *Architecture*, vol. 91, no. 12 (December 2002): 43.

28. Illustrated *New York Times Magazine*, September 8, 2002, 36.

29. See the account of this and other relevant films in James Sanders, *Celluloid Skyline: New York and the Movies* (New York: Knopf, 2001), 405–6.

30. Cited in Anthony Robbins, *The World Trade Center* (Englewood, Fla.: Pineapple Press, 1987).

31. Ada Louise Huxtable, "World Trade Center: Who's Afraid of Big, Bad Buildings?" *New York Times*, May 29, 1966; reprinted in Huxtable, *Will They Ever Finish Bruckner Boulevard?* (New York: Macmillan, 1970), 27–32.

32. Sabine Theil-Siling, ed., *Icons of Architecture, The Twentieth Century* (Munich, London, and New York: Prestel, 1998), 9. This is a typical mixed bag of usages of the concept of "icon," slipping between a building's having intensely concentrated value for the architectural profession and for more general publics.

33. Theil-Siling ed., *Icons of Architecture*, 96 and 122.

34. There is no mention of the WTC in such major, many-editioned textbooks as David Watkin's *The History of Western Architecture* (New York: Thames & Hudson, 1986, 1996, and 2000), or Marvin Trachtenberg and Isabelle Hyman's *Architecture: From Prehistory to Postmodernity* (New York: Abrams, 1986 and 2002).

35. William R. Curtis, *Modern Architecture since 1900* (Oxford: Phaidon Press, 1982, and Englewood Cliffs: Prentice-Hall, 1983), 373.

36. Ibid., 3rd ed. (London: Phaidon, 1996), 597.

37. Kenneth Frampton, *Modern Architecture: A Critical History*, 3rd ed. (1st ed. 1980; London: Thames & Hudson, 1992), 280.

38. Manfredo Tarfuri and Francesco dal Co, *Modern Architecture* (New York: Abrams, 1979), 308.

39. Ibid., 366.

40. Classics such as those by Gardner and Janson ignore the WTC utterly through their multiple editions, as do more recent contenders such as Wilkins, Schultz, and Linduff. See Helen

Gardner, *Art through the Ages* (New York: Harcourt, 1970, 1975, 1986, 1991, 2001); H. W. and Dora Jane Janson (later Anthony F. Janson), *History of Art: A Survey of the Major Visual Arts from the Dawn of History to the Present Day* (London: Thames & Hudson; New York: Abrams, 1970, 1971, 1973, 1977, 1991, 1995, 2000, 2001); David G. Wilkins, Bernard Schultz, and Kathryn M. Linduff, *Art Past, Art Present* (Englewood Cliffs, N.J.: Prentice Hall, 1990, 1994, 1997, 2001). The WTC is mentioned, scathingly, in the first two editions of Sam Hunter and John Jacobus's *Modern Art*, but dropped from the third and fourth: Sam Hunter and John Jacobus (and later Daniel Wheeler), *Modern Art: Painting, Sculpture, and Architecture* (New York: Abrams, 1976, 1985, 1992, 2000). Hunter refers to it in other texts, such as his *American Art of the Twentieth Century* (New York: Abrams, 1972), and his joint book with Milton Brown, *American Art: Painting, Sculpture, Architecture, Decorative Arts, Photography* (New York: Abrams, 1979). Similarly, Marilyn Stokstad refers to its height compared to the Empire State Building in the first of her survey books, but omits it from then on. Marilyn Stokstad, *Art History* (Upper Saddle River, N.J.: Prentice Hall, 1995, 1999, 2002). H. Harvard Arnason introduced it into a list of towers in the first and second editions of his mammoth *History of Modern Art: Painting, Sculpture, Architecture*, but dropped it in the third and most recent. H. Harvard Arnason, *History of Modern Art: Painting, Sculpture, Architecture* (New York: Abrams, 1977, 1986, 1998).

41. Sam Hunter and John Jacobus, *American Art of the 20th Century* (New York: Abrams, 1972), 521, and repeated in 1973 and 1979 editions.

42. Sam Hunter and John Jacobus, *Modern Art: Painting, Sculpture, and Architecture* (New York: Abrams, 1975), 298; 2nd ed. (New York: Abrams, 1985), 344.

43. Hunter and Jacobus, *Modern Art*, 2nd ed., 344.

44. Charles Jencks, *The Language of Postmodern Architecture* (New York: Rizzoli, 1977), 9. Of his use of the dynamiting of the Pruitt-Igoe apartments in lectures during the mid-1970s, Jencks said: "The idea of a sudden end, in conjunction with slides of the explosion, had an enormously liberating effect. During the following two years I used this formula in lectures around the world—death of modernity/beginning of post-Modernity, knowing that it was a symbolic invention. [I even made up a false date], and was still pleasantly surprised to see that almost everybody, especially the press, accepted it as the truth." Charles Jencks, *Postmodernism: The New Classicism in Art and Architecture* (New York: Rizzoli, 1987), 27–29. To Yamasaki himself, Pruitt-Igoe was "One of the sorriest mistakes I ever made in this business." Cited in Glanz and Lipton, *City in the Sky*, 95.

45. Charles Jencks, *Modern Movements in Architecture* (Harmondsworth: Penguin, 1973), 50, 190.

46. Ada Louise Huxtable, "The New York Process," *New York Times*, September 17, 2001, A.20.

47. Koolhaas continues: "Manhattan has consistently inspired in its beholders ecstasy about architecture." Here, I think his comment would apply more acutely to the citizens of Chicago. New Yorkers love the city as such, its buildings, its spaces, its movement, long before they pause to think about its architecture. Koolhaas's related point is, however, on the mark: "In spite—or perhaps because—of this, its performance and implications have been consistently ignored or even suppressed by the architectural profession." See Rem Koolhaas, *Delirious New York: A Retroactive Manifesto for Manhattan* (London: Academy Editions, 1974), 7.

48. *New York Times*, February 1, 1976, cited in Ada Louise Huxtable, *Kicked a Building Lately?* (New York: New York Times, 1976), 278, 279.

49. Michel de Certeau, *The Practice of Everyday Life* (Berkeley: University of California Press, 1984), ch. 7.

50. Jean Baudrillard, *The Spirit of Terrorism* (London: Verso, 2002), 43–44. For an elaboration of these ideas, see Valery Podoroga, "The Destruction of the Twin Peaks (Observations Concerning the Event)," trans. Dawn Seckler, in Jonathan Flatley, ed., *Warhol in Moscow: Essays on Art and Mass Culture* (Moscow: Logos Press, 2003).

51. See, for example, "Sacral Symbolism," in Catherine Bell, *Ritual: Perspectives and Dimensions* (New York: Oxford University Press, 1997), 155–59, which draws strongly on the work of Sherry Ortner.

52. Juhasz, untitled commentary, in *Contemporary Architects*, 3rd ed. (London: St James Press, 1994), 1071.

53. See Annabel Wharton, *Building the Cold War: Hilton International Hotels and Modern Architecture* (Chicago: University of Chicago Press, 2001).

54. Juhasz, untitled commentary, 1071.

55. W. J. T. Mitchell, *Iconology: Image, Text, Ideology* (Chicago: University of Chicago Press, 1986), 198.

56. Eric Darton, *Divided We Stand: A Biography of New York's World Trade Center* (New York: Basic Books, 1999), 118–19, with framing commentary in his "The Janus Face of Architectural Terrorism," in Sorkin and Zurkin, *After the World Trade Center*, 88–89.

57. Darton, "The Janus Face of Architectural Terrorism," 91. Mohamed Atta was born in 1968 in Kafr El Sheikh, Egypt, raised in a successful professional family, eventually taking a bachelor of architectural engineering degree in Cairo. In 1992 he commenced five years of study towards a masters degree in urban planning at Hamburg-Harburg Technical University. In a report to his German university on a study visit to Cairo in 1995, Atta deplored the fact that his country was turning into what he termed "McEgypt," bemoaned real estate speculation in the new cities, and despised the destruction of old buildings in order to create a fake reconstruction of the supposedly historic city wall of Cairo. Among Egypt's great riches, the "Islamic monuments" alone stood out for him. In a seminar at Hamburg he expressed the view that skyscrapers were symbols of a Western civilization that had relegated his own culture to the sidelines. He deplored their presence in Arab cities. He made a pilgrimage to Mecca in 1988. He completed his studies in 1999, achieving A-level grades. In his thesis he explored the conflicting presumptions about city planning held within Islam and modernity, applying them to the ancient city of Aleppo, in modern Syria: "Khareg Baben-Nasr: An Endangered Part of the Old City of Aleppo. Urban Development in a Section of an Islamic-Oriental City." Across the top of its title page he wrote: "My prayer and my sacrifice and my life and my death belong to Allah, Master of all Worlds." After graduation, Atta went to work for Plankontor, a German urban planning firm. He is thought to have received training at an Al Qaeda camp in Afghanistan in 1999, returning from there a committed Islamist. "Atta" means "the gift" in Arabic.

CHAPTER 6

1. Foucault's *Discipline and Punish: The Birth of the Prison* (Harmondsworth: Allen Lane, 1977), is the most concentrated statement of these themes. Foucault expanded them in many interviews. One specifically relating to architecture is "Space, Knowledge, and Power," in *The Foucault Reader*, Paul Rabinow, ed. (London: Penguin, 1984), 239–56. In this text, among other pertinent comments, Foucault refutes the banal equation of modernist city planning with "crypto-Stalinism," pointing out, rightly, that architecture only produces "positive effects when the liberating intentions of the architect coincide with the real practice of people in the exercise of their freedom" (pages 245–46). Foucault's ideas were widely influential among those concerned with these questions: see, for example, the special issue of the journal *assemblage* devoted to architecture and violence, edited by Mark Wigley (no. 20, 1993). My own efforts in this area include "Modernism and Visibility: The Power of Architecture," *Transition*, vol. 2, no. 3/4 (Sept./Dec. 1981): 16–22, and "A State of Seeing, Unsighted . . . ; Notes on the Visual in Nazi War Culture," in Paul Patton and Ross Poole, eds., *War/Masculinity* (Sydney: Intervention, 1985), 11–25; the latter is reprinted in *Block* 12 (winter 1986–87): 50–70.

2. Bernard Tschumi, *Architecture and Disjunction* (Cambridge: MIT Press, 1996), 259.

3. Cited in Yossef Bodansky, *Bin Laden, The Man Who Declared War on America* (New York: Prima, 2001), 296.

4. See Eve Sinaiko, "September 11 and the Arts", *CAA News*, November 2001, 4–5 (College Art Association).

5. José Clemente Orozco, *Textos de Orozco* (Mexico City: Imprenta Universitaria), 1955, 44. Fellow muralist Diego Rivera had had the same reaction on his trips to the U.S. during the same years. His fantasy was a Pan-American fusion of Mexican ancientness with U.S. modernity. See the discussion in chapter 6 of my *Making the Modern: Industry, Art, and Design in America* (Chicago: Chicago University Press, 1993).

6. Lewis Mumford, *The Brown Decades: A Study of the Arts in America, 1865–1895* (New York: Harcourt, Brace and Co., 1931), 153.

7. In the Museo de Arte Carillo Gil, Mexico City, INBA 17268. For background material and reproductions, see the essays in *José Clemente Orozco in the United States, 1927–1934*, Renato Gonzáles Mello and Diane Miliotes, eds. (Hanover, N.H.: Dartmouth College, Hood Museum of Art; New York: W. W. Norton, 2002).

8. José Clemente Orozco, *Autobiografía* (Mexico City: Secretaria de Educación Publica-Cultura-Era, 1984), 94–95.

9. See his *Poet in New York*, 192–93, cited in Mike Davis, "The Flames of New York," *New Left Review*, November/December 2001, 36.

10. H. G. Wells, *The War in the Air* (New York: G. Bell and Sons, 1908), 210–11. See also Alan Wykes, *H. G. Wells in the Cinema* (London: Jupiter, 1997).

11. Davis, "The Flames of New York," 34–50, now a chapter in Davis, *Dead Cities and Other Tales* (New York: New Press; New York: W. W. Norton, 2002).

12. *Contemporary Architects*, 3rd ed. (London: St James Press, 1994), 1069–70. The pyrelike implosion is discussed in Charles Jencks, *The Language of Postmodern Architecture* (New York: Rizzoli, 1977), 9.

13. See "The Skyscraper Theorists," in Koolhaas, *Delirious New York*, 93–109.

14. Oldenburg's comments on his proposal are illuminating: "The Lorado Taft *Statue of Death*, which I discovered in the Graceland Cemetery, has a shape like the Hancock Building, and the Hancock Building resembles the black slab against which the sculpture stands. I liked the contrast between such a romantic idea (almost comical) of a building and the machine-made cool of the Big John [the Hancock Building]. On the other hand, the Hancock Building, which I mostly saw before it was inhabited, is, in fact, a highly romantic funereal structure, an accidental result not calculated by the computer and, strangely enough, makes good company with the Taft. They both seem to link up across Chicago history; both radiate Midwest nostalgia that will not go away. Taft's sculpture signifies tradition." Cited in Barbara Haskell, *Claes Oldenburg: Sculpture into Monument* (Pasadena: Pasadena Art Museum, 1971), 68–69. Oldenburg also comments on the Hancock Building in Claes Oldenburg, *Proposals for Monuments and Buildings 1965–69* (Chicago: Big Table Publishing, 1969), 23–24.

15. An ink-on-paper drawing illustrating this conception is reproduced in Cossje van Bruggen, *Frank O. Gehry Guggenheim Bilbao* (New York: Solomon R. Guggenheim Foundation, 1997), 43.

16. The *Tilted Arc* controversy is extensively covered in Clara Weyergraf-Serra and Martha Buskirk, eds., *The Destruction of "Tilted Arc": Documents* (Cambridge: MIT Press, 1991).

17. *Frank Gehry Architect, 2002 Guggenheim Museum*, a calendar published on the occasion of the exhibition "Frank Gehry Architect," Guggenheim Museum, May–August 2001; text cited is the caption for the month of March.

18. See the discussion of "positive deconstruction" in Jacques Derrida, *Deconstruction Engaged: The Sydney Seminars*, edited by Terry Smith and Paul Patton (Sydney: Power Publications, 2001).

19. Another victim was his concept for a hotel on Astor Place, New York, for Ian Schrager, economically embattled promoter of a small and expensive hotel chain that emphasizes "buzz" design as a client attraction. This, too, featured an undulating, molten high-rise of rooms that wrapped around a collapsing central core. Gehry's one other viable skyscraper project (none of his earlier proposals have got beyond the first stages) is the *New York Times* headquarters for Manhattan, which has reached a developed design phase. At its structural core is a standard steel frame, slightly set-back skyscraper of neighborly size. Its façade flows in a distinctive Gehry manner, like a drape or sail billowing, fulsomely but gently. A dramatic note is the split in its lower skirt that allows entrance to the building. This is Gehry at his most restrained: a result, perhaps, of his tentativeness when it comes to designing skyscrapers, mixed with the demands of the client and overshadowed by the effects of aftermath. Just which factor has predominated is impossible to tell. Subsequently, Renzo Piano won the *Times* commission. For details as to Gehry's recent work, including these designs, see *Frank O. Gehry, Work in Progress* (Los Angeles: CIRCA Publishers, 2003). The related exhibition of models, drawings and diagrams—at the Los Angeles Museum of Contemporary Art, late 2003, early 2004—showed Gehry's greater comfort with the requirements of buildings across horizontally spreading sites.

20. See Allan Sekula, *Fish Story* (Düsseldorf: Richter; Rotterdam: Witte de With, centrum voor hedendaagse kunst, 1995), and his essay "Between the Net and the Deep Blue Sea (Rethinking the Traffic in Photographs," *October* 102 (fall 2002): 3–34, discussed in ch. 1.

21. Cited in full in Reporters, Writers, and Editors of *Der Spiegel* Magazine, *Inside 9–11: What Really Happened* (New York: St. Martins, 2001), 307–13, as is an Al Qaeda manual for the establishment and running of terrorist training camps and operation entitled *The Military Series*, 262–304.

22. See Joseph Lelyveld, "What Makes a Suicide Bomber?" *New York Times Magazine*, October 28, 2001, 49–58.

23. "Morbid Pleasures Found in Things That Fall Apart," *Guardian Weekly*, November 15–21, 2001, 23. In Riegl's terms, this would be the difference between age value and history value, brought, in 9.11.01, into a dramatic and deadly conflation.

24. See Christopher Woodward, *In Ruins* (London: Chatto & Windus, 2001).

25. "A Dialogue with Jacques Derrida," in Giovanna Borradori, *Philosophy in a Time of Terror: Dialogues with Jürgen Habermas and Jacques Derrida* (Chicago: University of Chicago Press, 2003), 93. I am grateful to Jacques Derrida for our discussions of these matters during the immediate aftermath.

26. Ibid, 187.

27. The neuroscientific basis and the political salience of common contractions between metaphor and reality have been thoroughly investigated by George Lakoff, notably in his books *Metaphors We Live By* (Chicago: University of Chicago Press, 1982) and, with Mark Johnson, *Philos in the Flesh: The Embodied Mind and Its Challenge to Western Thought* (Perseus, 1999). Of particular relevance to this discussion is his essay "Metaphor and War: The Metaphor System Used to Justify War in the Gulf," *Viet Nam Generation Journal & Newsletter*, vol. 3, no. 3 (November 1991), on-line at http://lists. village.virginia.edu/sixties/HTML_docs/Texts/Scholarly/Lakoff_Gulf_Metaphor_1.html, and his "Metaphors of Terror," in *The Days After: Reflections by Our Authors in the Aftermath*, University of Chicago Press, 2001, http://www.press.uchicago.edu/News/daysafter.html. See also the essays in *Architecture and Body*, a special issue (1988) of *Precis*, the Columbia University architecture journal.

28. The code words used by the attackers and their coordinators were "two high schools and two universities." The use of the code words and the nominating of the Capitol as the target is based on information given to Al-Jazeera London correspondent Yosi Fouda, by Khalid Shaikh Mohammed, chief of military operations for Al Qaeda, and Ramzi bin al-Shibh, Hamburg coordinator and associate of Mohamed Atta. See Peter Maass, "When Al Qaeda Calls: An Arab Journalist's Close Encounter with Terrorists," *New York Times Magazine*, February 2, 2003, 50. The targeting of the White House is based on information believed to have been given by Abu Zubaydah, senior operational planner for Al Qaeda, commander of the Khaiden camp in Afghanistan, where many of the 9.11.01 hijackers trained. He was captured at Faisalabad, Pakistan, in March 2002. Associated Press story, May 23, 2002, in the *Sydney Morning Herald* on that day. The most thorough account in English to date is *The 9/11 Commission, Final Report of the National Commission on Terrorist Attacks on the United States* (New York: Norton, 2004), which devotes ten chapters to a detailed narrative, and four to analysis and recommendation.

29. Mark Wigley, "Insecurity by Design," in Sorkin and Zukin, *After the World Trade Center*, 69.

30. Ibid., 71.

31. Ibid., 72.

32. Interesting studies of these events, and the recoveries from them, may be found along with others in Joan Okman, ed., *Out of Ground Zero, Case Studies in Urban Reinvention* (New York: Temple Hoyne Beull Center for the Study of American Architecture, Columbia University; Munich: Prestel, 2002).

33. Wigley, "Insecurity by Design," 74.

34. Ibid.

35. Ibid., 82–83.

36. Reporters, Writers, and Editors of *Der Spiegel*, *Inside 9–11*, xii.

37. Reuters, October 8, 2001, cited in Davis, "Flames of New York," 38.

38. For a detailed background to this event, see Jon Lee Anderson, "Letter from Kabul: The Assassins: Who Was Involved in the Murder of Ahmed Shah Massoud?" *New Yorker*, June 10, 2002, 72–81.

39. See Mohammed El-Nawawy and Adel Iskandar, *Al-Jazeera, How the Free Arab News Network Scooped the World and Changed the Middle East* (Cambridge, Mass.: Westview, 2002). See also Fouad Ajami, "What the Muslim World Is Watching," *New York Times Magazine*, November 18, 2001, 48–51, 76–78, and the documentary film *Control Room*, directed by Jehane Noujaim, released mid-2004.

40. "Islamist spectacular terrorism" is a well-defined category of analysis among commentators and policy makers. See, for example, Yossef Bodansky, director of the Congressional Taskforce

on Terrorism and Unconventional Warfare, in Bodansky, *Bin Laden*, 336 and throughout chapter 12. He offers a detailed coverage of the period 1998–99.

41. Slavoj Žižek, *Welcome to the Desert of the Real* (London: Verso, 2002), 11. This text is the best response by a theorist to 9.11.01 in its broader ramifications.

42. Susan Sontag, "Looking at War," *New Yorker*, December 9, 2002, 83. This essay is developed into her book *Regarding the Pain of Others* (New York: Farrar, Strauss and Giroux, 2003).

43. "Yes, This Is about Islam", *New York Times*, November 2, 2001, A21. Reproduced in his book of essays *Step Across This Line: Collected Nonfiction 1992–2002* (New York: Random House, 2002), 339–41.

44. David C. Lindberg, *Theories of Vision from Al-Kindi to Kepler* (Chicago: University of Chicago Press, 1976).

45. See Valerie Gonzales, *Beauty and Islam: Aesthetics in Islamic Art and Architecture* (London and New York: I. B. Tauris, 2001).

46. These questions are pursued in Finbarr Barry Flood, "Between Cult and Culture: Bamiyan, Islamic Iconoclasm, and the Museum," *Art Bulletin*, vol. 84, no. 4 (December 2002): 641–59. See also K. Warikoo, ed., *Bamiyan: Challenge to World Heritage* (New Delhi: Bhavana Books and Prints, 2002), and Matthew Power, "The Lost Buddhas of Bamiyan: Picking Up the Pieces in Afghanistan," *Harpers Magazine*, March 2005, 67–75.

47. Barry Unsworth, "Ambiguous Light," *New York Times Book Review*, February 2, 2003, 8, reviewing Kan Kalfus, *The Commissariat of the Enlightenment* (New York: HarperCollins, 2003).

48. Wahhabism has been the state religion (or, if you prefer, the official ideology) of Saudi Arabia since its founding in 1902. Muhammad ibn Abdul Wahhab, advocate of the spiritual cleansing and rehabilitation of Islam during the mid and later eighteenth century, was the ideologue of the original King Saud. A conservative form of Sunni Islam, it dominated Iraq during the early nineteenth century, and was revived throughout the region in the early twentieth. Yet Wahhabi antipathy to visual imagery has never been carried to the extreme in Saudi Arabia that it was in Afghanistan under the Taliban. Its code of conduct was structured around veiling, hiding, and purification.

49. For example, in July 1999 Mullah Omar issued decrees "Concerning the Protection of Cultural Heritage" and "Concerning Preservation of Historic Relics in Afghanistan." The latter included the stipulation that "the Taliban Government states that Bamiyan shall not be destroyed but protected." Cited in Juliette van Krieken, "The Buddhas of Bamiyan [continued]: A Turn-Around for Afghanistan's Cultural Heritage?" *International Institute for Asian Studies Newsletter*, no. 27 (March 2002): 15–16. It may have been during this period that Omar had the interior walls of his Kandahar compound covered with murals of paradisiacal gardens, and the interior rooms decorated with a flower motif. See photograph by Gilles Peress, "Kandahar in Ruins," *New Yorker*, January 28, 2002, 74–75.

50. Cited in van Krieken, "The Buddhas of Bamiyan [continued]," 15–16. Despite immediate and strenuous efforts by UNESCO and many other organizations and individuals, the Bamiyan Buddhas were destroyed in early March 2001. The Ministry of Culture and Information set about destroying all works in the Kabul Museum that represented a human form. This served the double goal of removing such imagery and obliterating Buddhist icons. The works live now only in the form of photographs and scholarly records. See Francine Tissot and Dominique Darbois, *Kaboul, le passé confisqué: Le Museé Kaboul 1931–65* (Paris: Editions Findahly, 2002). Officials from the ministry also destroyed many valuable works that had been kept in their own offices, for safekeeping from the religious police and other iconoclasts. Other items were discarded, left exposed to looting, or placed in the bazaars of Peshawar—among the 30,000 coins that disappeared were those from famous hoards at Mir Zakah, Chaman-I-Hazuri. These actions made systematic what was before then a sporadic eradication of traces of earlier civilizations in the area, although the vandalism increased rapidly under mujahadeen rule. The second-century Buddhist complex at Hadda has been pillaged, and the ancient Greek city of Aï Khanum—long excavated by French archaeologists—has been erased by illicit digging. See Osmund Bopaerachchi, "The Destruction of Afghanistan's Cultural Heritage," *International Institute for Asian Studies Newsletter*, no. 27 (March 2002): 13–14.

51. Nicholas Mirzoeff, "The Empire of Camps," *Afterimage*, vol. 30, no. 2 (Sept./Oct. 2002): 11–12. See also his *Watching Babylon: The War in Iraq and Global Visual Culture* (London: Routledge, 2005).

52. As shown at the International Center for Photography, New York, later months of 2002.

53. Paul Virilio, *Ground Zero* (London: Verso, 2002), 82.

54. Stockhausen cited *New York Times*, September 30, 2001, 28.

55. Contributions to "Talk of the Town," *New Yorker*, September 24, 2001, 29.

56. For example, see the collection *New York September 11 by Magnum Photographers* (New York: powerHouse Press, 2001).

57. "Jeff Marmelstein, Ground Zero, September 11, 2001," an exhibition at International Center for Photography, New York, in winter 2002.

58. "Bill Biggart, Final Exposures," an exhibition at International Center for Photography, New York, in winter 2002. The camera and the roll of film were recovered from the rubble.

59. On the U.S. televisual response see April Eisman, "The Media of Manipulation: Patriotism and Propaganda– Mainstream News in the United States in the Weeks Following September 11," *Critical Quarterly*, vol. 45, nos. 1–2 (spring/summer 2003): 73–84.

60. Sontag, "Looking at War," 93–94. Just one insight among many in this outstanding essay. Adam Gopnik, for one, noted that "the city has never been so neatly, so surreally, sectioned as it became on Wednesday and Thursday." "The City and the Pillars," *New Yorker*, September 24, 2001, 35.

61. A commonplace in ancient funerary practices in many cultures; see also Walter Benjamin, *Origins of German Tragic Drama* (London: New Left Books, 1977), 31.

62. Heinz Schütz, "Fame and Ruins," *Architectural Design*, November 2001, 54–57.

63. Michael Taussig, *Defacement: Public Secrets and the Labor of the Negative* (Stanford: Stanford University Press, 1999), 1.

64. Our earlier discussion of the WTC, its genesis and the various responses to it, accords with Taussig's account of faciality: "I take the face to be the figure of appearance, the appearance of appearance, the figure of figuration, the ur-appearance, if you will, of secrecy itself as the primordial act of presencing. For the face itself is a contingency, at the magical crossroads of mask and window to the soul, one of the better-kept public secrets essential to everyday life. How could this be, this contradiction to end contradiction, crisscrossing itself in endless crossings of the face? And could defacement itself escape this endless back-and-forth of revelation and concealment?" Taussig, *Defacement*, 3.

65. Some might discern here the specter of the doppelganger: a haunting by something that has the same qualities as that which has been destroyed, but is exactly not it, will not be it. The reverse mirror is at work, again. In its strange logic, this haunting return is a seeking for redemption. For both the haunted and the haunter, it takes the form of a turning back to see the beauty of the other, which is to lose it, and oneself, forever.

66. See James Glanz and Eric Lipton, "In Data Trove, A Graphic Look at Towers' Fall," *New York Times*, October 29, 2002, A1. The legal wrangle over the insurance payout is described in Charles V. Bagli, "Trade Center Developer Is Portrayed in Court as Calculating and Rapacious," *New York Times*, February 5, 2003, B4. A comment on the implications of the jury finding that the attacks were "one event" is Mary L. Clark, "A Fresh Start at Ground Zero," *New York Times*, May 5, 2004, A27.

67. See Lisa Belkin, "Just Money," *New York Times Magazine*, December 8, 2002, 92–97, 122, 148–49. Were they to read this, the 9.11.01 attackers might feel that their efforts were still being rewarded. They have forced the enemy to put aside their ideologies of freedom, civility, etc. and to acknowledge the materialism at the basis of their society.

68. "Reading 9-11-01," *Artforum*, November 2001, 36. These thoughts are elaborated in his essay "Democracy De-realized," in Okwui Enwezor et al., eds., *Democracy Unrealized, Documenta 11_Platform 1* (Ostfildern-Ruit: Hatje Cantz, 2002), 347–64.

69. William Langewiesche, "American Ground: Unbuilding the World Trade Center," *Atlantic Monthly*, an essay in three parts: July/August, September, and October 2002. The resultant book is *American Ground: Unbuilding the World Trade Center* (New York: North Point Press/Farrar, Straus & Giroux, 2002).

70. See Michael Thomasky, "Battleground Zero," *New York Review of Books*, May 1, 2003, 18–21.

71. Langewiesche's account of the theft by firemen is vigorously questioned by journalist and author George Black; see David Carr, "Research Challenges Account of 9/11 Looting by Firefighters," *New York Times*, March 23, 2003, A31.

72. Cited in Andrew Sullivan, "This Is a Religious War," *New York Times Magazine*, October 7, 2001, 45.

73. Jeffrey Goldberg, "Reverse Engineering: William Langewiesche Spent Months with the Crew That Dismantled the World Trade Center," *New York Times Book Review*, October 20, 2002, 9. This is a scenario familiar to admirers of Allan Sekula's art, especially his tracing of the movement of the world's materials within globalized capitalism's flows. See, especially, Sekula, *Fish Story*, and Sekula, *Dismal Science: Photo Works, 1972–1996* (Normal, Ill.: University Galleries, Illinois State University, 1999).

74. Herbert Muschamp, "Filling the Void: A Chance to Soar," *New York Times*, September 30, 2001, AR 1–3.

75. Herbert Muschamp, "Things Generally Wrong in the Universe," *New York Times*, May 30, 1993, 30.

76. Ibid.

77. *here is new york, a democracy of photographs*, conceived and organized by Alice Rose George, Gilles Peress, Michael Shulan, and Charles Traub (Zurich, Berlin, New York: Scalo, 2001). This book and traveling exhibition is perhaps the most concentrated and striking instance, among many others, of this effect, one that also serves as a detailed record of the outpouring of peoples' imagery. A related film is Steve Rosenbaum, director, *Seven Days in September* (CameraPlanet Pictures for A&E Channel, New York, 2002), which edits footage from twenty-eight filmmakers, both amateur and professional.

78. Mike Wallace, *A New Deal for New York* (New York: Bell & Weiland, 2002).

79. See Tracy Myers, Lebbeus Woods, and Karsten Harries, *Lebbeus Woods, Experimental Architecture* (Pittsburgh: Carnegie Museum of Art, 2004), 34–35.

CHAPTER 7

1. Wigley, "Insecurity by Design," 69.

2. Ibid., 70.

3. AISC press release, in *ArchitectureWeek*, September 12, 2001, H1.

4. Lee Gomes, "A Day of Terror: Jet Fuel Is Likely Cause of Buildings' Collapse," *New York Times*, September 12, 2001, A15.

5. For example, John Seabrook, "The Tower Builder," *The New Yorker*, November 19, 2001, 64–71.

6. Federal Emergency Management Agency, Federal Insurance and Mitigation Administration, *World Trade Center Building Performance Study: Data Collection, Preliminary Observations, and Recommendations* (Washington: Federal Emergency Management Agency, 2002). A number of investigations into aspects of the structural failures were undertaken, and continue. See, for example, James Glanz, "New Evidence Is Reported That Floors Failed on 9/11," *New York Times*, December 3, 2004, B3. And the relative merits of the different types of skyscraper form continue to be debated; see James Glanz, "Comparing 2 Sets of Twin Towers," *New York Times*, October 23, 2002, B1, on engineering comparison between the WTC and the Petronas Towers, Kuala Lumpur.

7. The list of causes are highlighted in the anniversary television documentary *Anatomy of September 11th*, produced by the New York Times and Granada Factual, USA, shown on A&E TV, September 9, 2002. An example of careful reconsideration by engineers is the computer-modeled simulation of the impact of the flight paths of the two jets through the buildings (the North Tower square-on, the South eccentric, causing a quicker collapse of the latter) leading to the conclusion that it was column failures caused by impact and intense heat from the fires that brought the buildings down, not failure of their floor systems. Evidence presented by Najib Abboud, Weidlinger Associates, New York, in the film *Building to Extremes*, directed by Veronica Young, Carleton International, New York, 2004.

8. Cited in Deborah Solomon, "From the Rubble, Ideas for Rebirth," *New York Times*, September 30, 2001, B37. The Team Twin Towers project is illustrated in Suzanne Stephens et al., *Imagining Ground Zero: Official and Unofficial Proposals for the World Trade Center Site* (New York: Rizzoli, 2004), 23–24.

9. James Howard Kunstler and Nikos A. Salingaros, "The End of Tall Buildings," www.planetizen.com/oped/item.php?id=30, September 17, 2001.

10. Ibid.

11. David W. Dunlap and Julie V. Iovine, "Tall Buildings Face New Doubts as Symbols of Vulnerability," *New York Times*, September 19, 2001, A20.

12. Ibid.

13. Ibid.

14. "Shanghai World Financial Center," Wikipedia, http://en.wikipedia.org/wiki/ Shanghai_World_Financial_Center.

15. Cited in David W. Dunlap and Julie V. Iovine, "Tall Buildings Face Doubt as Symbols of Vulnerability," *New York Times*, September 19, 2001, A20. In his response to reporters, Peter Eisenman was even more forthright. "You're telling me that a Harvard law graduate is going to work in an office 1,700 feet in the air? No way . . . There's no way we're going to design a phallocentric terrorist target." Cited in Michael Powell and Christine Haughey, "Out of the Rubble, Bold Visions: Architects Unveil Designs for the 16-Acre World Trade Center Site," *Washington Post*, December 19, 2002, A.01.

16. Traced in Paul Goldberger, *Up from Zero: Politics, Architecture, and the Rebuilding of New York* (New York: Random House, 2004), chs. 3 and 6.

17. Cited in Paul Goldberger, "Building Plans," *New Yorker*, September 24, 2001, 76.

18. Ibid.

19. Cited in Danny Hakim, "Watching a Creation from Infancy to Rubble," *New York Times*, September 14, 2001, 24.

20. Nicolai Ouroussoff, "Towers' Symbolic Image," *Los Angeles Times*, September 13, 2001, A32.

21. To Muschamp, the WTC was "Rockefeller Republicanism encoded in urban space." See his "Filling the Void: A Chance to Soar," *New York Times*, September 30, 2001, AR1.

22. Compare Paul Goldberger, "Buildup Plans," *New Yorker*, September 24, 2001, 75–78, to his essay "The World Trade Center: Rising in Sheer Exaltation," in Sonja Bullaty, Angelo Lomeo, and Paul Goldberger, *The World Trade Center Remembered* (New York: Abbeville, 2002). As he admits, Goldberger had described the Towers as "boring, so utterly banal as to be unworthy of the headquarters of a bank in Omaha," as "designed by people who did not understand that architecture could inspire love," but he came around as the buildings became more familiar as a landmark, a place of events, as postmodern pastiche paled, and as photographers rendered them as "benign objects" (all quotations from his 2002 essay, 23–27).

23. Ouroussoff, "Towers' Symbolic Image," A32.

24. Ibid.

25. Anthony Vidler, "Aftermath, A City Transformed: Designing 'Defensible Space,' " *New York Times*, September 23, 2001, WK6. Also in *Grey Room*, special issue on 9.11.01, no. 07 (spring 2002): 82–84.

26. Not so incidentally, Vidler here touches on the theme of José Saramago's novel *The Cave* (New York: Harcourt, 2002).

27. Vidler, "Aftermath," WK6.

28. Cited in Linda Hales, "Vision Rising from the Ashes," *Washington Post*, September 26, 2001, C.1. For this architect's "counter-proposal" see Bernard Tschumi, *Tri-Towers of Babel: Questioning Ground Zero* (New York: Columbia University Press, 2003).

29. Cited by Cathleen McGuigan, "Out of the Rubble," *Newsweek*, October 8, 2001, 12.

30. Cited ibid. See also Herbert Muschamp, "Filling the Void: A Chance to Soar," *New York Times*, September 30, 2001, AR1.

31. Subsequently a book, Max Protech, *A New World Trade Center: Design Proposals from Leading Architects Worldwide* (New York: Regan, 2002). The projects mentioned in the following passage were all illustrated in this book, and were accompanied by written rationales. The most comprehensive coverage of the internal politics of the process is Goldberger, *Up from Zero*. The most vivid and best-illustrated guide from an architectural point of view is Suzanne Stephens et al., *Imagining Ground Zero: Official and Unofficial Proposals for the World Trade Center Site* (New York: Rizzoli, 2004).

32. Set out in detail in Michael Sorkin, "The Center Cannot Hold," in Sorkin and Zukin, *After the World Trade Center*, 197–208.

33. See, for example, articles by Herbert Muschamp and Deborah Solomon, *New York Times*, September 30, and October 28, 2001; discussions *New York Times Magazine*, September 23, October 7, and November 11, 2001; Paul Goldberger, "Groundwork," *New Yorker*, May 20, 2002, 86–95.

34. John C. Whitehead, formerly deputy secretary of state under George Schultz in the Reagan administration, cochairman of Goldman, Sachs & Co., and chairman of the Securities Industry Association, was the founding chairman. Other members during 2002–4 were Roland W. Betts, operator of Chelsea Piers Sports and Entertainment Complex, which attracted 4.1 million visitors in 2001; Paul A. Crotty, head of public relations for Verizon; Lewis M. Eisenberg, chairman of the Port Authority; Dick Grasso, chairman of the New York Stock Exchange; Robert M. Harding, deputy major under Giuliani; Sally Hernandez-Pinero, an attorney who serves on many corporate boards; Thomas S. Johnson, chairman of Greenpoint Bank and the United States–Japan Foundation; Edward J. Malloy, president of the Building and Construction Trades Council of Greater New York; E. Stanley O'Neal, president of Merrill Lynch; Billie Tsien, architect and partner of architect Tod Williams; Carl Weisbrod, an attorney and president of the Downtown Alliance, the business improvement organization for the area; Madelyn Wils, chairperson of Community Board 1; Howard Wilson, attorney and chair of the New York City School Construction Authority; Deborah C. Wright, head of many housing development offices under Giuliani and Dinkins; and Frank G. Garb, chairman of NASDAQ until September 2001. Certain early members, including the wife of one of the victims, community representatives, and Silverstein himself have since resigned.

35. Ada Louise Huxtable, "The New York Process," *New York Times*, September 17, 2001, A.20.

36. Paul Goldberger, "Up from Zero," *New Yorker*, July 29, 2002, 29.

37. News, *ArchitectureWeek*, September 9, 2002, N1.1.

38. Rafael Viñoly, "Fill the Void with Beauty," *New York Times*, September 23, 2001, 2.29.

39. Herbert Muschamp, "A Visionary Has Become a Builder," *New York Times*, June 23, 2002, AR31.

40. Ibid.

41. Herbert Muschamp, "Thinking Big: A Plan for Ground Zero and Beyond," *New York Times Magazine*, September 8, 2002, 48–58.

42. Accounts of this pivotal meeting are offered by Michael Sorkin, "Critique," *Architectural Record*, September, 2002, 67–68, and Paul Goldberger, "Designing Downtown," *New Yorker*, January 6, 2003, 62–64.

43. For example, *Principles for the Rebuilding of Lower Manhattan*, February 2002, and, from its Growth Strategies Team, *Possible Futures*, May 2002. Available from www.nynv.aiga.org/reports/shtml.

44. See the LMDC website, especially www.RenewNYC.com for both the brief and the chosen proposals, which are presented through a statement of purpose and a slide show prepared by each entrant.

45. The chosen groups represented the cream of international architects, designers, and consultant engineers. Some included well-known contemporary artists. Starchitects working through their usual arrangements were London-based Norman Foster and Partners, and Berlin-based Studio Daniel Libeskind. U.S. starchitects Richard Meier, Peter Eisenman, Charles Gwathmey, and Steven Holl elected, exceptionally, to work together, with Meier taking the lead in the group's logo and, to all appearances, in the stamping of the overall design image. Long-standing New York firm Skidmore, Owings & Merrill, whose chief partners have had a major role in designs for the site since 9.11.01 and who are architects for developer Larry Silverstein, brought together a team including Field Operations of Philadelphia, Tom Leader and Michael Maltzan from California, Neutelings Riedijk from the Netherlands, and the Tokyo firm SANAA, as well as a number of contemporary artist associates: Inigo Manglano-Ovalle, Rita McBride, Jessica Stockholder, and Elyn Zimmerman. United Architects consisted of Reiser Umemoto, Kevin Kennon Architect, and Imaginary Forces, all from New York; Foreign Office Architects, London; Greg Lynn FORM, Los Angeles; and UN Studio, Amsterdam. Think was constituted of Shigeru Ban of Tokyo and Frederic Schwartz, Ken Smith, and Rafael Viñoly of New York, working with engineers led by ARUP. Experienced New York urban design firm Petersen/Littenberg completes the list. Among standout absentees: Frank Gehry (who snorted at the $40,000 fee), Rem Koolhaas, Zaha Hadid, and Santiago Calatrava.

46. Edward Wyatt, "Designs Unveiled for Transit Hub at Ground Zero," *New York Times*, November 13, 2002, B3.

47. See, for example, Edward Wyatt, "Planners Vow to Cooperate in Rebuilding Trade Center," *New York Times*, December 1, 2002, A49.

48. In a speech of December 12, 2003, Mayor Bloomberg recognized that the WTC was "an international icon. That's why the terrorists destroyed it," but nevertheless was inadequate as urban planning in that it never stimulated the envisioned jobs and growth in the area. See Goldberger, *Up from Zero*, ch. 9.

49. The process of developing a suitable memorial on the Ground Zero site has been less prominently reported than the search for an appropriate site plan and architecture, but is no less fraught and conflicted. A problem peculiar to this site is that the architectural plan as developed by Studio Libeskind is, as I will soon show, so profoundly memorializing in form and likely effect as to render any specific memorial minor, if not redundant. Whether an effective memorial can be achieved for the site depends, among many other factors, on this negotiating this paradox. For a report of useful expert commentary on memorialization as it relates to Ground Zero, see Kirk Johnson, "The Very Image of Loss, The Pit at Ground Zero as Icon of Absence," *New York Times*, March 2, 2003, 26. See also Kirk Savage, "Trauma, Healing, and the Therapeutic Monument," in *Terror, Culture, Politics: Rethinking 9/11*, Daniel Sherman and Terry Narelin, eds. (Bloomington: Indiana University Press, 2004), 103–20. Negotiations between Libeskind and those planning the memorial are reported in, for example, Edward Wyatt, "Spotlight Is on Wedge of Light, Symbol or Not," *New York Times*, May 2, 2003, B3. The designs of the eight finalists are extensively reported in Glenn Collins, "8 Designs Confront Many Agendas at Ground Zero," *New York Times*, November 20, 2003, A1. Not unexpectedly, the proposal that combined the most minimal aesthetic with the least intervention into the site's sacred limits, especially the tower footprints, won the day: Michael Arad's *Reflecting Absence*. The LMDC paired him with a landscape architect, Peter Walker, to bring his proposal to a final form. See David W. Dunlap, "A Ground Zero Memorial, Trying to Make Three Plans Work as One," *New York Times*, January 12, 2004, B1.

50. These range from the boosterism of Herbert Muschamp, "The Latest Round of Designs Rediscover and Celebrate the Vertical Life," *New York Times*, December 19, 2002, A27, through the chronicling of Paul Goldberger, "Designing Downtown," *New Yorker*, January 6, 2003, 62–69, to the healthy skepticism of Philip Nobel, "The Fix at Ground Zero," *Nation*, January 27, 2003, 27.

51. Baudrillard, *Spirit of Terrorism*, 50.

52. Cited in Edward Wyatt, "Design for Ground Zero," *New York Times*, March 2, 2003, WK2.

53. "The iconic skyline must be reassembled. We propose to celebrate New York's positive spirit with a unique twinned tower: the most secure, the greenest and the tallest in the world. The crystalline tower is based on triangular geometry–cross-cultural symbols of harmony, wisdom, purity, unity and strength. Its two halves kiss at three points, creating public observation platforms, exhibits, cafes and other amenities. These links also have a safety benefit, as escape routes from one tower to the other. They will break down the tower's scale into village-like clusters, each with its own atrium. These tree-filled spaces—parks in the sky—will purify the natural air that will ventilate the building. A state-of-the-art multi-layered facade will enable the towers to avoid energy-wasting air conditioning for up to 80% of the year. The building's raking corners offer the opportunity for funiculars to transport the public vertically up the building . . . Our plans meet the needs for remembrance, reconciliation and renaissance." Foster and Partners, www.RenewNYC.com/plan_des_dev/wtc_side/new_design_plans/firm_a/default.asp.htm.

54. Cited in Edward Wyatt, "7 Design Teams Offer New Ideas for Attack Site," *New York Times*, December 19, 2002, A1.

55. Daniel Libeskind, "Architect's Statement," LMDC web site, www.RenewNYC.com/plan_des_dev/wtc_site/new_design_plans/firm_d/default.asp.htm. Subsequent quotations in the text are from this statement. During the euphoria following his "victory" in the WTC design competition, Libeskind burbled that 1776 was "a date or number that will never be surpassed in history." Cited in Edward Wyatt, "Design for Ground Zero," *New York Times*, March 2, 2003, WK2.

56. A point not lost on many observers. See Edward Wyatt, "Designs Leave Blanks for 9/11 Memorial Contest to Fill," *New York Times*, February 12, 2003, B4.

57. Daniel Libeskind, "Architect's Statement."

58. Saskia Sassen draws the most positive message for "healthy density" in future cities from the specifics of some of the designs. See her "How Downtown Can Stand Tall and Step Lively Again," *New York Times*, January 26, 2003, AR35.

59. Herbert Muschamp, "Balancing Reason and Emotion in the Twin Towers Void," *New York Times*, February 6, 2003, E1. Muschamp went on: "It is an astonishingly tasteless idea. It has pro-

duced a predictably kitsch result." Muschamp plumped hard for the Think proposal in this and other pieces, for example, "A Goal for Ground Zero: Finding an Urban Poetry," *New York Times*, January 28, 2003, E1. A detailed defense of the Libeskind design was Marvin Trachtenberg, "A New Vision for Ground Zero beyond Mainstream Modernism," *New York Times*, February 23, 2003, AR54. Libeskind is attacked as a "philosophical prankster" and his design as one of "tragic incoherence, simultaneously swaggering and weeping, unable to resolve its display of commercial vigor at the skyline with a ghoulish obsession with the yawning pit below," by Michael J. Lewis, "All Sail, No Anchor: Architecture after Modernism," *New Criterion*, vol. 27, no. 4 (December 2003): 4–17.

60. See the report on the discussion of January 7, 2003, reported by Julie V. Iovine, "Appraisals of Ground Zero Designs," *New York Times*, January 9, 2003, B3. And other commentary, such as Witold Rybczynski, "They Rise, but Do They Soar?" *New York Times*, December 20, 2002, A39.

61. Nobel, "The Fix at Ground Zero," 27. Nobel has since published a trenchantly skeptical account of the process: *Sixteen Acres: Architecture and the Outrageous Struggle for the Future of Ground Zero* (New York: Metropolitan, 2004).

62. See Edward Wyatt, "Practical Issues for Ground Zero," *New York Times*, February 28, 2003, A1. Libeskind's was the only proposal that presumed a staged building program. A detailed contextual account of both Pataki's and Bloomberg's attitudes given in Goldberger, *Up from Zero*, chs. 5, 7, and 9. Libeskind emphasizes the string-pulling role of Ed Hayes, his go-between to the governor: *Breaking Ground*, 181–83.

63. The reflections in this paragraph followed a reading of W. G. Sebald, *On the Natural History of Destruction* (New York: Random House, 2003).

64. Eric Darton, "The Center That Would Not Hold," *Metropolis*, November 1995, 53.

65. These movements are detailed in, among others, Wallace, *A New Deal for New York*, 17–21.

66. Paraphrase by Pamela Williams, "The Diggers at Ground Zero," *Australian Financial Review Magazine*, December 2002, 43.

67. Ibid., 49.

68. Peter Lowy, CEO of Westfield America, commented in 2002: "It doesn't matter what you build—it won't be there for years, so it doesn't effect our income. Our investment was $27 million. Westfield America Trust has $8.9 billion in assets, so it is less than 1.5 per cent of our holdings. In terms of public profile, though, it was certainly the biggest thing." Cited in Williams, "The Diggers at Ground Zero," 49. Westfield's withdrawal was reported in Charles V. Bagli, "Retail Operator at Trade Center Is Pulling Out of the Deal," *New York Times*, September 16, 2003, B1. Rather than wait ten to fifteen years to begin to recoup profits, and believing that they would never reach the annual level of $900 per square foot that was returned in 2000, it sold its interests for $140 million.

69. See David W. Dunlap, "A Post-Sept. 11 Laboratory in High-Rise Safety," *New York Times*, January 29, 2003, C4. In January 2002 Skidmore, Owings & Merrill withdrew its "innovative" proposal for the entire site, leaving their partners high and dry and themselves in an untrammeled relationship with Silverstein.

70. After the fanfare of the December designs, the agencies and developers moved in to determine exactly what would be built, by whom, and when. A profile of this struggle is given in Charles R. Bagli, "Agencies Jockey for Control over Future of Ground Zero Design," *New York Times*, February 7, 2003, B1. Indicative of the kinds of pressures the developers bring to bear is the fact that in late January 2003 Silverstein wrote to the LMDC insisting that any architect taken on by the LMDC work under plans developed by his architects, Skidmore, Owings & Merrill. See Edward Wyatt, "Trade Center Leaseholder Says He Has Right to Rebuild as He Wants," *New York Times*, February 1, 2003, B3. And on March 14 Peter Lowy wrote to the Port Authority stating that his company would act against the reduction of below-ground-level retail space in Libeskind's design and against the fact that it allowed for less passing trade than expected. Westfield had 430,000 square feet before 9.11.01. It subsequently negotiated 650,000 in the LMDC specifications. Libeskind's plan offered 480,000. See Edward Wyatt, "Retail-Space Developer Balks at Designs for Ground Zero," *New York Times*, April 4, 2003, 6. Governor Pataki was active on behalf of both Silverstein and Lowy. Westfield was a Pataki donor. See James McKinley, "Westfield Big Donor to Election Campaign," *Sydney Morning Herald*, July 18, 2002, 7. On the pressures to modify Libeskind's concept, see Charles V. Bagli, "Vision for Lower Manhattan Is Still in Flux," *New York*

Times, February 28, 2003, B2, and David W. Dunlap, "Aspirations Bump into Practicalities at Ground Zero," *New York Times*, March 6, 2003, B3. For estimations of Libeskind's chances see Joyce Purnick, "An Architect with the Drive to Get It Done," *New York Times*, March 3, 2003, B1, and Paul Goldberger, "Eyes on the Prize: The Amazing Design Competition for the World Trade Center Site," *New Yorker*, March 10, 2003, 78–82. A detailed overview is Goldberger, *Up from Zero*, ch. 16.

71. Herbert Muschamp, consistent critic of Libeskind's master plan and its signature symbolism, saw in the appointment of Calatrava the first sign that "great things might grow" on the site: see his "Filling a Creative Void at Ground Zero," *New York Times*, August 1, 2003, B7.

72. Steve Brodner, "Rebuild Iraq? Daniel Libeskind Says, 'No Problem!' " *New Yorker*, May 5, 2003, 106.

73. Rem Koolhaas, "Delirious No More," *Wired*, June 2003, 168.

74. James Glanz, "High Anxiety: Designing the Safest Building in History for the Scariest Address on Earth," *New York Times*, March 14, 2004, AR1. Groundbreaking for the Freedom Tower occurred on July 4, 2004. Funding for the $1.5 billion edifice is in hand from insurers, as is that for cultural and memorial projects, as well as the transportation hub deigned by Santiago Calatrava, which comes from private and government sources. Funding for the remaining projects—including office towers by Foster, Jean Nouvel and Fumihiko Maki—is in doubt following the loss of the claim for $7.5 billion by developer Silverstein, who in mid-2004 looked set to realize no more than $4.5 billion, less costs. (See Jason Edward Kaufman, "Insurer Shortfall Threatens Building," *Art Newspaper*, no. 148, June 2004, 3.) Illustrations of each step in the design compromise that is Freedom Tower are in Stephens, *Imaging Ground Zero*, 31–35. She points out how close this result is to the tower in Concept Plan 4, designed by David Childs for the Skidmore, Owings and Merrill entry.

75. Cited in David Rennie, "Ground Zero tower aspires to be the world's tallest," *Sunday Age*, December 21, 2003, 12. Libeskind's journey through the Ground Zero experience is chronicled frankly throughout his autobiography, *Breaking Ground*. Despite everything, he remains hopeful.

CONCLUSION

1. See, for example, "Building for a Secure Future," special supplement to both *Engineering News-Record* and *Architectural Record* magazines, April 2002, and Purcell Carson, "Paranoid Architecture," *Architecture*, August 2002, 43–45.

2. See, for example, Nicolai Ouroussoff, "Art for Architecture's Sake," *Los Angeles Times*, March 31, 2002, F4, and Witold Rybczynski, "The Bilbao Effect," *Atlantic Monthly*, September 2002, 138–42. Ando has scaled up his restraint but with a sad loss of scale in his Museum of Contemporary Art, Forth Worth, Texas. It pales beside the precision and resonant elegance of its smaller neighbor, Louis Kahn's Kimbell Art Museum.

3. C. C. Sullivan, "Techno Towers," *Architecture*, December 2002, 56–57. See also Philip Nobel, "Diplomatic Immunity: A Defensive Buildup Highlights the Rift between Thinkers and Doers," *Metropolis*, October 2002, 84, 86.

4. On the Westin Hotel, see Herbert Muschamp. "A Latin Jolt to the Skyline," *New York Times*, October 20, 2002, Arts 2. See also Jean Baudrillard, "The Precession of the Simulacra," in his *Simulations* (New York: Semiotext(e), 1983), and James Traub, *The Devil's Playground: A Century of Pleasure and Profit at Times Square* (New York: Random House, 2004).

5. Nicolai Ouroussoff, "The New New York Skyline," *New York Times*, September 5, 2004, AR1, 22–23.

6. Chan Tien Hin and Khoo Hsu Chuang, "Petronas Tower Owner Plans $284m Raising," *Australian Financial Review*, July 23, 2004, 78. Pelli's account of his meeting with the Malaysian prime minister was given in an interview with Veronica Young, July 25, 2003, in preparation for the film *Building to Extremes*; see note 8 below.

7. Advertisements placed (in the December 8, 2003, *New Yorker*, for example) by the Republic of China (Taiwan).

8. *Building to Extremes* is a thorough and engaging exploration of the aspirations, concerns, and debate about these buildings among their developers, builders, engineers, and architects. Directed and produced by Veronica Young, this film was broadcast on PBS USA, February 8, 2004, and is distributed by Carleton Productions, New York.

9. See Robert Johnson, "A Local Dream of Global Trade," *New York Times*, April 25, 2004, 3.2.

10. Anthony Vidler, "Redefining the Public Realm," in "109 provisional attempts to address six simple and hard questions about what architects do today and where their profession might go tomorrow," *hunch, the Berlage institute report*, no. 6/7 (summer 2003): 469.

11. See Eric Höweker, *Skyscraper: Vertical Now* (New York: Universe/Rizzoli, 2003).

12. "109 provisional attempts to address six simple and hard questions about what architects do today and where their profession might go tomorrow," *hunch, the Berlage institute report*, passim. Another collection of intensely debated architectural ideas is Bernard Tschumi and Irene Cheng, eds., *The State of Architecture at the Beginning of the 21st Century* (New York: Monacelli Press, 2003).

13. Thomas Zummer, (*Rolling Waves of Lawlessness*), text/proposal for a pre-emptive architecture, 2004, a pencil on paper drawing exhibited at the Friederieke Taylor Gallery, New York, February 2004.

14. Michael Kimmelman, "An Artist beyond Isms," *New York Times Magazine*, January 27, 2002, 18–29.

15. Michael Kubovy and Rem Koolhaas, *Projects for Prada* (New York: Distributed Art Publishers, 2001). See also Aurora Cuito, ed., *Rem Koolhaas/OMA* (Düsseldorf: teNeus, 2002), 60–69.

16. "A Conversation with Rem Koolhaas and Sarah Whiting," *Assemblage* 40 (December 1999): 50, cited in Foster, *Design and Crime*, 61–62.

17. A clear example of rather desperately reinventing modernism is Hans Iberlings, *Supermodernism: Architecture in the Age of Globalization* (Rotterdam: NAi Publishers, 2002).

18. Italo Calvino, *Invisible Cities* (San Diego: Harcourt, 1974), 165.

19. Lebbeus Woods, *Architecture and War* (New York: Princeton Architectural Pamphlets, 1993), 6.

20. On the Djenné mosque, see Jean-Louis Bourgeois, *Spectacular Vernacular: The Adobe Tradition* (New York: Aperture, 1983), ch. 11.

21. Frank Gehry interviewed by Deborah Solomon, "Towering Vision," *New York Times Magazine*, Jan 5, 2002, 11.

22. Robin Pogrebin, "Gehry is Chosen to Design Ground Zero Performance Center," *New York Times*, October 13, 2004, A27.

23. Salman Rushdie, "October 2001: The Attacks on America," in his *Step Across This Line: Collected Nonfiction 1992–2002* (New York: Random House, 2002), 336; originally a *New York Times* column, November 2, 2001, A25.

24. Otto Karl Werckmeister, "Ästhetik der Apokalypse," *Frankfurter Allgemeine Zeitung*, January 8, 2002, 8, reprinted in Bazon Brock and Gerlinde Koschick, eds., *Krieg und Kunst* (Munich: Wilhelm Fink Verlag, 2002), 195–208. Werckmeister goes on to point out that imagery of the war against the Taliban and Al Qaeda was largely confined to archival footage of previous conflicts. Illustrated press reports began to appear after the war was clearly won; for example, the folio of images by Gilles Peress, "Kandahar in Ruins," *New Yorker*, January 28, 2002, 71–77. Reading Werckmeister's comment, allowance must be made for varying practices in the distribution of press agency imagery. In the U.S., photographs regularly carry the name of the photographer as well as that of the agency, whereas in Europe, this is less common.

25. A large number of scholars with convergent interests have elaborated these kinds of concerns into an interdisciplinary domain that is now reaching a certain maturity: see, for example, the essays in Nicholas Mirzoeff, ed., *The Visual Culture Reader*, 2nd ed. (London and New York: Routledge, 2003), notably those in the "Introductions/ Provocations/Conversations" section. Another art historian to comment perceptively on 9.11.01 and its implications for the larger visual culture is Al Boime. See his "The Fate of the Image-Monument in the Wake of 9/11," in Vincent Lavoie, ed., *Maintenant: Images du temps présent* (Montreal: Le Mois de la Photo à Montréal, 2003), 189–202.

26. Tom Kean, reported in Marian Wilkinson, "The Darkest Hours," *Sydney Morning Herald*, July 24–25, 2004, 29.

27. Icons included the Citygroup Center and New York Stock Exchange Buildings in New York, the International Monetary Fund and World Bank Buildings in Washington and Prudential Financial in New Jersey.

28. Douglas Jehl and David Johnston, "In Video Message, Bin Laden Issues Warning to U.S.," *New York Times*, October 30, 2004, A1, A9.

INDEX

Aalto, Alvar, 38
Abboud, Najib, 225n7
Aboriginal art, 46, 211n28
Abu Ghraib, 5
Acconci, Vito, 167
Adorno, Theodor: on aftermath of Holocaust,
    68–70, 172, 214nn7–8; Libeskind and, 74–75,
    85, 214n14
Advertisements for Architecture (Tschumi), 124
Aerospace Hall, Los Angeles, 62
Affair to Remember, An (film), 118
Afghanistan: Al Qaeda training in, 220n57,
    222n28; attacks on images in, 143, 144, 155,
    223n46, 223nn48–50; U.S. war on Taliban and
    Al Qaeda in, 1, 8, 11, 144–45, 150, 200, 231n24;
    World Trade Center in, 194
aftermath: contemporary architecture and, 190,
    203; difficulty of analysis during, 16; of
    Holocaust, 70, 71, 74, 75; Islamic fundamental-
    ists living in, 145; Jewish Museum Berlin and,
    83, 84, 85; of modernist spectacle, 196; of
    modernity, 7, 59–60, 85, 168; in Sydney Opera
    House and Uluru, 35, 47; of U.S. "victory" in
    Iraq, 2, 4–5, 8
aftermath of 9.11.01 attacks: building professions
    and, 160–62; chimeras of, 13, 154–59, 199;
    community spirit in, 157, 159, 166; compensa-
    tion for victims, 152, 154, 224n67; conse-
    quences for architecture, 7–8, 12, 13–14, 15, 16;
    designs for Ground Zero and, 13, 181, 182, 183,
    199–200; elements present in, 10; Gehry's *New
    York Times* headquarters in, 221n19; gigantism
    of, 152; infinite reverberations of, 154; legal
    cases, 150–52, 224n66; mass circulation of
    images and, 142; overreaching of WTC and,
    120; perpetual, 203; skyscraper limits in, 108;
    spectacle architecture in, 192; staged by hijack-
    ers, 146; traumatized architecture in, 126. *See
    also* Afghanistan; Ground Zero; Ground Zero
    development; Ground Zero memorial;
    September 11, 2001, attacks
AI: Artificial Intelligence (film), 129
Alhazen, 142
Al-Jazeera, 137, 141, 203, 216n6, 222n28
Al-Kindi, 142
Allende, Salvador, 14
Alofsin, Anthony, 61
Al Qaeda: ethical alternative to, 11; goals of, 137, 142,
    222n28; Madrid bombings and, 14; media

used by, 141; Mohamed Atta, 123, 220n57,
    222n28; political influence in Afghanistan,
    144; vs. state terrorism, 14; training manual of,
    221n21; U.S. pursuit of leaders, 15. *See also*
    Afghanistan; bin Laden, Osama; terrorists of
    9.11.01
al-Shibh, Ramzi bin, 222n28
"American Ground: Unbuilding the World Trade
    Center" (Langewiesche), 152–53
American Ground: Unbuilding the World Trade Center
    (Langewiesche), 155, 224n69
American Institute of Steel Construction, 161
Anangu people, 10, 42, 45, 46
Anatomy of September 11th (television documentary),
    225n7
Ando, Tadao, 181, 191, 230n2
Andre, Carl, 216n54
Anti-Oedipus (Deleuze and Guattari), 33, 208n31
Appadurai, Arjun, 205n6
Arad, Michael, 91, 228n49
Arcades Project (Benjamin), 214n17
Archi-Tectonics, 167
architects, reactions to 9.11.01 events, 160–61
Architect's Dream, The (Cole), 212n11
architecture: of aftermath (*see* aftermath; aftermath
    of 9.11.01 attacks); contradiction and, 57–58,
    89, 123, 172, 190; current trends in, 191–96; de-
    constructive, 65, 124, 132, 190; at end of twen-
    tieth century, 123; experimental, 194–96;
    Foucault on, 124, 220n1; Gothic, 39, 208n32;
    in iconomy, 6–8, 12, 15, 32; nonarchitectural
    values and, 89; Past-Modern, 55, 64, 84, 123,
    190, 213n13; power and, 7, 196; predestination
    and, 134; security concerns in (*see* security); so-
    cial contract of (*see* social contract of architec-
    ture); violence and, 6, 124–25, 220n1; war and,
    in Woods's approach, 91–94; "weak," 84, 88.
    See also classical architecture; contemporary ar-
    chitecture; destination architecture; modernist
    architecture; postmodern architecture; specta-
    cle architecture
"Architecture Intermundium" (Libeskind), 76
Arnason, H. Harvard, 219n40
Arquitechtonica, 192
Art and Objecthood (Fried), 216n54
Art Institute of Chicago, 53
ARUP, 227n45
Ascent, The (Woods), 159
Ashworth, Henry Ingham, 38